BELONGING

AUSTRALIANS, PLACE AND ABORIGINAL OWNERSHIP

This extraordinary book explores the feelings of non-Aboriginal Australians as they articulate their sense of belonging to the land. Always acting as a counterpoint is the prior occupation and ownership by Aboriginal people and their spiritual attachment. Peter Read asks the pivotal questions: What is the meaning of places important to non-Aboriginal Australians from which the Indigenous people have already been dispossessed? How are contemporary Australians thinking through the problem of knowing that their places of attachment are also the places which Aboriginals loved – and lost? And are the sites of all our deep affections to be contested, articulated, shared, forgone or possessed absolutely? The book cleverly interweaves Read's analysis (and personal quest for belonging) with the voices of poets, musicians, artists, historians, young people, non-European Australians, farmers and seventh-generation Australians.

Peter Read is an Australian Research Council Senior Fellow, Centre for Cross-Cultural Research, Australian National University. He has worked extensively in Aboriginal history and Australian places studies. He is the author of *A Rape of the Soul So Profound: The Return of the Stolen Generations* (1999) and *Returning to Nothing: The Meaning of Lost Places* (Cambridge University Press, 1996), which was shortlisted for several Australian literary awards.

It comes from the heart. May it go to the heart.
Beethoven, Missa Solemnis

BELONGING

AUSTRALIANS, PLACE AND ABORIGINAL OWNERSHIP

Peter Read

Australian National University

CAMBRIDGE UNIVERSITY PRESS

PUBLISHED BY THE PRESS SYNDICATE OF THE UNIVERSITY OF CAMBRIDGE
The Pitt Building, Trumpington Street, Cambridge, United Kingdom

CAMBRIDGE UNIVERSITY PRESS
The Edinburgh Building, Cambridge CB2 2RU, UK
40 West 20th Street, New York, NY 10011–4211, USA
10 Stamford Road, Oakleigh, VIC 3166, Australia
Ruiz de Alarcón 13, 28014, Madrid, Spain
Dock House, The Waterfront, Cape Town 8001, South Africa

http://www.cambridge.org

First published 2000

Printed in Australia by Australian Print Group

Typeface Palatino (*Adobe*) 10/13 pt.   *System* QuarkXPress® [BC]

A catalogue record for this book is available from the British Library

National Library of Australia Cataloguing in Publication data
Read, Peter, 1945– .
Belonging: Australians, place and Aboriginal ownership.
Bibliography.
Includes index.
ISBN 0 521 77354 7.
ISBN 0 521 77409 8 (pbk.).
1. Land tenure – Australia. 2. Aborigines, Australian –
Land tenure. 3. Australians – Attitudes. I. Title.

ISBN 0 521 77354 7 hardback
ISBN 0 521 77409 8 paperback

For Jessie and Bridie

CONTENTS

ACKNOWLEDGEMENTS

This book was written under the friendly roof of the Urban and Environmental Program, Research School of Social Sciences, Australian National University. My colleagues encouraged lively discussion, and Professor Patrick Troy in particular provided a happy and energetically stimulating working environment. Phillipa McGuinness, Senior Commissioning Editor of Cambridge University Press, believed in the book from the beginning. Elizabeth Wong and Richard Egan generously arranged school interviews, Mark McKenna suggested bands and singers, and Barbara Holloway suggested poets whose works I might consult. Pat Arthur provided accommodation for Dennis Foley and me.

I sincerely thank all the many participants who shared their feelings of belonging with me. Some of them, because of undertakings I made, cannot be named. My thanks to Damian Borgia, Monica Carroll, Elsie Chan, Manik Datar, Dennis Foley, Trina Gaskell, Abigail Gibson, Heather Goodall, Ian Green, Tom Griffiths, Bill Insch, Mandy Martin, Momo Miyaguchi, Henry Reynolds, Lyndall Ryan, Jennifer Vermeij, Marivic Wyndham; three anonymous students from Lake Ginninderra High School, Canberra; six anonymous students from an anonymous school, Sydney.

I am deeply indebted to Dennis Foley without whom the book could not have taken its present shape, nor reached its conclusions.

Jay Arthur as ever provided everything a writer could want.

The author and publisher would like to thank the following for permission to reproduce copyright material:

Aboriginal Studies Press (Geoff Page); Addison Wesley Longman Australia Pty Ltd (Bruce Dawe); Tony Birch; Wally Brummell; Rose Bygrave ('Spiritual Thing'); Carcanet Press Ltd (Les Murray, Judith Wright); CAAMA (Warumpi Band, Frank Yamma, Amunda, Sunrize, Coloured Stone, Wedgetail Eagles, Blekbala); Clive Newman Literary Consultancy (Coral Hull); Penny Davis and Roger Ilott; Pat Drummond; Ted Egan; EMI Music Publishing Australia Pty Ltd (Slim Dusty, Stan Coster, Ted Egan); Emusic/Matthews Music Pty Ltd (John Williamson); ETT Imprint (Gwen Harwood); Festival Music Pty Ltd (Michael Gant, Grant Luhrs, Tiddas); Fremantle Arts Centre Press (Alex Choate); Hale and Iremonger (Mark O'Connor); HarperCollins Publishers Australia (David Campbell, Geoff Page, Douglas Stewart, Judith Wright); Institute for Aboriginal Development (Molly Kruger and Kenny Laughton); Jacaranda Wiley ('We are Going', 'The Past', 'Son Of Mine' and 'Integration—Yes!, by Oodgeroo of the Tribe Noonuccal formerly known as Kath Walker in *My People* third edition 1990, published by Jacaranda Press and reprinted by permission of John Wiley and Sons Australia); Larrikin Music Publishing (International Copyright Secured. All Rights reserved) (Eric Bogle, Kev Carmody); Jimmy Little; Margaret Connolly (Les Murray); Margaret Scott/Vivian Smith (James Charlton, Jamie Grant); Molonglo Press (Adrian Caesar); Mushroom Group of Companies (Yothu Yindi, Archie Roach, Paul Kelly, Broderick Smith); Music City Music/Rosella Music Pty Ltd (Ceddy McGrady); Music Sales Group of Companies (Norma O'Hara Murphy, Michael Fix, Barry Moyses); Rosemary Brissenden (R.F. Brissenden); Eileen Ryan; Sheil Land Associates Ltd (Randolph Stow); Rondor Music (Australia) Pty Ltd (Graeme Connors, Colin Buchanan, The Flying Emus, Neil Murray, John Kane/Jenny Kane); Shane Howard; Slim Dusty Enterprises Pty. Ltd; University of Queensland Press (Robert Adamson); Warner Chappel Music Australia Pty Ltd (Lee Kernaghan, Big Red, The Bushwackers); Viscopy Ltd (Mandy Martin); Errol West.

Every effort has been made to trace and acknowledge copyright. We invite copyright holders whom it has not been possible to locate to contact us.

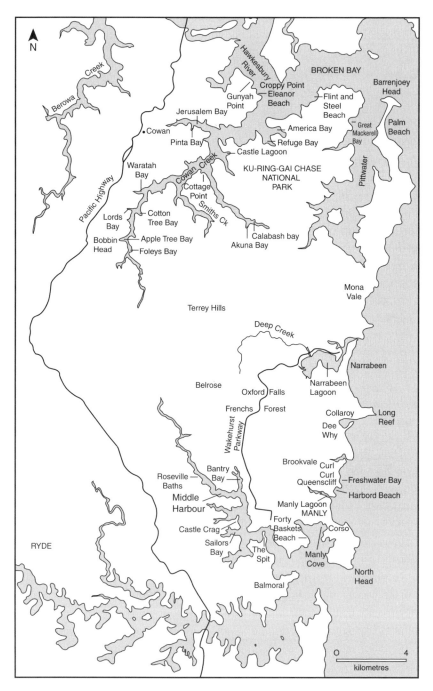

The Proper Country of Dennis Foley and Peter Read

INTRODUCTION

How can we non-Indigenous Australians justify our continuous presence and our love for this country while the Indigenous people remain dispossessed and their history unacknowledged?

My book *Returning to Nothing* explored the significance of places which we loved, and lost, and kept on loving. Savage were the emotions which we directed at the human destroyers of house, street or suburb, profound was the grief which we felt for sites gone forever.

Sometimes accompanying us on our journeys to nothing was the uninvited voice ever threatening to remind us that the land we loved was previously lost to others. We kept it at a distance. To invite conversation would have been to immobilise the mourning victims of lost place, then to paralyse the book itself. I wrote then:

> Some New Zealand farmers have argued before the Waitangi Tribunal that they, not the Maori claimants, are the true inheritors of the high country, for they have loved it and cherished it for 200 years. Australian farmers are beginning to advance their own sets of valued memories, attachments and histories over the same areas claimed by Aboriginal people. Having worked for many years with Aborigines deprived of their country, and more recently with non-Aborigines deprived of theirs, I am filled with anxiety at the complexity of such disputed attachments. They await a second study which will follow this book.[1]

Several reviewers of *Returning to Nothing* noted and welcomed my undertaking. They too seemed to feel that something unresolved, even illegitimate, clung about our attachments for as long as we ignored the skeleton at the feast. *Belonging* is the result. The problem which it confronts is this: those places which we loved, lost and grieved for were wrested from the Indigenous people who loved them, lost them and grieve for them still. Are such sites of all our deep affections to be contested, articulated, shared, forgone or possessed absolutely?

The usual starting point invites confusion and doubt. Let me demonstrate. We non-Indigenous cannot leave because we have nowhere to go and do not wish to go. Yes, but the Aboriginals have nowhere to go either. Yes, Aboriginals can return to the land which we have degraded. Yes, but firestick farming turned forests into grassland, surely that was environmental degradation? Yes, but Aboriginal land management was in harmony with nature. Yes, but Aboriginals have changed their nature and lost some of their skills; they too may degrade the land. Yes, but it's not the land we should be discussing but the nation. Yes, but the nation is composed of people of many ethnicities. Yes, but Aboriginals aren't like any other ethnic group, they were here first. Yes, but first doesn't matter: the equal ethnicities of multi-culturalism presuppose equality for all. Yes, but not all Australians are equally responsible for the dispossession. Yes, but the dispossession affected all Aboriginals. Yes, but the dispossession was aided by Aboriginal explorers, guides, stockmen and police. Yes, but today's police are filling the cells disproportionately with Aboriginal prisoners. Yes, but these prisoners are breaking not only our laws but Aboriginal law. Yes, but any Aboriginal arrested for assaulting police is a political prisoner. Yes, but our political masters refuse to use the word 'apology' to the stolen generations. Yes, but generations of self-identifying Aboriginals are also descended from the white settlers who killed their own ancestors. Yes, but not all of our ancestors killed Aboriginals: some protected them. Yes, but how relevant is the protection offered by such visitors who now refuse to leave the house of Australia? Yes, but every room in that house is not just occupied, it is shared. Yes, but the decision about who shares which room is made by the authority of the non-Indigenous alone. Yes, but the moral authority is held by the Aboriginals. Yes, but we conceded the frailty of our moral claim on the country last century, then forgot it. Yes, but selective forgetfulness can be a virtue in a modern homogenous state. Yes, but how can we forget when we do not yet know the whole truth? Yes, but surely there is no real truth, only partisans telling parallel narratives. Yes, but we do not allow the parallel narrative to be told. Yes, but theirs is a fundamentally different narrative of everlasting mythological and spiritual bonding with the land. Yes, but many non-Aboriginals also feel a spiritual bonding to the land. Yes, but the land isn't everything, we can bond with Australia independently of the land. Yes, but whatever the mechanism of bonding, equal citizenship implies equal responsibility for the past. Yes, but the past cannot be unmade. Yes, but while the past cannot be unmade it can be requited. Yes, but it is a bad principle of nationhood which acquits the dead by raising a levy against the living. Yes, but democratic living, which we accept, presupposes equal rights. Yes, but Indigenous rights, which we also accept, presuppose collective rights. Yes, but collective rights, which we also accept, may oppose individual rights. Yes, but Aboriginals are almost always prepared to sacrifice their individual rights for the good of the spiritual community. Yes, but many of us hold to some form or other of spirituality. Yes, but the modern rationalist state cannot privilege spiritual values over other values. Yes, but the old certitudes of rationalism are already moribund and should go back to Europe where they belong. Yes, but we cannot go back to Europe or anywhere else, we belong here and have nowhere else to go. Yes, but the Aboriginals have nowhere to go either. Full circle. What began as well-meaning confusion and doubt has led us to a painful intellectual and emotional impasse. It's clear that to advance our thinking we'll need to break from this constricting and self-defeating moral universe.

One way to begin is to reassess the self-denigration that portrays us as morally or spiritually deficient. In some cases we writers criticise ourselves more trenchantly than our Indigenous critics. The epigraph to the 1998 book *Seeking the Centre*, a study of the significance of the desert in Australian culture, asserts: 'At the heart of the book is the contrast between the European-driven notion of an empty, monotonous wilderness, and the profound spiritual relationship that Aboriginal Australians have with the desert.'[2]

The author writes: 'The poet Judith Wright has succinctly expressed the conceptual divide between European notions of a landscape derived from the perspective of an empowered observer, whose magisterial gaze calls an appropriately aesthetic prospect into being, and the Aboriginal understanding of a spirit-filled landscape through which individuals access their identity.'[3] The judgements are belied by the book itself, which presents many cultural affirmations of deserts by non-Indigenous Australians in terms anything but monotonous and empty. I ask myself, why do Aboriginals have relationships while we only have *notions*? Why do our notions *derive* while Aboriginals simply *understand*? I doubt if the magisterial gaze of European Australians any longer calls an 'appropriately aesthetic prospect into being'. Previous generations of anthropologists like Stanner, Elkin, and Ron and Catherine Berndt, who well understood Aboriginal civilisation, did not find it necessary to elevate its majesty through denigrating their own culture. David Tacey writes of the 'spiritually barren ... middle classes of white suburbia'.[4] I do not know anyone to whom I would apply that epithet. The whole of *Returning to Nothing* challenged Robert Dessaix's unlikely assertion that we Australians have no hearth to tell our stories around.[5] The art critic and painter Robert Levitus described his experiences trying to paint the landscape near Nimbin, NSW, as 'simply overwhelming'. He realised, he wrote, that he would never fit, and that probably no-one from a non-Aboriginal background ever does. White Australians did not have the benefit of many centuries of living in one place; but a relationship nevertheless existed, he continued, based on the diverse experiences of travel and exile. It was a transitory relationship to place and the landscape which did 'not allow for a deepening understanding of it or a symbiotic relationship with it, but which is coupled with a yearning to belong'.[6]

Why should it take hundreds of years to develop a relationship with landscape sufficiently to paint it well? Imagine such an assertion in the context that Australia actually was unoccupied in 1778 so that there was nobody to whom we could now compare ourselves. Surely then we would acknowledge spiritual diversity in the desert, a permanent home at the hearth, emotional strength in the suburbs, conviction and passion at the easel. The problem begins to emerge as one of self-perception, of whether, as non-Indigenous, one *should* paint landscape well.

It has not always been so. Bernard Smith observed that, a hundred years ago, 'To paint Australia you had to be Australian ... Unless you were born with "Australian" eyes you could not hope to "see" the Australian landscape.'[7] In the last quarter-century many of us have substituted 'Aboriginal' for (Anglo-Celtic) Australian. Confrontation with the role of the British in the dispossession brought not only a long overdue restraint and reflection to our national history, but to many of us, including myself, self-doubt and potential paralysis. Some of us took on the burden of guilt so earnestly that we half believed ourselves unworthy even to be here.

A second starting-point will be to allow that emotions and intuitions are part of deep belonging. Veronica Brady asks why the rationalists, distrusting the notion of sacredness and suspecting the metaphysical, fail to move 'across the boundary'. Some Australians seem trapped within what is left of the wholly rationalist mind-set, which is unable to cope with difference and, in relation to Aboriginal spiritualism, assimilationist. Our culture seems unable to deal with the Aboriginal 'other'.[8] Brady's own sense of belonging derives from many sources: from literature, awe, fear and fascination, respect for spirituality: listening rather than speaking, sharing rather than competing, the self flowing into and part of the whole, a sadness at the violation of what we first encountered.[9]

No, the reader might exclaim, stop talking on my behalf. I do not suffer any of your paralysing debilities. I love Australia, I embrace a spiritual dimension to my life! Just so. Everyone I have quoted so far, so far as I know, is like me: university-educated, urban, middle-class and Anglo-Celtic. Perhaps it is only this group which feels itself to be trapped. May it be that other Australians, older or younger, of other ethnicities, education, interests, culture, history and experience may not perceive the problem as they do? They may have different responses. They may not apprehend what I am presenting to be a problem at all.

I propose, then, to abandon the safe boundaries of reasoned self-doubt. To try to escape the ideological impasse I plan to encounter with book, map, camera, tape-recorder or CD player, Australians of every variety: young Australians, Asian Australians, foreign-born Australians, rich Australians, seventh-generation Australians, rural Australians, just-arrived Australians, poets, artists, country and western musicians, atheists, metaphysicians, spiritualists, those who have worked closely with Aboriginals, those whose land is under Indigenous claim, those who have yet to meet an Indigenous person face to face. What conceptions of belonging will they bring to this divided land, how will they place themselves in relation to the Indigenous past and present? I do not know what people I will meet or what arguments they will advance. In truth, I have no idea how this book will end. I confess to being a little apprehensive.

CHAPTER 1

DEEP IN THE SANDSTONE GORGES

The deep sandstone country just north of Sydney has inspired much creative art. Margaret Preston painted it; Douglas Stewart, Robert Adamson and David Campbell wrote poetry about it; Axel Poignant photographed it. The Ku-ring-gai Aboriginals carved rocks, danced corroborees and sang songs of creation and renewal. Cowan Creek and the lower Hawkesbury River have been compared to the Norwegian fjords because, like them, the bays and inlets are formed from drowned river valleys. The plunging gullies look like flowing watercourses, but they are not, the water is salt. The weathered sandstone cliffs tower hundreds of feet above the green-black water.

I made my first visit to Cowan Creek more than forty years ago at the age of nine or ten and have been coming back ever since. The local fisherfolk know every eddy, deep pool and outcrop by local names, but I know only the sites on the printed maps: Apple Tree Bay, Lords Bay, Smiths Creek, Coal and Candle Creek, Jerusalem Bay, Cottage Point, Church Point, Croppy Point, Foleys Bay. The origin of most of the names is obvious, but some remain mysterious: Croppy Point, Gunyah Point, Calabash Bay. Croppy is an old Aboriginal word for convict. A gunyah is an Aboriginal bark shelter. A calabash is the African equivalent of coolamon, the Aboriginal bark or wood cradle.

The tradition of an annual visit to this place of my childhood continues. Once a year I set out with a group of nine friends for two or three days. We embark at Bobbin Head in an ancient wooden cruiser hired from the grumpy staff whose company has held the franchise for generations. Usually we leave on a Friday afternoon at about 4.30, my friend Margot at the helm. We negotiate a passage through the moored cruisers, and head out past the people fishing on the rocks to Apple Tree Bay. Twenty minutes later Lords Bay is to starboard, Cotton Tree Bay to port. In mid-autumn the declining sun holds half the eastern sandstone cliffs in gold, the trunks of the angophoras are yellow-brown, and in the lower deep shade the darkening water slaps at the boulders and buoys. The crew congregate in twos and threes at different points on the boat to absorb the cooling afternoon. Spirits lift. These first thirty minutes after setting out is the most intense part of the most physically intense part of my year. Old-timers say that once the waters of Cowan Creek used to be cleaner and quieter, the fish enormous. What's it matter? Belonging to loved country is now, not then. It was quieter and cleaner still before the British invasion of Australia.

Cowan Creek is a place of my deep memory and experience. Castle Lagoon, where Jay and I spent the first night of our honeymoon; Eleanor Beach, known to us as Bridie's Birthday Beach (it was her tenth); Bobbin Head, where I just caught hold of my other daughter Jess as she slipped noiselessly overboard; Pinta Bay, where I celebrated a rowdy fiftieth birthday; the Coal and Candle Creek marina, where a sheet blew irretrievably from a makeshift clothesline; Calabash Bay, where the carelessly anchored cruiser rose on the tide and drifted away with Jess and her friend Chantal still aboard; Dangar Island, known to my family as Danger Island after a hair-raising adventure with a strong current; Jerusalem Bay, where such a boisterous gale got up one night that it blew the pillow from under the head of Margot's daughter Anna, sleeping on the deck. Sounds: I can still hear my mother's squeak of delight when she woke one morning in Castle Lagoon to see the bush swinging past our windy anchorage; Julia reading the poetry of her native New Zealand; the roar of the engine moments before a breath-taking dawn; the excited shouts as Con reeled in a huge hairtail at Smiths Creek; sounding a futile SOS on the horn as we drifted motor-less down the Hawkesbury into the gathering dusk; Ken's bagpipe rendition of 'Dark Island' to toots at first appreciative from far-away cruisers; Jane's songs from the north of England; the general execrations at an unnamed but often discussed place in Pittwater where a flounder (the only one we've ever caught before or since) slipped between the fingers of its scaler, then between the struts of the board-ing platform and vanished; late-night conversations with Trish on the roof of the cabin staring into a black and starry sky; the crash at Mackerel Beach when the drying rack hit the floor, breaking half the ship's crockery after the passage of a disobliging power-boat. Activities: night rowing in the magical phosphorescent waters; marooned on sandbanks; storms that woke the kids and set them crying for hours; half a metre of mast knocked off the sailing dinghy we were towing under the wrong arch of the Hawkesbury road bridge; a catfish bite for which the only known palliative appeared to be long swigs of rum; Julia's son Tom refusing to let his lunch interfere with the passage of a school of bream; Pat untangling a thousand childish fishing lines; hats pitched overboard by gusts; sundry emergency repairs to the ailing diesel systems; gliding to an evening anchorage at America Bay; Charlie Perkins, who had come out for the day, finding an Aboriginal stone fishing trap at Yeoman's Bay. My memory map of the area would take a day to draw.

Over many years I've explored the historic sites along and above the water. Windybanks boatshed, the remains of a paddle steamer at Waratah Bay, the walking track up to Cowan railway station. The waterway was much more heavily used last century; the remains of wharves, picnic kiosks and boatsheds are quite common. For those who know what to look for, evidence of the Aboriginal past also is everywhere.

The most common sites are shell middens, some 50 metres long; smaller ones occur every half a kilometre. I've found traces of substantial Aboriginal camps in overhangs and caves at the heads of little creeks, 50 metres above high tide. Often you'll find traces of smoky fires underneath the rock shelters, though the one behind the waterfall at Refuge Bay has been almost destroyed by the scrambling feet of three or four generations of visitors. The nineteenth-century enthnographers made much of the numerous sandstone carvings, but the absence of regular burning for more than a century has obscured most of them. In 1995 Anna, Jay and I, following a vanished track on an old map, went on a toilsome but futile search for one supposedly at the head of Castle Lagoon. I still don't know whether the site has been overgrown or if its whereabouts is now lost and forgotten. Precise information past the guidebook generalities is hard to obtain.

Knowledge about the post-invasion Aboriginal past seems to have disappeared recently but suddenly. As a lad in the 1950s I once set out from Bobbin Head with a friend of my father who pointed out to me what he called an Aboriginal corroboree ground, possibly a bora ring. I still have the black and white photo that I took with my Brownie Box, on which I wrote, in spidery red biro, 'Abos corobory place'. What fascinates me now are the questions—where exactly was that site? How did my father's friend know what and where it was? How did that information last until the mid-1950s, and then disappear so suddenly? No ranger or anyone else I have ever asked is able to help.

One sunny Saturday morning, the night after Con caught the hairtail, I left the others and walked up the steep slope from Cotton Tree Bay. Soon the angophoras gave way to grasstrees and dry sclerophyll scrub. I scrambled about a kilometre up the steep slope and there, half an hour after leaving the boat, in a silent and deserted clearing which looked as though it hadn't been visited for a century, I made a discovery that haunts me yet. Under a ledge of rock less than a metre high was a little pile of clam shells. By their remote position, the low shelf, and the finely discernible layer of dust in this serene and silent site, they were clearly Aboriginal, maybe 150 years old. The rocky ledge and its silent contents gave me a shiver of excitement that I still carry. In type it was not different from hundreds along the water line, but much smaller, the work of a single individual, more remote and isolated. I know of no others so intimate or so far above the water.

My discovery revived in me all the problems of wanting to belong in this breathtaking country of deepest personal and family memory. The hushed shell-pile reminds me that Cowan Creek is deep Aboriginal country also. I ask myself: Do I have the right to belong in this soul-country? Do Aboriginals belong in some deeper way than the rest of us, even though none as yet lays a Native Title claim to it? Would such a pre-emptive claim of belonging—if that is what a Native Title claim is—reduce or disqualify my own sense? If so, must it always? Considering those questions, and how non-Aboriginal Australians are grappling with them, is the subject of this book.

The mighty gorges and the dancing past whispered to the poet Douglas Stewart as insistently as they do to me. Close to midnight in the 1950s, fishing near a dark slope on one of those hushed and luminous nights, Stewart began to reflect upon a rock carving near his boat, and upon the artist who, like all artists, he supposed, spoke to future as well as present:

The moon lights a thousand candles upon the water,
But none for the carver of stone; and nobody comes
Of his own long-scattered tribe to remember him.
But he walks again for me at the water's rim …
And whoever laughs is a little afraid in the end,
For here is a swimmer in stone, and a 'roo that leaps
Nowhere for ever, and both can be touched with the hand, …
Centuries dead perhaps. But night and the water
And a 'roo and a fish on a rock have brought us together,
Fishermen both, and carvers both, old man …
Maybe it's all for nothing, for the sky to look at,
Or maybe for us the distant candles dance. …
The boat tugs at the kellick as it feels the ebb.
Good-bye, old wraith, and good luck. You did what you could
To leave your mark on stone like a mark on time,
That the sky in the mind and the midnight sea in the blood
Should be less of a desolation for the men to come;
And who can do more than you? Gone, you are gone;
But, dark a moment in the moonlight, your hand hovers
And moves like the shadow of a bird across the stone.[1]

A majestic invocation; yet the implications are worrying. Stewart, untouched by the post-colonial uncertainties that have afflicted many of us non-Indigenous Australians in the last quarter-century, created his art for the sake of art. His home was not *unheimlich*, that post-colonial condition which seems to render our own place unfamiliar and strange, alien and inaccessible.[2] He wrote in the comfortable assumption of the 1950s by which Aboriginal people—here the Ku-ring-gai—had simply gone away. The 'midnight sea in the blood', the dark, restless human spirit, was not fixed to this moonlit carving, not this quiet waterway, but to the world, not Aboriginal, nor yet Australian: but universal. An over-arching sensibility united poet and artist more strongly than the rather obvious—to us—discontinuity which divided them. My reaction is— *the Ku-ring-gai people just didn't happen to go away by themselves*. If the country was empty of Indigenous people a century after Governor Phillip's exploring party rowed up the Hawkesbury, surely they had been driven from their country by disease, hunger and despair. Maybe the absence of Aboriginal people in the Ku-ring-gai Chase national park didn't occur to Stewart at all.

We confront again that obsessive post-colonial nexus, the *fin-de-siècle* angst, which divides some of us contemporary Australians from previous generations. Our problem is this: is the midnight sea flowing in the blood of all human creatures a lambent poetic insight, or an arrogant ethnocentrism? Or is it both? Why did none of our reservations occur to Stewart and why do they so assail us now?

A second poet, David Campbell, learnt from Stewart a love of the spiky sclerophyll and inky-green waters of the sandstone gorges. In the 1960s he conceded that the Ku-ring-gai Aboriginals may not simply have wandered away:

> And if I thieved your [Stewart's] knowledge and your skill
> To find my voice again
> And walk these stunted hills with murdered men,
> Accept a live man's thanks, a friend's good will.[3]

Murdered? I doubt if more than a few of the Ku-ring-gai were. But it's not easy to be sure what did happen to them beyond smallpox and pneumonia. Historians of the first Aboriginal school at Blacktown have concluded that the Cadigal people, who spoke a language called 'Kuringgai', were the same people of Broken Bay. Although Berowra Creek evidently formed a linguistic division between the coastal peoples and the Cumberland Plains tribes to the west, it is certainly possible that some Ku-ring-gai-speaking children followed, or were taken, up the Hawkesbury–Nepean river to become inmates of the Native School at Parramatta in the 1810s and 1820s. Two of the nineteen children resident between 1814 and 1820 were said to be from the 'Hawkesbury Tribe'.[4] By the 1870s there was also an Aboriginal camp at Manly, a Sydney suburb. Does anyone now remember where it stood? Evidently the northern Sydney peoples could understand each other, which makes me wonder if some of the remnants who gathered miserably at the Manly camp in the 1880s, or their parents, had spent their youth at Cowan Creek.[5] From working in Link-Up, the Aboriginal organisation which reunites the stolen generations, I know that there were Aboriginal children still being taken from their families at Pitt Town, on the Hawkesbury, in the 1920s.

The Mitchell Library contains a photograph acquired in 1920 whose caption reads 'An Aborigine of the Hawkesbury River with his garden'. There he stands, probably in early middle age, tall and strong, in an old suit and hat amidst his maize crop and holding what looks like a bamboo pole; the height of his garden above the water level suggests the lower reaches of the waterway, maybe only 10 kilometres from my little pile of clam shells. So perhaps the Ku-ring-gai speakers survived in their country for a century. Why then did they vanish so rapidly?

Working with Northern Territory Aboriginals suggests to me that traditional people who bodily left their country never thought of leaving it forever, and continued to think of their 'proper country' as always theirs. Contemporary Aboriginals who cannot or do not return to the lands for which they have responsibility 'worry for country'; they mourn not only their absence, but their inability to carry out 'cleaning' (especially regular burning) and the rituals of renewal. Those Ku-ring-gai men and women worried for their country too. In fact there may not have been much overt pressure for them to leave their land before the 1880s so long as they kept out of the way. If they went hungry it was not because they weren't allowed to wander in the hills, which the fisher-folk and yacht crews avoid to this day; more likely the Sydneysiders refused to allow the Ku-ring-gai to come near favoured fishing spots. Or the white men started mining the shell middens for lime and chopping out the blue gums and turpentines. One or two Aboriginals probably worked on the fishing and timber boats in the 1840s and 1850s. I can imagine their families living for a generation or two, sometimes out of sight along the back creeks, sometimes appearing at dawn at isolated cottages to ask for flour or tobacco. When to the local Whites it seemed they had 'just vanished', it was because the Ku-ring-gai were dying out of sight of smallpox or pneumonia, or living at the now forgotten camp at Manly, or on their own gardens up the river; and when they 'disappeared' it was because they had been compulsorily shifted somewhere else. Some stayed along the upper reaches of the Hawkesbury. Still worrying for their country, the old people always planned to go back, but mostly they never did. Their allegiances and fading memories became merged with other Aboriginal and non-Aboriginal identities and regions. Today their descendants think of themselves as Dharuk or Eora or Tharawal. Their link to the Cowan Creek—so far as I am aware—is severed.

Such was my thinking in November 1996. Meeting a Gai-mariagal man from country adjacent to Ku-ring-gai some months later chastened my thinking and revolutionised this book.

What then, is the problem? What's my problem? With evidently no direct descendants of the coastal people, no current claimants on the Ku-ring-gai Chase National Park, no one to tell me that the land is not mine to belong to—why can't I, and all of us, just say and feel that part of our sense of belonging and identity is bound in Cowan Creek?

Consider the opinions of some of our own elders. I once interviewed Nugget Coombs on why he supported a treaty between Aboriginal and non-Aboriginal Australians. He cited the more obvious reasons of dispossession and injustice, but then he added a third:

> We've become accustomed to think of our occupancy of the land as legal, justified and secure. I think, again, each of those assumptions can be brought into doubt. And therefore I think we have to consider that the kind of security we feel in the occupation of the land at the present time may very well be called into question, certainly by Aborigines, perhaps by White people here, but also by nations overseas. ... And therefore if we wish to feel secure, and for our children and grandchildren to feel secure, then I think we have to establish the justification, the legitimacy of our occupation. And that means the legitimacy of our relationship with the original inhabitants, the Aborigines.[6]

Manning Clark remarked to his students at Yale University:

> Sometimes when I stand in the Australian bush on a clear windless day I am visited with strange thoughts ... I wonder whether I belong ... I am ready, and so are others, to understand the Aboriginal view that no human being can ever know heart's ease in a foreign land, because in a foreign land there live foreign ancestral spirits. We white people are condemned to live in a country where we have no ancestral spirits. The conqueror has become the eternal outsider, the eternal alien. We must either become assimilated or live the empty life of a people exiled from their spiritual strength.[7]

The historian Cassandra Pybus grew up at Oyster Cove in Tasmania, once an Aboriginal Station, now administered by the Tasmanian

Aboriginal Land Council. In her book *Community of Thieves* she tried to disentangle her own sense of belonging from that of the Palawa, the Tasmanian Aboriginals:

> It seems to me that the stories contained in the landscape I love so inordinately are critical to my self definition; to my pride in being Australian and a fifth generation of white immigrants born into this benign and lovely place. We are shaped by the past … and we need to know about it. We need to know how it is that we white Australians call this country home.[8]

Judith Wright is a poet who has agonised long over the Aboriginal dispossession, not least because her ancestors were actively involved. Perhaps she now feels embarrassed at the intensity of her own sense of belonging in the New England tableland, even though thousands of Australians like me have learned to love her verse, and through it, her blood's country:

> South of my day's circle, part of my blood's country,
> rises that tableland, high delicate outline
> of bony slopes wincing under the winter.[9]

Later in her life Judith Wright wondered at the cost: the country so despoiled by overgrazing that neither her own ancestors nor the Wadja people whom they dispossessed would now recognise it.[10] In 1981 she wrapped the meditation more closely about herself:

> These two strands—the love of the land we have invaded, and the guilt of the invasion—have become part of me. It is a haunted country … It was not 'wilderness' to the people who lived by it and through it, but the source of their very life and spirit; and to those of them who somehow survived our invasion, it remains so. And for us, too, it can be a place where we find some kind of rest, joy, and even forgiveness.[11]

Difficult issues flow from this apprehension—or, as the unsympathetic might describe it, this maudlin breast-beating. Surely the issue is not at all important to Aboriginal people themselves, whose serious contemporary problems do not include the sons and daughters of the invaders agonising that they don't belong. Is it possible, asks the political scientist Anthony Moran, to respect and honour difference without seeking to rush to incorporate it in order to benefit ourselves? Incorporation, he reminds us, is a kind of devouring, and envy is destructive.[12] The Jungian intellectual David Tacey notes succinctly that 'we have not only stolen Aboriginal land, destroyed the tribal culture, raped the women and the environment but we now ask for their spirituality as well'.[13] Timely observations, but not exactly germane to me or to the many Australians finding ourselves listening to the silences. I'm not envious, nor do I wish to incorporate myself spiritually into Aboriginality. I want to feel I belong here while respecting Aboriginality, neither appropriating it nor being absorbed by it. There may be millions to whom the issue is simply irrelevant to their lives. Non-Anglo-Celtic Australians, migrants or children of migrants, may well feel neither guilt nor responsibility, but dwell here in the belief that no racial or ethnic group has or should have a prior claim to the land. This young Vietnamese poet felt nothing but gratitude for the achievements of past British Australians:

> Saturday morning I went to the poll
> could not make up my mind who to vote for
> and the [candidate] voted for will be happy
> and the not voted for will be upset …
> The night came
> the winner had a big smile
> and the loser left the country power
> somewhere on the stage
> sported as big a smile
> waved to the nation and exited
> I just love Australian politics …[14]

Les Murray has argued that migrants never seem to be implicated as the agents of anything harmful; if some of the invaders are complicit, then all are.[15] It's possible that Italians or Greeks working around Manly in the 1920s may indeed have known about that lost Aboriginal camp. Giuseppe, the father of the artist Salvatore Zofrea, worked in the Brookvale market gardens, then a shanty town colonised by scores of single Italian men; later he worked at the Frenchs Forest brickworks. The poor and lonely Giuseppe, like the other Brookvale men of the 1920s, endured 'unspeakable trials' in what seemed a barbaric country poorer than the one they had left; they perched on the banks of the North Manly Lagoon in 'makeshift dwellings between a saltwater swamp and a forest swarming with giant mosquitoes', whose eucalypt forests sheltered 'strange animals and madmen with matted hair hanging over their eyes'.[16]

Within a year I will have cause to remember these madmen.

Typical of the generosity of spirit of the Indigenous people, many Aboriginals have pondered if, when and how the British and non-British newcomers have attached themselves to the land. They never confer belonging lightly: there is always a price. Mick Dodson, formerly of the Human Rights and Equal Opportunity Commission: 'I don't think they're excluded but I do think they've got to grow up and be part of the spirituality that's based on the law of the land. You just don't extend that to people unless they've demonstrated their maturity for it.'[17]

Noel Pearson asked why, if neither Aboriginals nor most non-Aboriginals wanted guilt, 'has it been alleged that Australians have been urged by the black armbands, through a delirium of political correctness', to feel guilty about the past: surely it was enough that present-day Australians should be responsible for present-day infidelities. Our collective consciousness should include all the past; if Gallipoli is 'ours', so should be the relations with Indigenous people.[18] The theologian Dr Ann Pattel-Gray wrote: 'Our spirituality begins from the day we are born. Let us share with you some different aspects of our spirituality and how they are engrained in our Aboriginal way of being in relationship with God.'[19]

The Aboriginal Reconciliation Council, pursuing Manning Clark's anxiety, urged non-Aboriginal Australians to share the country's history as well as its land because any immigrant people will, for a time, experience a degree of historical discomfort in a 'strange' and 'new' land. One way of coming to terms with an adopted country is to view the land through the eyes of the Indigenous owners.[20]

Owners? There's a sticking point. Like Stewart, many Australians have assumed that the trust of ownership had passed from Black to White, or at the least, from Aboriginal to shared. While intellectually we may acknowledge dispossession, emotionally the land is ours and our love for it seals the union. In *The Little Company* Eleanor Dark depicts

Gilbert Massey in 1942 standing in the bed of a droughty creek, absorbing the heat through his boots, listening to the curious dead silence, the 'patient enduring stillness of the bush'. Threatened by the danger of Japanese invasion, he ponders how the bush has 'captured the imaginations and the love of its step-children'—the Whites—and imagines it owned and loved by the enemy. Maybe they would treat it better than his own people had done. Then he rejects the intellect: 'His mind could tell him that the aborigines were the real Australians, just as the Red Indians were the real Americans; his conviction still said: No, The country is here inside my body, and its air is the breath out of my lungs.'[21]

Gilbert Massey's received intuition following upon reasoned doubt to me is longer tenable. Having worked closely with Aboriginal people for more than twenty years and having recorded maybe 1500 interviews, I'm weighed down by my knowledge of a truly terrible past. And yet, while I once was shouting slogans at an Aboriginal rally, someone took out an Australian flag and burnt it. I was so distressed I had to leave the rally. *We always knew that the dismantling of the colonial paradigm would release strange demons from the deep.*[22] I don't believe that we will never belong, nor necessarily that we don't now. But we are required to undertake some very hard thinking, talking and learning.

I'm not yet using the word 'sacred', though I am at one with David Tacey and Veronica Brady in not rejecting the non-rational. Tacey wants us to strip away our self-doubt and sense of personal inadequacy, but I can't accept his suggestion that the British invasion can be seen 'in a larger sense as the intrusion of a progressive spirit that had to arrive in the Aboriginal psyche in one form or another'. I'm no Jungian. I do not want to sacrifice to my own inner depths, to the nature within myself.[23]

Much of the recent literature of belonging concerns the need for non-Aboriginals respectfully to avail themselves of Aboriginal traditions. Eugene Stockton, a Catholic priest, sees non-Aboriginal Australians as the living tips of a tree. Each newcomer is grafted on to the trunk 'growing in the soil of this land'. If we are willing to be grafted on to their spirit, 'Then we can read our story as the fuller history of human presence on this continent. We have been here 50,000 years or more … Over that immense span of time we have grown spiritually attuned to this land. … The sacred story of the first comer becomes the sacred story of the latecomer.'[24] The earth becomes the holy land for both. But grafting ourselves into the tree without a knowledge of the ancient or recent growth may sit us beside Douglas Stewart in his fishing boat in the Ku-ring-gai Chase National Park. Sidney Nolan, of that same generation, visited Lake Mungo: *I had the feeling it was right that we came here. You see, I feel I belong here, and while I'm here I'm happy.*[25] Was Nolan prepared to share Lake Mungo with Aboriginals? Too many Australians, wrote the archaeologist Isabel McBryde, think of Lake Mungo as belonging to Aboriginals of past millennia rather than to today's.[26] Assertion is not belonging; that's possession, without knowledge. Miriam Rose Ungunmerr of the Daly River region of the Northern Territory believes that what Australians need is 'inner, deep listening and quiet, still awareness'.[27] My 'quiet still awareness' includes outrage at the death of the Sydney Koori David Gundy, shot by mistake while he lay in bed in a bungled police raid in Redfern in 1988. The Royal Commission into his death found that the police raid was unlawful, that instructions and legal requirements were ignored, and that some search warrants had been illegally obtained and executed.[28]

The Reconciliation Council takes the opposite position from Miriam Rose Ungunmerr in arguing that we need to *understand* the past: that 'unless positive steps are taken to come to terms with these scars, the burden of the past will continue to weigh heavily on both Indigenous and non-Indigenous Australians for many years to come'.[29] At La Perouse, Sydney, where many Aboriginals still live near the former reserve, the historical and contemporary confrontations are much more obvious. The histories do not meet at La Perouse, they clash.[30] The Wurundjeri Aboriginals of Melbourne have established parallel histories beside the British-Australian monuments throughout the city, those 'places where historical events of importance to both Aboriginal and European people occurred' and 'intended for those who want to share in Aboriginal heritage by visiting reminders of their past so that we can build a future together based on respect and understanding'.[31] Yet the story of the dispossession of the Ku-ring-gai speakers is almost unknown.

Veronica Brady has written:

> It seems to me, then, that being a non-Aboriginal Australian means being somehow cut off from where we belong. We no longer belong in

the place from which our ancestors came to this land, but we do not quite belong here either because the events of the last two hundred years have created a gap between us and the people of the land who lived so intimately with it and still holds its secrets. Partly this gap comes from the rivers of blood and tears which have flowed between us, but partly, too, it comes from our loss of the sense of the sacred which is of the essence of Aboriginal cultures and of their relations with the land.[32]

The rivers of blood and tears. That's what has been omitted by so many seeking to belong beside or through the Aboriginals. We must understand what happened before we argue through our responsibility. And yet I have to ask myself what my knowledge of Aboriginal history actually has brought to my own sense of belonging. So many massacres, so many homes destroyed, so many children stolen, so many daily insults to the Indigenous people that I sometimes feel overwhelmed by the sadness of our history. If anything my sense of moral belonging has been weakened by so many years of painful interview and conversation. Nor is it a matter of historical knowledge alone. The geographer Richard Baker feels the lack of traditional knowledge of country:

> I've got perhaps ten per cent of the feel; so it does give you more of a respect, but it's an unknown book that you don't know how to read. Intellectually and emotionally I know the [Borroloola] area quite well, and I know how rich the stories are of that place. The extraordinary thing is to think of all of Australia being like that. And that's the extraordinary indictment on western people in Australia that maybe forty per cent of Australia's left with stories intact. … It gives you an emptiness driving to Sydney down that freeway—even the European history has been obliterated. No one now knows what the full level of those meanings were.[33]

Other Australians by reading and listening have now come to share that anguish carried by those scholars lucky enough, like Richard Baker, to work closely with a single group of Aboriginal people over a long period. The Wik decision, in Noel Pearson's words, threw the country into the social, political and psychological turmoil it always had to have.[34] Legally and emotionally what had been ours might now have to be shared, or even given back. Neither possession nor dispossession are any longer realisable categories; authority is arbitrary, the binary dissolves, and all of us are in place and out of place simultaneously.[35]

To whom can we look for advice? African-born intellectuals like Doris Lessing and Nadine Gordimer have wrestled with a sense of belonging in their own rapidly changing countries. Gordimer reasoned that people like herself in de-colonising Africa wanted to be members of a multi-coloured, any-coloured society, freed from both the privileges and the guilt of the white sins of their fathers. Her difficulty was that belonging implied wanting to be accepted several generations before Africans would accept them. She and those like her would have to learn to be immigrants in the country of their birth. *I speak for people like myself, who think almost too much about the whole business and hope to arrive at an honest answer, without self-pity for the whites or sentiment about the blacks.*[36] We can recognise some common threads, especially concern about ancestral sins and privileges; but the differences are too great. Aboriginals are a tiny minority; too much has happened here since 1950 for anyone born here to have to learn to be a migrant.

Gordimer wondered if she and her friends thought too much about the whole business of belonging. Perhaps I do too, but it's no bad thing. The secure identity I had, say, as a twenty-year-old youth was built on very unsure foundations. The Read side of my family only arrived here in the 1870s; my great-grandfather must have spoken English with a London accent. My grandfather, born in Sydney, did not, so it seemed to young Peter of the 1950s that the Reads had been here not just four generations, but for ever. Migrant families arriving more recently, especially if their origins are Celtic or Jewish, may divide their loyalties more sharply. Many thousands of Australians have returned to the birth countries of their ancestors to find spiritual renewal or forgotten ruins. One hundred and thirty years after my family's exodus from England I have nothing and nobody to return to.

The White New Zealander Michael King wrote *Being Pakeha*, a rather sad book about his experiences in writing and making films about Maori history. (I wish we had a word like 'Pakeha' for Australians who call this country home but who are not Aboriginal.) The mid-1980s' renaissance in Maori pride and culture not only impelled the Pakeha to examine their own consciences but the Maori people to demand that no-one should write their history but themselves. Though King was forced to cease his activities, his years had not been wasted. Working amongst the Maori, King's Celtic ancestry allowed him the more readily to absorb the deep values of which his English education had kept him in ignorance:

> a feeling of connection between living and dead; the sense of spirituality which recognises that people and places are more than mere physical presences; the conviction that the consequences of behaviour remain somehow embedded in the ethos of places, just as they do in the lives of people; a belief in the power of psychic communication in those who are open to such faculties; a need for ritual and tradition; emotional honesty; the fierce warmth of friendship and a lack of physical inhibition in the physical expression of it; an equal lack of inhibition in the expression of anger and grief.[37]

I have no Celtic ancestry to draw me towards such liberating theologies; what I possess I have learned mostly from mixing and working with many hundreds of Aboriginal people for half a lifetime. I belong but I do not belong; I seek a solemn union with my country and my land but not through Aboriginality; I understand our history but it brings me no relief.

This unsatisfactory dialectic was as far as I could take my dilemma at the time I met Dennis Foley, an academic at the University of Queensland's Aboriginal and Torres Strait Islander Studies unit. In early 1998 Jackie Huggins, the Murri (Queensland Aboriginal) historian and I had been carrying out some interviews with young Indigenous people for the Oral History unit of the National Library. At lunch we strolled across from the unit to the staff centre where Dennis joined us for lunch. The next hour jolted my thinking, and this book, to a new dimension.[38]

Dennis began by telling me that he was a Sydney Koori, a Gai-mariagal, who are part of the Eora people. Eora country runs from Botany Bay north to the Hawkesbury River, bounded in the west by Toongabbie Creek and the shale ridge beyond Parramatta. Dennis's proper country is this northern section: the Parramatta River at Ryde, the Lane Cove River, Middle Harbour, the northern beaches of Manly, Freshwater, Curl Curl, Dee Why and Narrabeen. His most intimate country is southern Gai-mariagal country, at Manly. The Gai-mariagal identified not by country and kin structure alone. When he was born in 1953 at the Royal North Shore hospital in the heart of suburban Sydney, Dennis's grandmother obtained the placenta, burnt it and spread the ashes in the trees nearby. On listening to his description my heart quickened. I spent most of my school holidays at these northern beaches. Dennis's dreaming country was also my country of association and memory.

The hairs on the back of my neck rose as Dennis began unfolding his living Gai-mariagal culture on site after site of my own childhood. The Lane Cove River, two kilometres from where I grew up: the rocks underneath the concrete weir marked the ancient divide between salt and fresh water, dark and light, danger and safety, the serpent from the serpent-free. I'd had dozens of picnics by the weir, always swimming on the high side. 'You know the big white housing tower on the left of the ferry as you leave Manly for Sydney Cove? Well, just beyond the gasworks were the gunyahs of Nanna Watson and other members of our extended family, all removed during the 1950s because the council thought the tower tenants would be offended by the view.' So that's where that Manly camp was! I've explored that area looking for signs, of all things, of the gasworks. The rocky ledges behind the Manly art gallery where Dennis's mother and grandmother took Aboriginal people to talk out of sight of the welfare and the police: I'd been there on picnics by tram or ferry with my own grandmother in the 1950s. The Corso, scene of a hundred cappuccinos: that was once a sandy spit sometimes covered by the ocean. Forty Baskets Beach to the east of the Manly pier: often I've looked at the walk marked on the map and stared at it from the ferry. That beach and the gasworks site, Dennis said, were the summer camps of his family. He remembers helping older men hunt for taylor there with bamboo fishing spears. In winter the old people—there were usually very few children—walked three or four kilometres up to the Manly Lagoon beside what is now the Queenscliff golf course. I've often stayed just up the road and driven past it often. Round the spit and up Middle Harbour for a few kilometres is Roseville Baths: a no-go area, a dangerous men's place. I'd swum there, stung by jellyfish, dozens of time in the 1950s, usually taken by the dad of my next-door neighbour of my own age. Dennis's mother lived at Freshwater, the next beach north after Manly, a women's place: Mum used to take us kids every second day in the summer holidays. I don't remember ever going there with my dad. Every suburb which Dennis described was intimately familiar to me. He was taken by his older male relatives to a stone bora ring at Frenchs Forest. He was told of stone dwellings at Brookvale, destroyed by the British after the smallpox plague in the 1790s.

Despite their ancestry, their stories and their growing up, Gai-mariagal people are not accepted in their own country. They have had no land returned to them, either under the New South Wales Aboriginal Land Rights Act or under the Native Title Act. Their claims have been largely ignored by the non-Indigenous and challenged by other Sydney Aboriginals.

Up the coast at Narrabeen, on Deep Creek, was the third of the 1950s Gai-mariagal camps. Dennis went there several times, only once to stay the night. The old people gave him a loving welcome, for no children lived there: 1950s child welfare officers were horrific. *They just came in and tore us apart.* Because young Dennis was so fair they called him 'Wulghi', the little white ghost. His clearest memories of the Deep Creek camp are the many campfires, kept smoky to drive away the mosquitoes, lots of mongrel dogs, tinned food, broken glass. *The only thing they could look forward to was a bottle.* They spoke in English and used a variety of Sydney Aboriginal words, for Ku-ring-gai people as well as Gai-mariagal lived at Narrabeen. Where was the camp? Near three sacred trees in this place of men's business, accessible by a foot track along the creek or down the old dirt road which in the 1940s became the Wakehurst Parkway. What happened to the camp? Oh the council came in and got rid of the lot; God only knows where they went to. When was that? Towards the end of the 1950s. And where was the Deep Creek camp? Where the National Fitness Camp is now. *Probably that's why they hunted everyone off the place, they wanted to build that camp.* But I used to stay there in the middle 1960s coaching football teams. One magic dawn I'd crewed a heavy surfboat being rowed from the Fitness Camp to the surf club. That must have been only a couple of years after the Gai-mariagal camp was destroyed. Why didn't I realise that? I've worked in Aboriginal history for most of my adult life and never once suspected that Sydney Aboriginals were still living together in their own country—and my own country—when I was a teenager. As Judith Wright had told her friend Oodgeroo,

They didn't tell me the land I loved
Was taken out of your hands.[39]

Dennis's clearest memory of the Narrabeen camp people was of
Uncle William, William De Serve, who supposedly took his name from
a crew member of the French explorer La Pérouse. Uncle William in
1960 was a very old man, always clad in a suit coat and pants, with
big shoulders, over two metres tall. His skin was marked by cicatrices,
the only Sydney man Dennis ever knew so scarified. *His eyes were
glistening, smoky and milky-looking, but when he talked about the old days
they sort of danced.* Uncle William, like Dennis's grandmother, was a
Kouradgee, a clever-person, who summoned spirits and spoke with
the wild creatures. Uncle William was an Eagle-man. He spoke with the
sea-eagles.

Young Dennis was in the particular care of his two uncles, his
mother's brothers, Garfield and Alwyn. They took him to Pittwater and
told him to keep away from the picnic area near Palm Beach, that was
strong country, and dangerous. So was Flint and Steel Beach on the way
up the Hawkesbury, powerful men's country which even his uncles did
not fully understand. Dangar Island: there was a strong creation story
from that place. They talked of catching penguins and whales, and
dolphins helping the Old People to fish. They showed him how to light
fires in the pouring rain, how to dive for the 'beautiful big mussels' of
Bobbin Head. In Foleys Bay.

Foleys Bay? Bobbin Head? In the Ku-ring-gai Chase National
Park? My own country of deepest memory and affection! Oh yes; see
though, we were traditional enemies of the Dharuk, and spoke to them
in the old days only in sign language, we were very friendly with the
Ku-ring-gai. So Uncle Gar and Uncle Alwyn used to take me every year
up to where Uncle Willie had lived a few years before. Maybe he was a
full Ku-ring-gai elder. Where did he live? Oh, at Coal and Candle Creek,
opposite where the big marina is now. In the 1950s. *The marina was where
we had picked up Charlie and Eileen Perkins. The site must be exactly the spot
to which the cruiser had drifted with Jessie and Chantal aboard by themselves
before I rowed across to rescue them!*

Now my heart was pounding. Dennis, could you tell me more
about Uncle William's place? Well, we used to get one of those old
chug-chug boats from Bobbin Head or Pittwater and went round to

Coal and Candle Creek. As we got close my uncles would start calling out in Gai-mariagal and English to find out whether it was all right to come on up the creek. We circled until we saw a sea-eagle, and if we didn't see one, we didn't go in. Most times we did. Uncle William had a little place there, though it was in ruins; by the late 1950s, he'd stopped going there. Just above the water it was, and he had another little hut up the top where he kept his tools and seeds. He used to grow melons, pumpkins and corn, and maybe—so went the story—a bit of barley for the still. At the end of the fishing we'd always throw one or two of the best fish into the water for the sea-eagles. I thought of Debbie Rose's classic exposition of Aboriginal land attachment, *Nourishing Terrains*. Discussing the inter-relatedness of species, she remarks:

> A 'healthy' or 'good' country is one in which all the elements do their work. They all nourish each other because there is no site, no position, from which the self-interest of one can be disengaged from the interests of others in the long term. Self-interest and the interest of all of the other living components of country (the self-interest of kangaroos, barramundi, eels and so on) cannot exist independently of each other in the long term.[40]

But Dennis, I go to Cowan Creek quite often with my friends. Would it be okay if we went and explored the place? Sure it would be.

Amongst my like-minded friends the effect of the news was almost as profound as it was on myself. The trip to Uncle William's camping place became the focus of our boating expedition of March 1998. On the Sunday near Looking-Glass Rock, in exactly the place where I've always imagined that Douglas Stewart addressed his old wraith the rock engraver, Con found a carving of a whale about a metre in length in an overhanging and protected ledge. On Monday, while the temperature of that tempestuous summer approached 38 degrees, we set out to find what surely was the last camp of a Ku-ring-gai Aboriginal still living, 170 years after the invasion, more or less continuously in his own country. There was the inlet, the shallow freshwater creek of Calabash Bay, the only place where Dennis had been allowed to swim. In the blinding heat we explored a flat area five metres above the water level. Clearly this land had once been cleared and probably farmed. No hut. Wasp stings and the remains of a Shelley's soft-drink bottle were the result of half an hour of prickly scrub-bashing. Margot, rowing round the corner towards the end of the creek, gave a shout. She had found some steps.

The remains of a jetty, rusting iron pipes set in square kerosene drums, which Aboriginal people also used to flatten out as walls for their huts. Seven steps cut into the rock. In the undergrowth, three metres above the water, square foundations of a hut three metres by four. This was it! A dozen steps cut into the rock at the eastern end of the flat area we had just explored. The remains of a shell midden encircled the hut. Maybe the hut was built on one. How long had the Ku-ring-gai been living here? This was no midden abandoned in 1860. Uncle Garfield and Uncle Alwyn and Dennis were adding to the pile a whole century later:

> and nobody comes
> Of his own long-scattered tribe to remember him.
> But he walks again for me at the water's rim …

While Douglas Stewart was writing these beautiful but ignorant lines, perhaps Uncle William De Serve was sitting over his campfire not 3 kilometres away, enjoying his oysters and home-made whisky in the heart of his traditional country. Maybe he sometimes waved at Stewart the fellow fisherman. Maybe on the night on which Stewart weighed those powerful words, Uncle William was fishing in the next boat! And I too was boating in the same area in the 1950s. Maybe I saw Uncle William too. Now I know why that friend of my father was able to point out the corroboree site to me in 1955. It was still common knowledge! All the locals knew something of the Aboriginal sites because Aboriginals connected to their own past were still visiting and living in their proper country. My little pile of clam shells was not 10 kilometres away, only 4. As we upped anchor a sea-eagle flew over the boat.

In the days which followed, I remembered that Mitchell Library photograph and rang Dennis about it. Yes, of course he knew of it, he had seen it in his mother's house, and the family had always assumed that it was Uncle William. The man in the photograph was wearing an old suit and hat like Uncle William always wore; the bamboo pole was of course a fishing spear. Yet the Mitchell Library's annotation is 'about

1890'. Enquiring further of the provenance of the picture, I found no further information. Suppose, though, 1890 was the guess of an archivist as self-deceiving as myself, who had thought, *It couldn't have been 1920 because everyone knows there were no Aborigines on the Hawkesbury by then!* In fact the date may just as likely have been the time the photograph was acquired, 1920. Uncle William would then have been about forty, which is about the age of the man in the photograph. His large frame, the curve of the bank and the distance above the water seem to match his campsite.

I pondered the significance of these events. A Public History student working in the Blue Mountains, and visiting the Gundangara Land Council at Katoomba, told me of a Gundangara camp at Catalina Park on the way to the scenic railway from Katoomba station.[41] So the Gundangara also had continued to live together until the 1950s. I'd spent much of my youth walking those trails of the upper Blue Mountains. We must have driven past the camp often, and never noticed it. How many times had I cautioned students not to assume the local Aboriginal population had disappeared. A whole chapter of my PhD thesis on the Wiradjuri people had been devoted to the 'Town Housing Scheme', whereby the NSW Aborigines Welfare Board tried to evict the Aboriginal communities, with varying degrees of success, from both the official and unofficial reserves and town camps. I had been taken to one called the Murie on the Lachlan River near Condobolin. The council had alleged that the camp was polluting the town water supply; the Wiradjuri thought the decision had something to do with the water-skiing then gaining popularity. In 1981 virtually nothing remained of the Murie. All my guide could show me were gravel heaps and a few wild roses. In the official reserve at Yass only sheets of rusty iron and one or two broken toys remained. What Dennis had told me was surely the same stick-and-carrot assimilation enacted in cities.

What process makes us descendants of colonists so blind to those displaced from our own proper country? In Wiradjuri country, and at La Perouse, the Aboriginals were more numerous, so they had regrouped in new towns or suburbs or streets. But in northern Sydney the Gai-mariagal had been scattered, presumably forever. *God only knows where they went to.* Surely the dispersal of the adults was no accident, because the 1950s was also the peak period for the removal of Aboriginal children. That was for their own good too. These last

Gai-mariagal camps at Deep Creek, Manly, Manly Lagoon and Forty Baskets Beach had also been destroyed in the name of assimilation, all in the late 1950s. We can understand the anger of Judith Wright's friend Oodgeroo Noonuccal at the destruction of the Aboriginal suburban camp at Acacia Ridge, Brisbane at the same time:

> White men, turn quickly the earth of Acacia Ridge,
> Plough the guilt in, cover and hide the shame;
> These are black and so without right to blame
> As bulldozers brutally drive, ruthless and sure
> Through and over the poor homes of the evicted poor.[42]

The past is never simple. Sometimes Aboriginals left their camps voluntarily. The Wiradjuri living 8 kilometres from Narrandera in rural New South Wales abandoned their camp of extended kinfolk to move voluntarily, to the edge of the town. An elderly resident told me, *The simple reason was we were progressing in our own way. We weren't forced. And the white people here gave us a chance.*[43] Indigenous history is more complex than simple heroic struggle against the invader: Aboriginal men in the 1950s pretended to be Maoris in order to get a drink in a pub and laughed about it.[44] Camps were destroyed for more reasons than brutal forced conformity: members of assimilation organisations which flourished in the 1950s thought it wrong for Aboriginals to have to live in dark ramshackle tin humpies without water, sewerage or electricity while other Australians had Housing Commission bungalows. It's not all colonial hatred: Dennis remembers the principal of Chester Hill primary school asking the Koori boys to conceal their identity to prevent them being removed from the school by the Education Department at the request of certain parents. Yes, Zofrea Salvatore's father Giuseppe endured 'unspeakable trials' on the banks of the 1920s North Manly Lagoon;[45] but the 'madmen with matted hair hanging over their eyes' were surely the Gai-mariagal, the uncles and great-aunts of Dennis Foley, the Indigenous people of northern Sydney at their penultimate community encampment.

Judith Wright wrote to her friend Oodgeroo Noonuccal:

> Let us go back to that far time,
> I riding the cleared hills,

plucking blue leaves for their eucalypt scent,
hearing the call of the plover,

in a land I thought was mine for life ...

But we are grown to a changed world:
over the drinks at night
we can exchange our separate griefs
but yours and mine are different ...

The knife's between us. I turn it round,
the handle to your side,
the weapon made from your country's bones,
I have no right to take it.

But both of us die as our dreamtime dies,
I don't know what to give you
for your gay stories, your sad eyes,
but that, and a poem, sister.[46]

For what will be the final chapter in this book I've invited Dennis
my shadow brother to explore together our own proper country and
our separate griefs. Before then, we must travel many miles.

CHAPTER 2 | VOICES IN THE RIVER:
THE POETRY OF
BELONGING

I start by reading some recent Aboriginal poets. At once I am struck with how almost all intimately involve the injustices Aboriginals have suffered at the hands of other Australians. Consider these themes drawn randomly from thirty or forty contemporary or near contemporary poets. The first is equal rights:

> They give Jacky rights
> Like the tiger snake gives rights to its prey
> They give Jacky rights
> Like the rifle sights on its victim.[1]

Finding Aboriginality after forced separation:

> Where do we belong is the question we ask
> Too white to be black—too black to be white
> Too little evidence to prove where we're from
> Only the memories of our childhood minds
> And those of our elders, who may still be alive
> Waiting to claim us, their poor little lost souls.[2]

Urban life:

> Flecked with the gentle dreams of another time of scents and
>   feelings,
> Country dog in the city, endure, it was this life or a country bullet.[3]

Aboriginal deaths in custody—and those chilling but magnificent final lines:

> Can't see the stars from my place
> can't hear the telephone or the human race
> can't hear the radio
> can't see the flowers grow …
> that's all we know, no other way
> and all we know is how to disobey
> I do it now, I did it then
> I almost became one of them
> but no need to fight
> no need for fists
> just a razor itching at my wrists
> and another night without stars.[4]

Racism:

An old saying goes, 'When you're white you're right.'
When you're black, to a lot of folks you're outside the light
I wish the situation would come to a halt
But how do you stop a racism cult?

Monkey see, monkey do—hey monkey, we're the same
It's how the racist white boys learnt, they are not to blame
It's in their families, they will never change—
A change for the good is way out of range.[5]

Alcoholism:

> Please don't drink—said my old man—
> The grog is eroding the strength of the clan
> Please don't drink—said my dear mother
> You know it's killing our sisters and brothers.[6]

Environmental damage:

> Then the other came
> and ripped the soil

and plagued our hearts
yours and mine
the benediction became a curse.[7]

Being saved:

Daisy—Government Spy
hunting Yella-fellas
light-skins
blue eyes
she counts them
for government men
licking their lips
in the city of churches.
…
Nungar women remember
'Crazy Daisy'
they remember those
saved and those
taken away.[8]

Potential rape:

i never had a woman like you
what woman do you mean?
you know,
no,
i mean a black woman.
oh.
they say they're better than white.

who? do we say, or men who've seen the light?
other men, white men black men, what do you say?
i don't know driver, you see I've never had
a woman black or white.

i take a drag
exhale
my words are gone.

here it comes, he's gonna ask
about my men ...

why should I pay [a cab fare] and submit
to cabbage minds like that
when I smell I can tell
a violent racist bait?[9]

Destroyed land:

> mist which lies over the country
> dynamite which exploded
> the place becoming cleared
> I had to sing about
> my father's father's country
> dynamite which exploded
> a bulldozer nosing into Guymay-nginbi
> mist which lies across the country
> dynamite which exploded.[10]

Prison:

> Have you ever been ordered to strip
> Before half a dozen barking eyes,
> Facing you against a wall
> ordering you to part your legs and bend over? ...
> Have you ever laid on a wooden bed
> In regulation pyjamas
> And tried to get a bucket to talk
> In all seriousness.[11]

The most that the more generous of Aboriginal poets are prepared to concede is that not all White Australians were bad. Here Jack Davis appraises the work of the anthropologists Ronald and Catherine Berndt:

> We owe you much
> as much as any race
> can owe the members

> of another
> Thank you for the fight
> together you will always
> be to us
> Our father and our mother.[12]

Many Aboriginal poets explore their sense of belonging, mostly connecting to the spiritual forces which they feel or absorb when revisiting ancestral land. The past is never shared; always it is a time without Whites:

> I have seen corroboree
> Where that factory belches smoke;
> Here where they have memorial park
> One time lubras dug for yams.[13]

GRANDFATHER GRANDMOTHER SING SWEET TUNE

Central Australian Aboriginals revere 'grandmother time' or 'grandfather time' as a time of serenity. Grandparents—meaning older kinfolk, whether living or dead doesn't matter—are assumed to care for the living in their own country. This lyric by the Aboriginal singer-songwriter Ruby Hunter leads me to ask what we can learn from our own older generations of poets.

I don't find so much help in the poets of my own grandparents' generation. Katharine Susannah Prichard and Eve Langley were strong and thoughtful poets. Prichard imagined that the physical Australian earth was not necessary to link one's soul to the eternal. She is content to die anywhere, her soul and body united in the whole globe itself from which Aboriginals are not only absent but irrelevant:

> Let me lie in the grass—
> Bathe in its verdure
> As one bathes in the sea— …
>
> For I am an earth child,
> An earth lover,
> And I ask no more than to be,
> Of the earth, earthy,
> And to mingle again with the divine dust.[14]

That won't help. I'm a child of Australia, not the world. So was Langley, who in her 1940s poem 'Native Born' gathered to herself all the Australian biota except—specifically—Aboriginals! She writes of ritually cremating a kangaroo which she has found dead. Lamenting that she has no 'native song' for such a rite—as do, so she conjectures, Italians in their own country—she invokes her own essential Australia by linking Anglo-Celts with the native fauna, flora and the natural elements. She ignores Aboriginal spirit forces not because she thinks them alien, but because the relevance, perhaps even the existence of the Aboriginal 'native-born', has not occurred to her:

> Beside her in the ashes I sat deep
>   And mourned for her, but had no native song
> To flatter death …
>
> Incarnate lay my country by my hand:
>   Her long hot days, bushfires, and speaking rains,
> Her mornings of opal and the copper band
>   Of smoke around the sunlight on the plains.
> Globed in fire-bodies the meat-ants ran
>   To taste her flesh and linked us as we lay,
> For ever Australian, listening to a man
>   From careless Italy …
>
> I burnt her with the logs, and stood all day
>   Among the ashes, pressing home the flame
> Till woman, logs, and dreams were scorched away,
>   And native with night, the land from whence they came.[15]

Langley's essential Australia is as impenetrable as the lament of the Aboriginal singer-songwriter Archie Roach: 'We cry, the native born'. His 1980s song—also called 'Native Born'—excludes non-Aborigines just as comprehensively. Neither Langley nor Roach (in this song) have anything to learn from or offer to the other.

In the 1970s poets cogitated more painfully on the meaning of responsibility for the past. They usually began at Langley's position that Aboriginality as spirit-force was extinct, even if Aboriginals themselves were not. To Gwen Harwood at Oyster Cove, Tasmania, the Aboriginals already were doomed while living:

Dreams drip to stone. Barracks and salt marsh blaze
opal beneath a crackling glaze of frost.
Boot-black, in graceless Christian rags, a lost
race breathes out cold. Parting the milky haze
on mudflats, seabirds, clean and separate, wade.
Mother, Husband and Child: stars which forecast
fine weather, all are set. The long night's past
and the long day begins. God's creatures, made
woodcutter's whores, sick drunks, watch the sun prise
their life apart: flesh, memory, language all
split open, featureless, to feed the wild
hunger of history. A woman lies
coughing her life out. There's still blood to fall,
but all blood's spilt that could have made a child.[16]

Randolph Stow blamed the pastoralists:

The dark women go down to the haunted pool.
They speak to the women, the spirits, the yet-unborn …
I have robbed the starving women, I have gone down

to the pool of children stolen, I have conceived
a tall blond son, and the pool and the land are his …

     The dark women come up
barren from the dark water. The spirits die.[17]

To David Campbell, the Whites were a kind of Pied Piper:

They dance on the cliff shelf under the sacred mountain
Where all the footsteps lead.
Why? Who? There is no reply.
In middens
The camp-fires blacken under forty thousand years.[18]

While not assigning guilt, R. F. Brissenden understood Aboriginality as 'yesterday':

We didn't climb Ayer's Rock.
Our sacred sights are elsewhere: Marathon, Glencoe, Gallipoli …
But none so old as this great rock

Where yesterday snake-man, goanna-man
And wallaby-man emerged to make the world.
The web of tracks is torn, the words are stolen.[19]

The myths both of 'the last of his tribe' and of lost history lie deep in White Australian poetry:

Above the snowline, the wind hums
shreds of the old clan songs.
Canberra's early history never thaws,
forever sealed in libraries of stone.[20]

Canberra's Ngunnawal, like Tasmania's Palawa and Sydney's Gai-mariagal, are in reality formidably alive.

The continuity of Australian occupation, first Aboriginal then others but linked by a common humanity, remains a theme common to many amateur poets:

The man who crouched beside the fire
To warm his hands this way
Felt the fanning gale blow higher
That blows my back today.[21]

More pointedly, David Campbell apprehended the continuity of human characteristics, in this case, aggression:

In 'the war to end all wars', an obsolete tank
Patrolling the blue littoral
From Gabo to York, pitted the rock
And unearthed from moss a boomerang.[22]

The physical presence of shell midden or exposed boomerang signals the familiar metaphorical continuity of people 'passed away' rather than forcibly dispossessed—or not gone at all.

THE PAST EMBEDDED IN THE LANDSCAPE

Judith Wright is one of the few poets to acknowledge the continuing integration of physical and spiritual Aboriginality. Past and future, individual and artefact and land are one. An elder awaits death:

Age and life lived unchain him. Set before him
his time of silent freedom. What need now to be human?
The rose, the river shade him. He is a stone.[23]

Wright's huge contribution was to awaken us to the continuing
presence not only of Aboriginality but of real Aboriginals. Though
I cannot embrace her closed-off pessimism which we met in the first
chapter, I rejoice in her intuitions. It is the heart, not the brain, of
Wright's casual horse rider which senses at an abandoned ceremonial
ground a continuing Aboriginal spirit force tinged with unrequited
violence. The man:

> halts at a sightless shadow, an unsaid word
> that fastens in the blood the ancient curse
> the fear as old as Cain.[24]

Local Aboriginality may be finished, or yet to revive, but the
spirit forces which it created remain. The unlaid violence of dispossession lingers at the sites of evil or old magic. Death will unchain the
old man, but old violence will enslave us, evidently forever.

That was as far as the most advanced thinking of 'grandfather
grandmother' time can take us. I'm not prepared to wait for death
to unchain me. We of the new millennium must unchain ourselves
while living.

Randolph Stow, who is also still living, understood the land as a
living organism which, as to Judith Wright, had no need to bleed to
declare its ancient pain. The land pulsed. Yet not every casual heart
started at the sightless shadow. To Stow it was only those of the cursed
sons and daughters of the first invaders. That generation, neither single-
minded true pioneer nor forgetful true inheritor, alone knew what the
alien surface of the land concealed:

> My father has faltered in nothing: his hearth is established,
> his sons are grown; we shall reap the predicted harvests.
>
> Only I, riding the flat-topped hills alone,
> feel in the inland wind the sing of desert,
> and under alien skin the surge, the singing,
> a wisdom and a violence, the land's dark blood.[25]

Surges 'the land's dark blood': an unextinguished, unrequited, throbbing life force which is wholly Aboriginal. Yet Stow implies that the 'alien skin' will in due season cease to be alien.

R. F. Brissenden bore no alien skin because the past was his own time transfigured. He pondered continuity not dichotomy, succession rather than dispossession. 'Blood' was no metaphor but the physical fluid shared by humanity. All of us humans are occupiers. What united Aboriginals and Whites at a particular beach on the New South Wales south coast was the physical sharing of that place—first them, then us, exactly here, on this soil, by that tree. The stars are detached from human art—and to feelings of belonging—as indifferent as Stewart's sky in the mind. Amidst cosmic desolation, it is not the spiritual forces of the earth, nor of the land Australia, nor the psychic power of Aboriginals, which make connections: it is the human observers of this precise site.

> But there are other places. This was yours,
> Old people: humbly we seek to share it. Blood,
> Semen, sweat, dung, tears; bones of the fish,
> Fur of the beasts we've killed and eaten; Ashes
> Of cooking fires that warmed us while we talked
> And touched, slept, wrestled with love and grief,
> Cried out or wept beneath indifferent stars
> Cold dawns and leaching rains: these—yours and ours—
> Have mingled with this soil. There, by that tree,
> Naked under the sun in simple joy
> We found our love; there on the sand our children
> Laughed, licking sea-salt from naked skin.
> We cannot ask forgiveness—but this site
> Bears our name now, our mark, as well as yours.[26]

Brissenden here makes no further connection, but he forges an almost-metaphysical bond between Aboriginals Past and We Now in a second powerful poem written for the same location. In 'Sea Beach and Cave Durras', on the beach or in the cave a young couple swim, fish, eat, make love, sleep. At night the present touches the past and the past the present, not genetically, psychically or spiritually: but physically. The cave-floor of time past 'minutely shifts and settles' beneath the sleeping bodies of time present. It is physical earth which makes this magical imaginative response between them and us.

> The fish-bones smoulder in the cooling fire.
> The spear shines in the moonlight. In the cave
> Behind the sleeping lovers the earth floor
>   Minutely shifts and settles,
>
> Drifts over the other bones, the other spears—
> The fish-hooks carved from shell, the flakes of stone,
> The bones of birds and animals and fish,
>   The blood, the long-dead fires.[27]

Brissenden's shells at Durras drift under the sleeping bodies imaginatively to unite aeons of history, present and past. James Charlton's midden shells at Cape Barren Island will abrade and grind forever. Cape Barren Island's Dan Smith will find no forgiveness, none of us will. 'Koonya, a black girl' haunts all of us. Reconciliation is unimaginable.

> They fed her well in the sealers hut,
> changing the leash after each month's
> work. Still she coughed up oyster pulp;
> and those white barnacles she grew
> inflamed Dan Smith with their hot rasp.
> He buttoned up his trousers,
> trussed up her legs,
> took her out the back,
> fired a flintlock in her ribs.
> There in the Cape Barren dunes,
> under the midden shells,
> her chipped nails claw
> the evasive sand.[28]

I need to pause a moment before I go on.

Even if a poet rejects superficiality or purposelessness or guilt, the weight of illegitimacy is not extinguished among those whose who still sense the surge and pulse of past malfeasance. Judith Wright's land is haunted.[29] Her poetry implies the questions of the first chapter. Can the ghosts be laid? If so, how? Will true belonging follow absolution? Can non-Aboriginals find forgiveness? Should they have to? Will they ever be granted the right to belong here? Who will grant it? Despair at wickedness which cannot be undone is almost unbearable.

Not all non-Aboriginal poets agree that we should heed the voices at the edge of hearing, as Geoff Page put it, nor that the voices are there at all. In 'Custodians No Longer', Alec Choate questions whether contemporary Aboriginals are the true inheritors of the spiritual past. Travelling near Mt Russell in the Northern Territory, and encountering some impressive rock art at a waterhole, he is unimpressed by the Aboriginals who arrive to greet them:

> we at once accepting they belong here,
> the true custodians of this art and water.
> Or are we wrong?
> Their anyhow attire, its unthinking flourish
> dims the age-old innocence we look for. ...
> They say they are mission natives going bush.
> They ask for cigarettes, and as we leave
> our farewell view of them is through wry smoke
> that wreathes their brittle speech, no one remarking
> we have trespassed a sacred site.
> If, as it seems to us, they do not care,
> a half-wrecked car, a rifle, some cigarettes,
> skirts, overalls, and headgear
> merge into a rubbish art that fits their loss.[30]

Choate was not born in Australia, but the opposite reaction also is possible amongst those alienated from their own birthland. The British landscape, to Adrian Caesar, seemed a foreign language. He migrated to Australia to find

> a place at last,
> I told myself that I could call familiar.

Caesar went camping in the Flinders Ranges:

climbing those ancient ranges
where the wedge-tailed eagle haunts
the thermals, …
listening to a friend explain the Aboriginal
and settler history of the place,
I am an intruder once again
as if one can't cut off the past
of colony and empire with neat saws:
'you can't inherit guilt,' I've told
myself a thousand times, but
when I hear the Adnyamathanha
have been mining ochre hereabouts
for thirty thousand years,
I'm put in my stranger place,
returning to suburbia
try to know more nearly where it is
I both belong and don't.[31]

Why should, indeed, Anglo-Australians not relate themselves to their own Anglo-Australian past? Reviewers were cool to Les Murray's recent work *Subhuman Redneck Verses*, detecting in his verse, among other departures, an uninterest in Aboriginals. I think Murray is not so much uninterested in or hostile to Aboriginals; rather, he is perplexed and angry that Anglo-Australians have abandoned their own history and achievements in ignorance or shame in favour of the indigenous. Murray condemns the poetic drift from the bush to the land, from productivity to mystic spirituality:

Well
below in the struts of laundry is the four-wheel drive
vehicle in which to make an expedition
to the bush, or as we now say the Land,
the three-quarters of our continent
set aside for mystic poetry.[32]

No poet has traced the connection between Anglo-Celtics and the land with more passion and insight than Murray. Here his 'earth floor', like Katharine Susannah Prichard's, is one of universal humanity, not Australian alone, still less Aboriginal:

> I am striding on over the fact that it is the earth
> that holds our mark longest, that soil dug never returns
> to primal coherence. Dead men in the fathoms of fields
> sustain without effort millennial dark columns
> and to their suspension, the crystal centuries come—[33]

'Soil dug never returns/to primal coherence.' The past is entrapped in the soil, the earth is never again the same, but Murray does not suggest that the deeds themselves remain. Even the evasive sand at which Koonya's chipped nails forever claw is metaphysically enriched, the physical land retains no memory of suffering.

More commonly, Murray correlates the exterior Australian landscape with a specifically Anglo-Australian past:

> Abandoned fruit trees, moss-tufted, spotted with dim
>   lichen paints; the fruit trees of the Grandmothers,
> they stand along the creekbanks, in the old home paddocks,
>   where the houses were …[34]

This is the more tangible bequest of grandmother time. To Murray, the more purposeful the former activities of (British) Australians, the more immediate conjunction they made and make to the present. In 'The China Pear Trees', the grandchildren of a settler on the northern New South Wales coast return to work at the earlier farm whose contours of building, clearance and exotic trees are still discernible. The changes in the landscape are not only inevitable, but logical and natural. The exotic—but equally useful and appropriate—vegetation Murray does not lament but celebrates:

> And they called lush water-leaved trees
> like themselves to the stumpholes of gone rainforest
>
> to shade with four seasons the tattered evergreen
> oil-haloed face of a subtle fire landscape …

It was this shade in the end, not their coarse bottling fruit
that mirrored the moist creek trees outward,
as a culture
containing the old gardener now untying and heaping up
one more summer's stems and chutneys.[35]

I read this as not the same as Brissenden's smooth continuity between generations and ethnicities. New and different 'water-leaved' people do not just happen to be here: they have earned a right to belong. 'Shade' implies protection; the rainforest has been replaced by something equally legitimate. The distinction between 'exotic' and 'indigenous' is arbitrary and ideological:

But so far as treetops or humans now alive know
all these are indigenous beings. When didn't we have them?
Each was born on this continent. Burn-off pick and dusty shade
were in their memory, not chill fall, not spiced viridian.[36]

ONLY DESPAIR

My reading and discussion keep turning on the meaning of the trodden land. It's worth returning to the Aboriginal poet Oodgeroo Noonuccal, who grew up on a real reserve and found its total destruction both physical and spiritual. Here was no metaphysical continuity, only despair. 'We [Aboriginals] belong'—but for how long?

Notice of Estate Agent reads: 'Rubbish May Be Tipped Here'.
Now it half covers the traces of the old bora ring.
They sit and are confused, they cannot say their thoughts:
'We are as strangers here now, but the white tribe are the strangers'.
We belong here, we are of the old ways …
The bora ring is gone.
The corroboree is gone
And we are going.[37]

Analogously to Murray, Oodgeroo's land is real and exterior. The central consequence of dispossession is palpable: the absolute deprivation of land and culture. Any achievements of the 'pioneers', and whatever else Anglo-Australians may inherit from their ancestors, is of no moment. Oodgeroo's 'blood' is race memory, not earth memory, nothing discarnate embedded in the land.

> But a thousand thousand camp fires in the forest
> Are in my blood.
> Let none tell me the past is wholly gone.
> None is so small a part of time, so small a part
> Of all the race years that have moulded me.[38]

The pessimistic Oodgeroo holds that the past, once erased, cannot be deciphered. The spirit force is extinguished. As the people depart, their existence dissolves within the dust of those bulldozed reserves and camps. The past is in her blood, not the land. Belonging is biological, not terrestrial.

THE FRINGES OF OUR RESTLESSNESS
Let's take another direction, to investigate how poets have understood the violent past to impinge upon individuals as well as land. David Rowbotham describes the moral calcification of the settler 'Mullabinda Campbell' which followed Campbell's murderous role in a 'punitive expedition':

> The target-circles of black brats, glistening, hung
> Thick-nippled-centred over the billabong …
> The legends ricocheted with each report;
> Till stone thoughts filled the well of his heart, and age
> Made a crumbling woolshed of his slab-hard rage.
>
> Time grooved him like the bloodwood; but deep
>   in the dried
> And channelled country of his being where pride
> Once flooded to the full, whispered and grew
>   the fig-tree,
> Fruitless, but a wild, green and rooted memory,
> Growing on, long after the vengeful spear,
> Thumping his shoulders out of the quiet air,
> Acquitted him of hate, and of tree, shed, well—
> Mullabinda Campbell's estimate of hell.[39]

The perpetrators inflict as much suffering on themselves as on those they harmed. This is the poet Ian Mudie describing another Campbell-like pioneer:

> Half-blind from sand; the tribe he stole from, dead;
> the land he raped made barren as his mind.[40]

David Campbell, clambering over the same country where Douglas Stewart wrote 'Rock Carving', invoked the contemporary spiritual desert:

> The kangaroo has a spear in his side. It was here
>   Young men were initiated,
> Tied to a burning tree. Today
>   Where are such cooling pools of water?[41]

Before long the poets draw us back to the correlative of desecrated Aboriginality and desecrated land. Dorothy Hewett's family inheritance was degradation compounded by corruption, the rape of land and woman:

> No wonder I cannot count for the sound of the
>   money-changers,
> The sweat and the clink, the land falling into
>   the cash register,
> Raped and eroded, thin and black as a myall
>   girl on a railway siding.[42]

Judith Wright advanced a conjunction of destroyed people and destroyed country more explicit and of greater anguish:

> And in those days
> there was one of him and a thousand of them,
> and in these days none are left—
> neither a pale man with kangaroo-grass hair
> nor a camp of dark singers mocking by the river.
> And the trees and the creatures, all of them are gone.

But the sad river, the silted river,
under its dark banks the river flows on,
the wind still blows and the river still flows.
And the great broken tree, the dying pepperina,
clutches in its hands the fragments of a song.[43]

What may the land reply? Mark O'Connor imagines a bequeathed corruption diseased and venal:

I am the spirit of this land;
I walk in leprous white.
I am the cousin of the crow
And sister of the night.[44]

ESCAPING THE BURDEN OF GUILT

A few poets have taken refuge in shared dispossession. In this poem about the flooding of the Burragorang valley, near Sydney, for a dam, the author invokes the joint calamity of country lost to both Blacks and Whites:

So now the white folk too have gone
And kangaroos will romp
In freedom on the luscious grass
Around Gumbeding swamp.[45]

This won't do at all. Aboriginals lost not only a beautiful valley but a whole country, and violently. Judith Wright, while conceding that all Australians have lost their inheritance through greed and despoliation, explicitly rejects the union of shared loss:

But we are grown to a changed world:
over the drinks at night
we can exchange our separate griefs
but yours and mine are different ...[46]

Guilt can paralyse. Bruce Dawe concludes that a guilty heart thundering at the killings of Kalkadoon warriors in central Queensland is far from adequate.

> We cannot call the Turrbul back
> and guilt's a slippery thing
> if all it feeds is speeches
> and songs the poets sing …
> And we who wrote their finish
> must turn and write a start
> if *we* would turn from running
> and face our thundering heart.[47]

Jamie Grant writes such a start in arguing that guilt is inappropriate. His pioneer past is no more than particles of dust. Visiting the house of his great-great-grandfather near Bothwell in Tasmania, he contemplated the homestead's ruined shell, 'verandahs propped by beams and joists of sunlight', the orchard run to seed, willows and rabbits in the garden.

> Inside the abandoned house, sour clods
> of light, the same brilliance curdled on sturdy
> farmers, clumsy with muskets, hustling
> to the gun slits—ready for genocide.
> Believing in self-defence, they'd picture God
>
> bearded like Darwin, smiling *Natural*
> *Selection*. I can't inherit the guilt
> of such innocent men, as guilt's an abstract
> like blood, replaced throughout the body,
> changing in shape all the time; those human skulls
>
> were mashed years back, reduced to bracken spawn
> atoms, fragile moth dust, sun motes.[48]

Robert Adamson, challenging Aboriginal deaths in custody during the Bicentenary of the European invasion, offers but does not answer this observation:

> The Uniforms are finding the dead: young hunters
> who have lost their hunting, singers who
>
> would sing of fish, are now found hung—
> crumpled in night-rags in the public's corners; …

slumped on the thousand grooved, fingernailed walls
of your local Police Station's cell— ...

Meanwhile outside the count continues, on radio
the TV news; like Vietnam again, the faces

of mothers down across the screens—
And the poets write no elegies, our artists

cannot describe the shape of their grief, though
the clean-handed ones paginate dossiers

and court reporters' hands move over the papers.[49]

And for those who acknowledge vicarious guilt—what then? Bruce Dawe's guilt was not enclosed by the nineteenth century. Guilt concerned the present generation: his 'exiles' in this poem were probably the Aboriginals evicted from the same destroyed settlement at Brisbane's Acacia Ridge that Oodgeroo mourned. Bulldozers and dump trucks at Acacia Ridge—and Deep Creek—were more likely to attract the observer than refugees 'slowly moving'.

Whereas the engines of our endless spoilage
mould the horizons to our foreign dream,
and they, from their last sanctuaries, are turned out,

Who that observes them slowly moving now
along the fringes of our restlessness
could see them as they were before we came.[50]

Geoff Page's remorse was painfully personal:

He was my best friend for a while
    and sent a letter once,
my second year at boarding school
    when he'd left the school six months.

The hand, well-spelt, had worked the roads
    some time before his beard.
I'm sure I must have written back
    before he disappeared.[51]

Guilt was the dominant voice of the Anglo-Celtic poets of the 1980s. Bruce Dawe's 'Beggar's Choice' is his strongest poetic attack upon his own people, and probably the strongest of the decade. It is 'we', not 'they', who share, and inherit, the fruits of this appalling history.

> We said, We'll let you choose:
> there's syphilis, there's booze,
> trachoma, early death
> long sentence for short crime
> (just to name a few)
> —they're all there just for you
> with every living breath
> *Hurry up and take your time.*[52]

At that point in the mid-1980s our poets seemed to be emulating the most severe that the most trenchant poetic critic of White society, Kevin Gilbert, was able to pen.[53]

There were and are alternatives. Let's return to the meditative Oodgeroo, who by no coincidence spent many years working closely with like-minded and supportive Whites, and on occasions found light within darkness. Here in the 1960s she debates with herself which history of Australia she should relate to her young son Denis:

> I could tell you of heartbreak, hatred blind,
> I could tell you of crimes that shame mankind,
> Of brutal wrong and deeds malign,
> Of rape and murder, son of mine;
>
> But I'll tell you instead of brave and fine
> When lives of black and white entwine,
> And men in brotherhood combine—
> This would I tell you, son of mine.[54]

No non-Aboriginal poet except, once, Bruce Dawe wrote like this in the 1980s. Most were too preoccupied with guilt to offer themselves a choice in interpreting our history and our sense of belonging. Now Oodgeroo is dead. No major Aboriginal poet at present writes with such generosity or thoughtfulness. Though her depiction of non-Aboriginal society is less than comprehensive, Charmaine Papertalk-Green offers no relief:

> Your world is not mine
> Your belly has always been full
> violence was seen on the telly
> not down the street
> Your mother was hit behind doors
> where she was too ashamed
> to scream for help
> What would the neighbours think!
> They had all this from you.[55]

That's one element which the non-Aboriginal have not absorbed from the Indigenous poets. We desecrated the land, yes, but not one poet claims that White Australians do not love it. Les Murray might have answered Papertalk-Green:

> After the war, and just after marriage and fatherhood
> ended in divorce, our neighbour won the special lottery,
> an amount then equal to fifteen years by a manager's
> salary at the bank, or fifty years' earnings by
> a marginal farmer fermenting his clothes in the black
> marinade of sweat, up in his mill-logging paddocks.[56]

James Charlton implied that the Whites had relinquished their right to Australia through wickedness. To the Aboriginal Jack Davis matters were more simple: the land was and is Aboriginal.

> This is Our Land
> you cannot dispute it
> nor can you refute it
> this is Our Land
> You can gouge at our heart
> tear us apart

> kill forests and grasses
> but through life as it passes
> this is our stand
> in pain or in splendour
> we will never surrender
> the claim to Our Land[57]

The acerbic poet Ouyang Yu reinforced the alienation of exile from his homeland:

> I stand on this land that does not belong to me
> that does not belong to them either.[58]

ESCAPING THE RHETORIC

Aboriginal and non-Aboriginal poets have discussed, sometimes in some very fine poetry, the themes of guilt, dispossession, murder, enforced labour, Black deaths in custody. In this chapter we have not considered much positive remedy—for in the poetry there is very little. Judith Wright, the pre-eminent post-war poet of indigenous relations, offers no more than a deep personal and general desolation.

The most creative recent poetic voices break from this rhetoric of bleakly irresolvable guilt and pain. One of the most original Aboriginal poems reflects on the Hamlet-like dilemma of the author. Fully conscious of his people's past, Errol West holds no particular desire to take up its burden:

> They had no resistance to the legacy of the white invasion—
> or so they must have thought
> I am their legacy and I'll not disgrace them

> But there is no one to teach me the songs that bring the
> Moon bird, the fish or any other thing that makes me what I am …
> I do not want blood—just opportunity—to be.[59]

Les Murray savagely rejects the elevation of Aboriginal and recent migrants at the expense of Anglo-Celtic Australians:

> Our one culture paints Dreamings, each a beautiful claim.
> Far more numerous are the unspeakable Whites,

the only cause of all earthly plights,
immigrant natives without immigrant rights.
Unmixed with these are the Ethnics, absolved
    of all blame.[60]

Murray indicts 'climaxing native self-hatred' for the desire to eliminate exotic animals like feral pigs.

Us against species for bare survival may justify
the infecting needle, the pig rifle up eroded gullies,
but this luxury massacre on landscapes draining of settlement
smells of gas theory. The last thing brumby horses hear
is that ideological sound, the baby boom.
It is the hidden music of a climaxing native self-hatred
where we edge unseeing around flyblown millions towards
a nonviolent dreamtime where no one living has been.[61]

Repudiating climaxing self-hatred, Bruce Dawe at least acknowledges process. His 'Phase to Phase' is one of the very few works of the period to acknowledge that the apparently unretractable violence of dispossession can be negotiated, maybe resolved. He sets his poem at a public function, perhaps a book launch. Pondering the question of the Asian visitor, 'Why do you Australians sit there and let yourselves be insulted ...?', Dawe answers himself that meek acceptance is a phase which must be suffered by all prepared to do so. Temporarily, he and his generation must endure 'bad' (inaccurate) history for 'bad' (evil) history:

    This is the collective race-guilt phase.
    During this phase non-Aboriginals can generally
      be expected to be insulted.

    Our role is to sit there and take it.
    The fact that we are supportive will not save us.
    Here we get bad history for bad history.
    This is known as the payback system ...
    —for us the scourge and the automatic hand-clap
    are basic ritual instruments, interchangeable.

This future is not altogether to be welcomed, but at least it will release those ensnared by self-righteousness on one side and guilt on the other:

> Already the traps and snares of compromise are set.
> Good sales and follow-up titles will bring on
> the evil spirit of sophistication. Art must then
> compete on terms of equality with art. In that phase
> we will regain our freedom.
>   Then we will really meet
> —the masks put off, the last
> paternalism ended.[62]

Of all the hundreds of 'belonging' poems that I have reflected upon, the one which best advances a shared and requited future is Geoff Page's long blank verse poem 'Bandjalang', in his book *The Great Forgetting*. Significantly, his book is illustrated by an Aboriginal artist, Poorarar. In the northern New South Wales of his own deep familiarity, Geoff invokes those 'voices in the river', the 'voices at the edge of hearing', the 'rapids in the darkness' which never cease to speak shared past and shared future to those able and prepared to listen: and negotiate. The violent history of the Bandjalang people is extinguished neither morally nor physically in the present. It is immanent and now and must be released.

'Bandjalang' ends with a confrontation between members of a White family and an extended Bandjalang clan about how a site of past violence in the Lismore district is to be preserved and remembered. These lines are taken from the last few pages:

> 'Land rights, sure,'
> says Bobby, 'but not right here, not now,
> The law doesn't run to that.
> More like a kind of recognition.
> Some sort of plaque maybe, a headstone.
> Something laying out the facts.' ...
>
> Long Ted says: 'I think the bones
> can stay right 'ere. They in the soil

they ought to be in. You call it Whitby
land right now but you blokes are only
possum skin. It's Bandjalang
deep down. We'll leave 'em where they are.'

'Let's do the wording here and now',
says Ray, and reaches for the paper.
Bobby Watson goes to speak,
looks once at Ted, then takes a drink. …

'How would it go now? Just the facts.'

There is a further silence now.
Six people sitting at a table,
three white, three black, their separate breathing
the rapids at the edge of hearing. …
'A man, a woman, and a child',
Long Ted insists. 'You got that, mate?' …

'And that fence to keep off stock',
says Tommy. 'Or we take it to the papers.'

'And what about this book of Ray's?'
says Lyall. 'It says the same damn thing.'

'The book is full of deaths already',
says Ray. 'I could leave three aside.' …

Lyndall grabs her husband's wrist.
'And the truth of what we've put
in since, let's not forget', she says.

… And once more in a final silence,
before the scraping back of chairs,
before the wary net of handshakes,
they hear the rapids in the darkness,

the voices in the river.[63]

The power of these final lines is this. Geoff Page's people do not
rely solely on Western adversarial law. His white Australians insist

on recognition for what they have achieved, the deep significance to them of the land Australia, and of their own proper country. They don't commune with spirits in the landscape: they negotiate with real, self-confident Aboriginal people, and what they exchange is passion and knowledges and history and a love of the land. And they know that the voices in the river will never be silent.

CHAPTER 3 | GROWING

I've just finished interviewing a dozen young Australians about the Aboriginal dispossession and their own feelings of belonging. Their responses occupy a very wide continuum. I asked a Year 11 high school student, What if Aboriginal people couldn't remember actually being on a piece of land, but read that it once belonged to their grandfather. Would they have any kind of claim to it? She replied, *Too bad. We shouldn't have to pay for our great-grandparents' mistakes.* What if they wanted the reserve back they used to live on? *Too bad. Too bad.*

That's one end of the continuum. To explore the other, I asked another young woman, Do you think we'll ever really belong here? She replied, *Well, we're a culture based on financial gain, which doesn't show itself to be very complex or deep; and until money isn't number one priority I think we will never deserve, in the Aboriginal sense, to live here.*

These young Australians can disentangle dispossession from feelings of guilt:

Monica, aged 24: I can't understand why Australians feel so guilty at the moment for previous happenings. I understand that it happened and I understand it's very bad and that it's wrong and that it shouldn't happen again, but I can't understand why this generation should feel guilty, as if they've done something.

They are conscious of their own rites of passage:

Trina, **aged 27:** *I'm in two minds about my sense of belonging. Sometimes I feel like I'm developing a stronger sense of belonging. I used to want to just get up and leave Australia and go and live somewhere else, and I still do for the experience, but I think I'm kind of growing roots. I don't know if that's a kind of normal age/space development thing, or if I've actually changed my mind. It's probably normal to start putting roots down.*

They may be irritated by their teachers:

Anonymous, aged 17: *We had a discussion in class, and the teachers all expect you to think Aboriginals here, they had a great history and they're all great and they're all sitting out there and living in the land still, and I'm sitting there thinking, 'But they aren't all doing that,' and as soon as you bring up the fact that half the town's on the dole and none of them are working and they don't have any idea about the culture, they say, 'that's a bit of a racist comment'.*

Damian, born to Italian and Greek-Slovenian parents, supports Aboriginal land rights, but believes in a shared Australia: '"Always was, always will be Aboriginal land?" It's a tough question. It is their land, because it's a part of them, but by the same token because I'm a first-generation Australian, this is all I've ever wanted, it's all I've ever known.'

And their last sense of belonging may be quite different from that of older Australians. Abigail, aged twenty-six, says, 'I think I'm a world citizen first, not an Australian. That's my ultimate responsibility.'

What senses of belonging occupy this middle ground? What common senses of belonging are shared by young Australians growing?

IDENTIFYING

I start with the conservatives, a group of students from 'Orley School' in Sydney. To my proposal to interview some of the boarders from country New South Wales the headmaster reluctantly agrees, provided that their housemistress is present (whether to restrain my questions or the girls' answers is not clear) and that neither school nor students may be identified.

The first group gathers in the housemistress's flat after evening prayers on 27 October 1997. The first Year 12 English exam has taken place that morning; none of the girls has another exam for a couple of days. We introduce ourselves. The students come from Brewarrina, Manilla, Yass, Port Macquarie, Dubbo, Merriwa and Gulargambone; all but one (who lives by the sea) come from properties ranging from 100 to 65 000 hectares.

Within the first few minutes the girls reveal themselves implacably opposed to what they take to be Aboriginal privilege. In education:

[Aboriginal specialness] that's all crap. They should belong as much as any Asians. There's not Chinastudy is there, or Italiastudy, there's Austudy and Abstudy. And Abstudy is a joke. Because, they want to be treated as equals, so fight for Austudy just like everyone else has to. So they've got a right to say that, but I've got a right to say, well, I'm special.

In land:

I think we should be all treated as equal, so how are we going to make them equal if they're going, 'Give me more land, give me more land' or 'I'm black so therefore give me more money'? I know that's a really harsh way of saying it, but I don't know, I just get really frustrated by it all.

In housing:

And at home, like they get like, houses and everything built for them. And it is so obvious that when they get sick of the houses they live in, they drive cars through them. And that's not fair. And that's just wasting our money.

And in society:

That's why people become so racial about them, because they get these special exceptions and we don't, and we hate them for that.

But they're creating the segregation. I don't get this whole blackfellow whitefellow yellowfellow brownfellow, it's absolutely staggering that we can live in such a multicultural society and still have a race debate.

The girls talk over each other, recounting Aboriginal hearsay: Well, this mother had had her eighth child and she just got up and walked away, just left the child there. It was raised by a white family in town, and then the mother just turned up and wanted it back. Well, up at Purfleet, I heard that the Aboriginals were given new houses but within two weeks one was burnt down and the rest had their floorboards ripped up. Well, another lot up the coast somewhere had got the land back and then sold it straight back to—to—to whoever you sell it to up there. Well, a mob walked onto our property wanting to borrow fuel and while Mum was getting some they robbed the jackeroo's quarters. Well, a lot of Aboriginal boys that I was in primary school with are now breaking in to the shops. Well, I heard that the other day they had some kind of housing inspection because they're so awful now, and they walked in and found two emu legs sticking out of an oven. They'd just chucked the whole emu in there, it was just so disgusting.

A dozen other young people of rather less privileged backgrounds whom I interviewed were less certain, more aware of the inconsistencies in their thinking, much more sympathetic to Aboriginals. *Why should it be their culture that's making concessions, why shouldn't we change ours?* Most thought it morally right that Aboriginals should make claim to land that others could not. Three students from Lake Ginninderra College in Canberra, Josephine, Dale and Scott, thought that the prime minister should apologise to the stolen generations. They were worried by latent racism; they regretted that non-Aboriginal Australians used the land only for commercial purposes. They admired the apparent Aboriginal characteristics of 'peacefulness and forgiveness and caring for the country'. I asked them to name the achievements that White Australians could be proud of. The extreme position was *I can't think of a thing.* Dale was proud that Australia had created its own culture from the best of around the world; Scott admired Sir Douglas Mawson—perhaps significantly, I thought, an explorer outside Australia.

Abigail, whom I spoke with in Melbourne with Trina, offered a more cautious appraisal. She has lived overseas for most of her adult life:

It seems to be a bit black and white that the Aborigines are good and the White people are bad, and I don't think that. Yes, we need to see and recognise all the bad things we did, but also recognise that we have a lot of good qualities; and the same with the Aboriginals on a personal level. Western culture isn't in itself bad, but there needs to be a balance, preferably between both; because it's here, and there's no point [in saying] 'get rid of it, it's wrong' because it's here; and it has a value as well. Technology isn't all bad.

The Canberra students approved of Cathy Freeman carrying the Aboriginal and Australian flags at the Commonwealth Games. *We owe them something*, Dale summarised the feeling of the group:

We can learn from the Aboriginals and they've taught us a lot, we've adopted a lot, and a lot of Aboriginals have been accepted in the White Australian culture. Why can't the White man learn from the Aboriginal culture? I'd love to go up and learn what they do and live the way they do.

To those who are striving to find a place for themselves, a relationship with the Indigenous is not of the first moment. Elsie Chan, born in Canberra, is a medical student at the University of Sydney. While her father, after twenty-five years' residence here, thinks himself still Hong Kong Chinese, Elsie is emphatically Australian. Does she belong? As a child, though she ate Chinese food and spoke Cantonese, she thought herself no different from any other Australian. *To be honest, the fact that I was Chinese, and there was probably only a handful of Asians in the whole school, really did not occur to me. I just never noticed the difference.* Attending the Canberra Girls Grammar School, where all her friends were Caucasian, she had no reason to doubt her Australian identity until she walked in to the first lecture at the University of Sydney:

I remember walking in on the very first day and suddenly I saw this mass of black hair and I just saw so many people, and I was honestly shocked myself, even though I was Asian and I was staring at the whole crowd of Asians and I was just so shocked. And then gradually through the year, I think probably more the influence of actually living in Sydney rather than being in medicine where the majority are Asian, I just noticed that some people just expect you to be friends with the Asians, they're surprised if you hang around with a group of non-Asians. It's as if in my own mind the issues of discrimination and the issues of racism have suddenly come up when I'm eighteen rather than when I'm five or six which you might have expected at school.

Elsie says of herself, 'I still think I'm very Australian, but I'm redefining what Australian means.'

BONDING

Places of the heart. The Orley School students are convinced of the moral strength of a rural upbringing. *Yes! Definitely! A place to raise five kids! That's why I want to go back to the land! You grow up a little bit tougher and a little bit better able to handle things. You learn more common sense. Better perception of life—of what's really important.* Someone's sister at a job interview, asked what she would take while walking in remote Australia, chooses a blanket and water, while the other girls ask for mobile phones. Sister gets the job! A better perspective on money. *You're not going to prance around in a cute little short dress and a pair of high heels in the bush.* One answer was especially intriguing. *The things that you're in control in—jodhpurs and riding boots—are things I'd never ever wear in the city.* In control? Do city students ever think of themselves in control of anything? The Orley School girls believe that the bush brings physical and emotional toughness. During the drought someone's dad had to shoot 900 sheep: *Seeing things like that, the fact that you don't have a boyfriend and don't have the clothes you want really pales.* These Orley School girls are more secure, more certain of their values than any other young Australians that I have met—except for a few young Aboriginals! Orley School boarders are self-possessed, articulate, intelligent, confident, in control.

None of the others drew such moral strength from either place or lifestyle. To Monica, Black Mountain in Canberra was one of several sites of great significance. *They're part of who I am, certain places in Australia which make life not 'not worth living', but give me positive experiences, and I don't know if I could live without them.* What if Aboriginal people denied her access to Black Mountain? Monica's consciousness of the dispossession framed her answer: *I'd be very sad if I couldn't do that for the rest of my life. Not intolerable but really sad and I'd probably always miss it and think about it.*

Momo Miyaguchi's sense of belonging to Australia was shaped by her being the child of Japanese and Irish-American ethnicities. She felt an affinity with dispossessed Aboriginals:

I understand the feeling that this is my country and everyone else who's come here has come from somewhere else; but my view is that being a displaced person in your own country you share some common ground with [other] people who don't fit in with society completely as well. Certain issues of belonging and place and identity.

Momo's attachment to the land was comparable, she thought, to Aboriginal feelings, even though European civilisation had 'moved quite a way from nature'. An essential humanity was more important than cultural or historical difference. As she entered her twenties she reflected that the Hobart landscape where she grew up was increasing in importance to her. What if her loved country was debarred from her by a land claim? Unlike Bob Brissenden, who understood history to be a succession from Aboriginals to Others, Momo's Australia was shared affection:

It depends on how [access] was going to be if it was just a matter of who owns it: it doesn't really matter if you can still use it and still share it. I guess you'd hope for a compromise where it's not just one person's concept of the land and how it should be used, but it should incorporate how other people use it as well, because we can't help being here and we can't help. … You'd hope to work in conjunction with the owners.

The Orley School girls at home in their land, confident, articulate, physical, sensual: *I think of golden wheat crops. The air, it's quiet and it's still. I feel at ease. Everything drops. Here [in Sydney] there's always this roar, even in the middle of the night.* Attachments narrow: *Just looking over the hills and knowing exactly what's over that hill, you know what trees there are and there's a river down the end of that valley. It's knowing all that. It's a question of familiarity.* A friend adds, *When I've been to stay with you, it can remind you of home but it's never the same.* A girl from Gulargambone says: *I go on walks out the back where there's no-one around at all.* I think of how many interviews with city people I had made who, when pressed for a more precise location for their favourite location of 'gum trees', reply 'gum trees—anywhere'.

Memory forms and releases attachments still more precise. *Everywhere you go you've done stuff.* On the tallest place on the property where some pigs came and the workman fell off the horse and I was running up the tree. Family Christmases in the dining room. Yabbying: the whole family treks out to the dam, *there's one place where you pull up.* Swimming in the dam. Remembering exactly where she and Mum were standing in the kitchen when the news broke that a friend had died. Being thrown over a fence by a Brahman bull. Lying in an empty bath while smoking and looking at the stars. *I think it's the association of memory.*

How do you say hello to your place when you come home? Just jump in a ute and drive around. *Oh yeah, Mum's planted some new things.* Check out the house paddock. *I always notice what Mum's wearing.* Take the horse. Go by bike. *Whatever the weather's like, Toyota. Drop my bag, grab my board and go to the beach. Going for a ciggie is really a good way to get back to nature.*

A hubbub of affectionate belongings is linked to people: when you go out to help your father, that's very important. *When I go back my mum and dad have usually let my dog off, so I pat that and walk straight into my room.* Does the country know you've come back? A thoughtful pause. *Well, no. My dogs know. A tree can't know you. A tree gets hurt if you drive over a branch.* Everyone laughs. I tell them how Aboriginal people formally introduce strangers to country. Another quizzical silence. They find it interesting rather than odd. *Well, when you bring people to the country you explain every single thing, why the tree looks like that and why the grass grows like that, but not introducing you directly to the country.* Less certainty now; fewer jokes among the considered silences. *I see it more as a rediscovery, I don't see it as a greeting.* Another opinion: *There's a degree of endearment that's—I won't say normal. You can—I can comprehend why they do that.* Dads more than Mums figure in memory and story, usually as the source of hard work, the ultimate expression of land and depth of feeling. *If my dad's been away for a while he walks along and he'll say hello to everything. That's just him.* Would he actually use the word 'hello'? *Sometimes if he's in a strange mood—but you can sort of tell that's what he's thinking.*

And how, at the end of the holidays, do the girls say goodbye to the land? *To the house, the dog, driving out the gate, I always look back.* Saying goodbye to the goat, the horses, the yard dogs. *My lamb.* Saying goodbye in one's head. For one student returning to school involved going into town to catch a bus, then riding back past the property. *I hate it when you go past and you're not going there. It's a negation of your identity. There's no recognition of the fact that you were there.*

Young people growing, at the edge of the intuitive, restrained by education, by peers, by rationality. Does the country say goodbye to you? *It's always sunny when I leave.*

SHARING

Monica's willingness to sacrifice her own special places is distinctly a minority voice among these growing Australians. The majority opinion is 'I'd sort of insist on sharing'. Most, like Trina, accept the classic rationale for supporting Aboriginal land rights, that:

Basically the land was stolen, which is no different from burglars, you'd kick up a stink and demand that it would be returned to you. On a grander scale, the same thing happened, and in an ideal world they demand it back and demand that they have the right to determine who can come on or not.

Now Trina hesitates, conscious that she might react differently if her own loved places were actually threatened:

I think maybe I idealise the situation and I don't have to worry about it. I don't know how I'd feel if I really did feel strongly about [a particularly precious place to which she was denied access]. I have a sense, and it's maybe too idealistic, but Aboriginal people are interrelated and interconnected with the land that it's almost one and the same—not that they were all peaceful people, I know that. Maybe I'm a bit scared to think I would put up a fight to challenge my ideals.

Jennifer, Monica's friend, is, like her, a graduate anthropology student. Her objections to exclusively Aboriginal land are practical as well as rational:

If you shut them up and say either side can't go there, you're not going to learn anything about each other any more. Through understanding we make progress. If it's open, [they can] teach the non-Aborigines about it. I find that my contact with Aboriginal people is very minimal and a lot of assumptions come out of that.

Elsie Chan does not distinguish between sites personal to her and more distant locations. *Aboriginals in the Northern Territory deserve to have their land because so much was taken away. For me it's like, 'why not?'* But still land must be shared. She respects Aboriginality as she does a Japanese temple, but would be wary of the imposition of rules on photos or special permits. *Sometimes I'm not sure that what they say is what they culturally believe or whether they're just taking advantage of the situation in which they say 'We're Indigenous, we've been suppressed, we want this, we want this.'* It is a matter of principle to her that she retain the same rights in the western desert as she holds in Sydney. If these areas

of personal attachment—like the Ku-ring-gai Chase National Park—
became Aboriginal land she would reject any attempt to refuse her
entry because she hopes that Aboriginals, like others, 'want to integrate together rather than having separate patches of land that different
people own that we exclude each other from'. *I feel I have as much
right to the land as anyone else does.* I ask about her exclusion from
men's sites.

*Oh it's like an orchestra that doesn't allow females, to me it's the same sort of
issue. In a sense I think, 'No, there should be nothing when you exclude one
sex or the other', but on the other hand I do have in my mind a certain respect
for other people's religious beliefs. Ideally I don't like to think there is anything
exclusive to any one sex, but for a cultural or religious belief I will respect it if
I have to.*

Motivation to Elsie is critical. She does not disassociate herself,
though of Chinese descent, from the past misdeeds of the White
Australians. *It was a bad thing that we did, as a community.* Yet sympathy
can be very dangerous. *To do things for people, because you feel sorry for
them is the wrong way to do it. You'll end up making the wrong decisions, and
believe what they say rather than what was actually true. People will take
advantage of you.* While historical awareness is essential, it is a mistake to
be 'overly sympathetic' or consumed with guilt because the majority
culture may find itself exploited. Land claims should be arbitrated on
the principles of natural justice, not sympathy or politics. *They've been
suppressed for so long, we'll give them a bit of land here and there.* Ultimately
isolated communities are not solving anything, *It's just a temporary
solution.*

I recite to the Orley School girls the last lines of Marjorie Pizer's
poem, 'On Revisiting My Childhood Home after Many Years',

> Ghosts of my childhood walk around with me
> Though strangers work in every room I knew.

They understand the emotion of losing country perfectly.

*I remember when we left our property and went back to visit half a year
later and it made me so angry seeing other people in my house and kids my*

age. Like we went and played with them because I was only little, and it made
me angry thinking, 'this is my place'. And it still makes me angry.

Hardest of all to bear is farmland turned into suburbs.

We live right near Murrumbateman [a Canberra 4-hectare commuter area,
once a separate village]. It just seems they're encroaching on you. It pisses me
off no end. It's just that it used to be pastoral land, I hate that, and all that land
around Gungahlin [another Canberra suburb] which was the most stunning
pastoral and grazing land, now they've just stuck all these revolting suburbs
on it.

KNOWING
Not everyone has spoken with an Aboriginal! Monica had a sharp
experience, from which she drew a painful conclusion:

I went to a conference in Adelaide, called 'Women Power and Politics', and
there were some Aboriginal women from Adelaide and they helped open the
conference, 'Welcome to our land' and stuff. I went to a few of the sessions
they gave, and they were so angry, they were saying 'We feel really sorry for
you white people' and they were swearing a lot. That really made me re-think
how I regarded Aboriginal Australia. Because I'd always had an attitude,
I guess 'cause I'd never seen anyone so angry, it was very confronting. Up to
that point I'd been really committed to doing anything people wanted me to do.
I thought I had a really clear direction in what I wanted to achieve in the world,
to devote myself to something that needed a lot of attention and I didn't think
I'd be entirely welcomed at this point. People were angry at me and I had to
rethink it.

She realised the difficulties of a position sympathetic to Aboriginals but which implied an exclusion of wider human experience. *It's*
really frustrating because everyone's been fucked over in their life, and you
should use it as a connection rather than a barrier.
None of the students at Lake Ginninderra had ever spoken with
an Aboriginal at the time we met. The concept of Aboriginal specialness made all three thoughtful or uncomfortable. All were aware that
the notion of Australia as an equal and ethnically impartial country
does not altogether sit with Aboriginal specialness. Dale believed that

'special privileges' meant only recognising that in some areas Aboriginals were very disadvantaged, Scott that economic concessions are a problem, but 'on the other hand the Aboriginals were here first and we've gotta see their religion and their culture'. They wondered why Aboriginal passports were necessary as some Aboriginals demanded. *It just takes away the Australian identity.* Josephine holds out for an Aboriginal flag for the Olympics Games as well as passports. Her friend objects, 'But aren't we all equal?' and continues:

We're all the one nation so we all should have equal opportunities, and that comes down to other decisions like the land—why should they have their certain place when the rest of Australians can't have it? What's stopping one religious group coming up and saying well our god has told us that the Majura range is a sacred place, why can't we feel that? So that's what it comes down to, Aboriginals are going to be getting special grants, special rights, then why can't different other people?

In her first year of medicine Elsie Chan visited an Aboriginal settlement some distance from Tamworth, NSW, to find a society both excluding and excluded. The adults seemed hardly ever to leave and few strangers entered. Mothers told her of a few joint activities with the non-Aboriginal children. *The kids'd get along fine, they'd be happy to see each other, they'd be good friends, and yet it's the parents who would somehow get in the way somewhere.* The children on either side were often not allowed to go to each other's birthday parties. *Asians and Aborigines can be racist too.*

These young Australians have not met many Aboriginals, and have had fewer direct experiences. They are sympathetic to Aboriginal suffering. They know the generalities, but not much of the detail, of Australian history. They do not wish their own place to be compromised, either in the nation or at a site of attachment, not least because that exclusion conflicts with the deeply set sentiment of a culturally equal Australia. None expressed any desire to be spiritually at one with Aboriginals, though most contrasted a spiritual culture with what they took to be their own shallower society. *'In most people's case it's probably a parallel track.'*

I'm sure that the Orley School girls are wondering why I haven't yet asked them about race relations. Partly it's because I've been surprised at their passionate articulation of their own senses of belonging, and partly because I want to establish a friendly relationship with them before we begin what I expect to be a difficult topic. Now it's the end of the first side of the cassette. I invite them brightly, 'Okay, well, it's time to consider the other major group with a claim to the land—the Aboriginal people. So first, everyone, tell me about your experiences. Do you know any Aboriginals?' The tension rises perceptibly.

One student particularly has been waiting for this cue. She announces almost triumphantly:

I've been hit by one.

Oh yeah? Tell me about that.

I went to a dance, and a girl in year eight no less, at the Catholic disco, this girl was on Abstudy at our school. She didn't like the look of me, she thought I was too white, so she punched me in the face.

Were there mainly Kooris in the pub?

No, she was the only one, but she had a lot of standing at our school, she was really scary. Big girl, big girl. I got back up again and that was it. And she was suspended.

Now everyone wants to tell their Aboriginal story:

At Merriwa there is one Aboriginal which is a half-caste who's our pig-worker's girlfriend, and she's not very nice whatsoever.

I live half an hour from an Aboriginal camp site which is called Weilmoringle, we have Aboriginals that come and work on our property all the time, we're not really fazed by them unless they start stealing stuff; and we also have Brewarrina which probably consists of three-quarters Aboriginal, most of them are now half-castes. Actually all the properties employ Aborigines as for crutching and shearing. No-one's really that bothered by them that much.

In Barraba there's probably about five or six, there's not many, but I know one quite well, she works in community service in the nursing home. I think she's lovely, I wouldn't see her as, what—being an Aboriginal from what I've seen lately. Compared to the others, nothing like them. Then the other half of the family is alcoholics, they don't do anything and they're on the dole.

I went through the park in Dubbo one time with a friend, and they came up to us and were going, 'what are you doing here, you know, you're white, blah'. They swore at me and lots of stuff and made you feel, like; well, we hadn't done anything to them, like I was going to swimming training and was just walking, cutting through the park. And ever since those sort of situations, and then what was really funny was that they had someone who was white with them as well.

I've only ever had a—hardly ever known any Aboriginals at all and the very few experiences were really so shit. One time I had to ride my pony past, I wasn't very big, I was only about twelve, I had to ride my pony past, there's like an area of town in Yass where all the Aboriginals live, there's about six or eight houses in a row and they all just choose to live there. It's not that they have to, but it's just they choose to stick together, I guess. But to get to the vet's you have to go past sort of where they live. And I'm just riding past, you know, little horse, and there was a guy sitting on his front porch, I guess, he picked up a bottle, smashed it on the side of his verandah and pegged it at me, and it hit the fence behind me horse and we were out of it real quick.

Yeah, my cousin was cotton chipping up in Ruena and anyway, she went to the pub one night, like on a Saturday night, and all the Aboriginals must have ganged up and the whole pub was, just it was covered in—

A friend: *Surrounded?*

yeah, just surrounded with Aboriginals, and pub had to be closed down or locked up and they had to stay in there for the night, before the police could control the Aboriginals outside. And they were throwing rocks and God knows what—

I went to the Come By Chance picnic races last holiday and there were a lot of Aboriginals there, and one tried to pick a fight with me, and luckily I had two very very big strong boys next to me, but I mean that was, it's not necessary and the next morning after the races, there were two, two black women and they were going round smashing everyone's tail lights in, for no reason, they were all very intoxicated.

A friend: *They were stealing as well—*

A friend of mine, they were coming up to his car, and he said, 'Look, don't, stop it', and they turned around 'want a fight eh?', and he gets aggressive and he's in for a fight—but he wasn't—he was extremely hung over. And they, because they'd been smashing the tail lights with broken bottles, they'd broken some bottles, and they lunged at him and cut him on his chin. And he just went straight to this big police van and Aboriginals are now up for attempted manslaughter. And they were so angry, and they were chained to the van, and they looked like wild animals trying to get away, and they were cutting themselves because of the handcuffs, I mean, that's really unnecessary.

The friend: *And people had to be breath-tested as they were leaving, and as they were driving up to be breath-tested they were yelling at all of us, and saying 'all you white rer rer', and at the police, and they were trying to hit them. Really violent.*

The conversation remains serious, tense, angry. Could the girls share their properties with Aboriginals visiting sacred sites or occasionally camping? Clearly it is a subject that they have often discussed. Again everyone wants to speak. *'Fine!' 'It's cool!' 'It depends!'* Almost forgetting the microphone, they argue entry rights among themselves:

It depends on what your land's being used for, if you've got crops there you don't want—

Aboriginals trooping through—

Yeah, it could be perfectly good crop land.

Could you then come to some sort of agreement okay, right now?

Of course you can. Yeah right now we've stripped, we've done our bit, so could you do it the times of the year that we're …

No that's fine—

But if they demanded to march on, I mean, you'd have to negotiate, but I mean, I can't see a problem with it.

I don't think we'd have any problem with it. If they've got specific religious reason, I mean not religious but cultural reasons for going, that's fine.

I think it'd be cool to have people wandering round.

If they respected it for what we had made it now—well, we don't make much of it now—but if they didn't leave rubbish around, and they did have the respect to ask for it as a sacred site, I don't see any problem. But only if they were doing it as a serious claim, not if they had just read something and thought, 'Oh that's what we can get'. Because I don't think they'd know about it.

I ask about entry not for cultural reasons, but because of memories of growing up along the river when the elderly people were children. What if they had been forced from their land and trucked hundreds of kilometres to a run-down government settlement? *Well, it wouldn't have been my family that would've taken them.* Yes, but would requests for entry through such associations be more problematic? No:

If I'm approached as a rational person then treated as a rational person, yeah, sure. I'd know that if I'd lost my land then I would want to go back. Yeah. Yeah.

I mean you can understand that.

Like we go fishing all the time.

A few ground rules—don't leave the gates open and things like that. As long as you've got rules laid down and they obey. Well, it's not a question of rules. If everyone mutually understands.

I don't think, honestly, when you look around the town, that the Aboriginal people there that you're seeing, would know anything about their background.

What if they read that it belonged to their grandfather?

Too bad. We shouldn't have to pay for our great-grandparents' mistakes.

What if they wanted an old reserve back, at Port Macquarie?

Too bad. Too bad.

Other students understand better the supposed historical ignorance of the Aboriginals:

Well, if they could get some proof, I'm not doubting it would be, that would be fine by me. I'm not saying that my father would let Aboriginals—

They don't care, they're getting money from being half and quarter Aboriginal.

Would some of the pastoralists in your district oppose Aboriginal land claims?

Definitely, yeah.

For sure.

Oh yeah.

My grandfather would. You'd get the really old school conservative type.

I think it's got a lot to do with a lot of, how much land the Aboriginals already have, to how much people accept more Aboriginal title. Because I think people are more scared of at the moment, that if we let the Aboriginals back on to our land to do these sacred ceremonies and everything …

All my land is being claimed by Wik, so pretty angry at the moment. They've claimed it all along the river. Well, we're pretty angry because actually we're trying to sell one of our properties which we've been unable to do because of the Wik uncertainty, we haven't been able to get loans from the bank or anywhere else. I agree with my parents that that's unfair on us, because this isn't going to be decided for a couple of years yet, and so we can't sell anything till it has been decided.

Is there any talk of negotiation?

It's too hard because we really don't really know who it is. They've been pretty quiet about it, because they've claimed a lot of the land.

How then, I asked, were we to solve these problems?

It's too hard!

I don't know how to fix that one!

Can't help you there, honey!

It depends really on whether the Aboriginals actually want it or whether they're after the money.

If you're genuinely using the land and the Aboriginals claim it, then you don't want to see them, you don't want to see it go to ruins—

But at the same time there's this whole kind of other thing, that they've been here like for so much longer than we will ever probably be here in a way, that—

Okay, sure, we're using it for agricultural purposes, but I guess under their culture they should be allowed to use it for their cultural purposes which might not necessarily make much money—

A student asks her friends, 'But how much do we have to give them before they—?'

Exactly. Exactly. But I mean, yeah, they deserve, well at the moment it's like, they're not claiming my property, so yeah, they definitely deserve some land, but they're not treading on my toes, so go ahead.

DELIBERATING

Monica the anthropologist is deeply aware of the Aboriginal past history and that some of her own relations are 'incredibly racist'; in a negative sense, she thinks, she defines herself against them. The initial dispossession changed everything:

I dunno 'pay for', but recognise it. It's not just giving back land and paying back money, you have to recognise something, and if you recognise something then you can realise where people are coming from, and therefore have empathy, you can relate; but that's where people find it really difficult, to recognise that because if you grow up in mainstream Australia then you don't actively seek out to find out more about what you learn at school or read in the paper, then you're not going to get that background.

Monica admits to feelings of guilt which are surrounded by conflict. *Yes, I do. I can feel remorseful. I don't want to but I do.* Her friend Jennifer, born in Belgium, contributes, 'And it's probably not very helpful.' Monica replies, 'That's okay, I'm young.' Jennifer evidently feels that she belongs nowhere, yet that Australia holds still part of her. She treasures certain parts of the land in affection which, though neither as precisely remembered nor as located as the Orley School students' land, remains of great importance. *It would be very difficult if [Aboriginals] said to me 'you can't go through'.*

Trina feels that she belonged to parts of Melbourne:

I feel that on a much smaller scale within Melbourne. Like when I'm in Beaumaris [where she lived till she was twenty] I just feel that things are familiar, I recognise—but I don't feel like I truly belong; and when I go away from it sometimes it's really important [to know] that's where I grew up, that's where I came from, that's where my roots are. Like when I'm away from it it's important, like two countries almost. I'm developing a sense of belonging in Fitzroy after three years.

Momo emphatically rejects the notion that she has no right to be here, that 'exclusionary sense because you're not Aboriginal it's not your land and you have no right being here, it's our land, go away'. Non-Aboriginal Australians may have arrived recently, but that is out of her control: *We have to make a living here as well, we can't deny the existence of the last 200 years. We're not the first ones here, but what does it matter?* Trina argues that her family, arriving in Australia in 1852, belongs no differently from an Italian family arriving a century later. A hundred years is nothing. I ask, then aren't we illogical in insisting that Aboriginals being here first is of primary importance? Trina replies that the distinction is the point of invasion:

Not in my mind, because as far I can gather, the White people invaded a pristine culture that had been going on for thousands of years, and I don't know that Anglo-Saxon people ever invaded another culture equally pristine. Asian people are no different to me in that sense, they're newcomers.

Monica is troubled by the implications of 'firstness':

That's really interesting, I've been thinking about that and a lot of the time when we talk about this, it's based on the fact that Aboriginal people were here first, and it makes me wonder why we privilege firstness—it's sort of mixed up with a sort of trend in our society: the person who wins the race, you never know who comes second, and I think perhaps the importance of firstness might not always be as important as it is now; I don't know if we'll ever change our ethic of competition. I can't understand why Australians feel so guilty at the moment for previous happenings. I understand that it happened and I understand it's very bad and that it's wrong and that it shouldn't happen again, but I can't understand why this generation should feel guilty, as if they've done something.

Jennifer has no doubt: *Because it's still happening, that's why. It's still happening.*

BELONGING

Though Momo Miyaguchi and Elsie Chan feel sometimes rejected by their fellow Australians, they emphasise that they feel, and are, Australian. Momo thinks that young Australians of mixed parentage like herself have a unique contribution: *You've got the benefit of seeing how different cultures work and the values that work for them and how they shape your understanding of situations.* They more easily conceive of different values. Otherwise: *You're not consciously aware of the values you have.* She sees the specialness of Aboriginals less in their spirituality, more in their environmental knowledge. Yes, we have indeed a lot to learn; if Aboriginals are willing to share that knowledge then Momo is happy to be taught. I persist—do Aboriginals have a firm moral authority as the first, or more spiritual, Australians? In terms of belonging, it doesn't matter:

If [Aboriginal] people are saying, 'you're a second-class citizen and you haven't been here and there's no chance of you ever making up for it and don't try', well, I don't think that's very constructive. Sure, we come from such different backgrounds, but we can all work towards the situation where we can all co-exist. My place too? Yes, because it's inside your head, it's inside your concept of maybe home, or where you belong, and you can't help it, and you're here in this country as well.

Elsie studies in a divided medicine course and lives in a divided Sydney. While she knows 90 per cent of her fellow students, the Asians and non-Asians frequently keep apart.

It's partly because the non-Asians in the course just don't go out of their way to socialise with the Asians much, which stems from the upbringing they've had. The Caucasians were too groupy, too disinterested and exclusionist, and they still are, they're very much, well, they think they're different and they obviously have no need to get to know everyone else.

Now Elsie seldom finds herself amongst all-Caucasians except when in Canberra. Yet she does not mix well with the majority Asian group who arrived within the last five years. *At times I feel a bit in the middle, then I realise that that's another group in itself, the people who are not [either]. My really close friends here [in Sydney] have all come from a very similar background to myself.* Physically Elsie belongs to Australia.

Socially she belongs to Chinese Australians born in this country. *Now I feel I may be missing out on a bit of Chineseness, I don't have the best of both now.* In Sydney she has not been allowed to forget her Asian descent. *I'm increasingly aware of how segregated Sydney is.* Against such urgent preoccupations, Aboriginals are less significant, essentially no more than another valued Australian ethnicity. Greeks and Italians contribute their close family values, the Chinese an ethic of hard work. Aboriginals, she is certain, will contribute too—herbal medicine? As to many other Australians born overseas, Elsie's belonging is primarily not a matter of land, but of social relations. The obverse of the question 'Do you belong?' is 'Are all individuals and all ethnicities accepted as equal?' If so, then Elsie belongs to Australia physically, culturally and socially.

Belonging can mean more than care for the nation, more than the acceptance of all Australians. Young Australians' responsibilities Trina sees to extend to the global environment; true citizenship may be international. Not one of these young Australians would agree with Robert Levitus' gloomy prognostication that 'probably no-one, at least from a non-Aboriginal background, ever does' fit.[1]

Out west belonging in body and mind derives forever from the land and the rural lifestyle. The sense of attachment of the Orley School girls is rooted in the perceived moral worth of themselves and their families which flows from the land and the lifestyle and, in truth, of historical and contemporary ignorance of Aboriginality; in return they bestow on their land love, strength and affection formed out of memory and association. Aboriginals challenge that belonging. Unlike Indigenous people elsewhere—anywhere—*their* local Aboriginals they describe as corrupted by special privilege, forgetfulness, ignorance, their less than total Aboriginal descent, their dissipation, their desire for easy gain, their high place on the government list of 'disadvantaged'. Yet they concede that Aboriginal belonging can be accommodated under certain conditions. Sharing under controlled terms is fair, and greatly to be preferred to legal alienation. Sharing may take place for two purposes, not unlike the girls' own senses of belonging—through cultural and personal association. Not through the original dispossession and not for commercial gain.

Orley School girls distinguish themselves from the more conservative older generation. The police should not have chained up the drunken Aboriginals to the police wagon like wild animals. They concede that the past is problematic:

We originally created the problem, it festered in the middle and now it's being swung back at us like the complete opposite. I suppose it's no correlation to what they had to face when the first white settlers came in, but the unfairness has come back on us now.

As is the present:

But at the same time—I don't know because I've got no idea—is it harder for them? I mean, what sort of racial prejudices exist, like, does prejudice exist to make it harder for them to get to university and stuff, without these kind of programs. Does it?

And the future:

I hope the Aboriginals do get their compensation they are looking for, but not my land. I do respect a lot of the Aboriginals from home, there's a lot of Aboriginals work very hard.

One speaker conceded Aboriginal specialness:

In spirit. I think in spirit they are. 'Cause I mean, in a bit, well they founded the land.

Who, if anyone, was responsible? One Orley School response had been firm:

My parents have enough money for my family, and my education and my clothes—and why should they have to pay for their clothes because my great-grandfather made a mistake? It's just absolutely ridiculous.

I recall Charles Perkins once telling me how as a young man he walked up dance halls in Adelaide in search of a partner, constantly ignored or told, 'I don't dance with Aboriginals, you know.' I ask the girls a related question. 'Could you have an Aboriginal boyfriend?'

Oh yes. These girls are not their parents: there is room for compromise, there may be common ground.

LIVING IN THE HOUSE OF AUSTRALIA
Think of Australia as a house, I suggest. Morally and physically—who owns it now? As ever, Orley School jumps in enthusiastically:

I can't agree with that!

It should be everyone's house!

It's not but they think it is!

It shouldn't be but at the moment it is, because that's the way society is, in terms of law.

No … Oh that's sentimental. I mean, I'm not saying they let us in the country, but I'm saying, like now there's other people that are coming in … But we can all share, I really don't see why there's such a problem.

Look at America, they had their native blacks, and now white people have moved in, and they're not kicking up a huge fuss about it.

But we've got to accept that we've got to become a lot more tolerant and make it easier for Aboriginals to live in society as they choose to. But at the same time they've got to accept that it's got to be a compromise. Yeah, they've had to give the most all the way along, but you can't revert to that as it was. History has moved on. It can't go back. And so the only way for them, I think in a way it's sad, but they're probably going to have to work within our society in order to achieve the things they want.

Monica accepts that the Australian house is still Aboriginal: *I'd ask 'How much is the rent?' It's entirely reasonable. I feel we're definitely in arrears.* To most others, Australia has ceased to be a solely Aboriginal house, even morally:

I think it's everybody's house, we all come here.

I don't think so. It's a long time since we first came here. It was the Aboriginals' house, but right from the start we didn't consider it as their house, we considered it as land, these people are here, we should share the land. They didn't share the land at all, we took it over, killed the Aborigines, the Aborigines didn't know what the hell was going on. Maybe for a while or for a very short time it would be the Aboriginals' house, but from there on the entitlements changed.

We changed the culture so much that if it [still] was the Aboriginals' house, wouldn't it mean we'd have to change back like to a different culture, back to Aboriginal culture?

You can't really say that it's the Aboriginals' house any more because they have been forced out of it basically.

It's still all our house, and the Aboriginal house all shoved into one little corner of the attic, very small possessions.

We sort of kicked them into the attic, and when they went they sort of shut up, now they've come out and the problems are rising, and they're asking for things and want right to the kitchen and the toilet and the bathroom—but where's it stop? I don't think this is going to happen, but they're going to say 'jump' and we're gonna say 'how high?' I don't think that will happen, but when's it going to stop? How much are they going to claim?

We're not going to get up and leave, it's just about recognising, in some areas the Aborigines are obviously very disadvantaged, and that's not really part of a working society.

Damian, the first-generation Italian/Greek/Slovenian, is as torn between his head and his heart by this question as to whether he supports the slogan 'Always was always will be Aboriginal land'. His head says: *You don't want to say it's not an Aboriginal house because it is.* His heart says: *I've been born here, all my knowledge is Australian, and why shouldn't I have my section of it?* Damian was as distressed at the prospect of Aboriginals burning the Australian flag as I was when I witnessed the act outside Parliament House. It would be desecration to burn any country's flag, still less his own. He is sickened at the prospect. *I can see why you do it but it doesn't mean that I like it.*

Young Australians growing. The first project of those who feel themselves excluded by the mainstream society is to achieve social belonging in their own right. *It's not so much the land that is in my mind at all, it's more just the general community attitude.* Those raised on rural properties are much less troubled by the past than the Anglo-Celts of the cities, who are unconvinced of the value of the society which dispossessed the Aboriginals. All whom I spoke with, I think, place themselves somewhere on the spectrum that Aboriginality once was, or may be still, a rich and spiritual society. But it is one ethnicity among many. Aboriginality is to be valued, respected, tolerated and encouraged. Aboriginals may be brought to a level playing field, there must be an end to discrimination. Ultimately, though, all are equal.

This is the common ground. Australia must be shared less by individuals than by ethnicities. The Orley School girls put this negatively: while Aboriginals have not exactly forfeited their right to a prior moral or actual claim, as their parents and grandparents might have believed, it is now a matter of fact that the house of Australia is also occupied by others who by their presence share in joint possession. *You can't set aside 200 years. We belong here too.* At the other end of the spectrum others put the same position positively. The overarching value of Australia is multicultural equality, skewed though it may be away from some and towards certain other ethnicities. Multiculturalism is the ultimate Australian value:

That defines us. Our multiculturalism is our identity. Mistakes in the past? We're here now. We're all Australian, whatever else we are. It's a growing multicultural culture!

Does Aboriginal prior belonging, if that is what it is, weaken that sense of equality of culture?

Oh no!

Does the 'first Australian' claim irritate you?

No! No! I acknowledge it. Their identity [as the first Australians] is different from mine as a first-generation Australian. But we're all equal. We're all here now, aren't we?

| MEN'S BUSINESS

I NEVER FELT I HAD A STRONG SENSE OF BELONGING
UNTIL I WORKED WITH ABORIGINAL PEOPLE

I met Ian Green twenty-five years ago at Tindal, outside Katherine in
the Northern Territory. We were both teachers, he at the Area School,
I at the School of the Air. Our children were the same age, we played in
bands together, we had our ears pierced on the same day. While staying
with him in 1989 at the Aboriginal reserve Papunya in Central Australia, and picnicking a few kilometres into the bush, we were in deep
discussion about Aboriginal and Western conceptions of country. From
nowhere a willy-willy descended to punctuate the still point of a pretty
serious conversation, blew for twenty seconds and scattered our lunch
for 50 metres. A coincidence? I thought of the words of Peter Sutton the
linguist-anthropologist, who knows traditional indigenous country as
intimately as any non-Aboriginal alive today:

> I don't believe in any great thing up there governing things, and I don't
> have an architect-of-the-universe view of the world, but I do think
> you've got to be opportunistic about gaining meaning, to link things that
> may appear to be unlike to each other, or linking things which in fact
> are like each other but which you've tried to forget are like each other.
> It's the connecting sensibility, and that's what Aborigines are doing
> talking about the dreaming and land. … Connect Connect Connect. We
> [Westerners] tend to compartmentalise much more in a linear way.[1]

I am going to try to release some competing realities to connect three
men and their relationships to land. Men's business.

Ian describes himself when an undergraduate as young and cocky, not belonging anywhere in particular. He had enjoyed, in the Adelaide suburb of Fullarton, a 'wonderfully secure and sheltered childhood and family life', but never as an adult had he a feeling of permanent attachment to one place. If his parents died, he thinks, he would no longer visit the family home, nor Fullarton. Returning to any of the many places he rented in Canberra touches intellect rather than emotion. *I feel I'm just looking at memories.* In a BA Honours degree in English literature and an MA in linguistics, Ian learned that the world worked according to the ways of the classroom. Theories could explain all perceived phenomena: *You can get away with that sort of thing when you're a bit of a smart-arse lefty hanging around with your ideological mates in Canberra.* If he had belonged anywhere generically, he thought, it was not to houses or suburbs, but to unlocated country, mostly gleaned out of Wordsworth and lectures about landscape poetry in English I. As an angst-driven young undergraduate he would go to and sit down by Lake Burley Griffin and 'think that was marvellous and tranquil'. Ian does not think that at this time he ever felt landscape powerfully.

In 1980 he selected the barely known Marrithiyel language of the Daly River region in the Northern Territory as the subject of his MA thesis. Knowing nothing of the country, and having hardly ever spoken seriously to an Aboriginal person before, he set out for the Daly River in an Australian National University four-wheel-drive Toyota. Ian drove up the Stuart Highway from Tennant Creek and Katherine. The country was beautiful, not least because of his heightened emotions as he arrived.

You get on to the Daly road, and there's a particular point when you come around and as you come up one of the rises you can see the smaller hills that flank the river and you can see the beginnings of the road up to Wooliana where the Malak Malak people are; it's more or less coming into the inner valley of the river.

Ian made a first acquaintance with the older man who became his principal language teacher, Bill Parry. One of Bill's Aboriginal names, the mythological context of which remained mysterious at this time, was Watjen Gusribek, 'The Dingo Howls Out'.

The first cultural shock was simply living in an environment so alien as to be a foreign country. The Western clock was irrelevant. *You just learn to sit around and enjoy being with people, take things in.* He began to absorb the Aboriginal village Nambiyu, the old Catholic mission of Daly River: the drinking and the feuds, the fun and the gossip, the invective and the passions of ordinary Aboriginal life. Ian had arrived as the self-confident professional linguist, the prospective Master of Arts who now found that it took six or seven days to put together his first complex verb. They could speak four or five Aboriginal languages and do a good job in English. Simultaneously dawned on him the immense learning of the older men and women which no-one had explained to him at university. Ian's non-Western education had begun. He did not yet realise his luck in learning the stories of country from men who themselves learned them from their grandfathers on the exact and appropriate sites. On the Daly today that is no longer possible.

A White man working with Aboriginal men is expected to take part in the large-scale hunting and fishing trips rather than hunting turtle or gathering lily roots with the women. As the possessor of a four-wheel-drive vehicle, Ian's patronage was useful. He learned to shoot, winch himself out of bogs, mend punctures, weld a cracked chassis. As an outsider he was supposed to observe all the complex rules of politeness but was forgiven (the first time) when he did not. He soon became embroiled in factions impossible to avoid: *if you're with any group you're very soon identified with their political interest; men are expected to come in boots and all, get dirty.*

He learned first the social rather than the religious stories of the land. In the rocky ridge country dwelled the *menumemeri*, Marrithiyel-speaking little pygmy men, quite black, who were felt, or heard, at night or who twinkled at the edges of vision. They are dangerous. A man travelling by night or camping in their country is liable to be enslaved, a woman to be raped. Amongst the men of Bill's generation, stories were told of Marrithiyel who had found themselves surrounded in the ridges, but who had talked their way out of trouble by speaking to *menumemeri* in Marrithiyel and by giving gifts of flour, tea or sugar. In the months that followed three or four of Ian's friends told him how on different occasions, stopped by *menumemeri*, they had spoken with them, offered supplies and been let go. Their absolute conviction in the stories left Ian in no doubt that they believed that they had seen the *menumemeri*. This was a puzzle never adverted to in linguistic lectures. His friends were not drunk, they were not hallucinating. Absolutely they had experienced something. What did that mean?

Ian had been taught, like all linguists of Australian languages, that land is central to the most basic Aboriginal senses of being. It appeared that on the Daly River in the early 1980s, land was principally inherited by men through the patriline, sometimes through wife or mother. Knowledge of location and the stories associated with sites were a fundamental part of the initiation of young men and their later education. He understood intellectually that the relationship between land and its sacralised sites, sometimes unspoken but never absent, was the *sine qua non* of the moment and of the whole of life. Aboriginal land was thronged by the presence of the creators, the spiritual guardians and of the dead. It sang, it cried out, it assumed multiple forms simultaneously, it knew when it was respected or violated, cared for or abandoned. Country knew, and knows, newcomers; it looks to visitors to identify themselves; in return, country will care for its children. In the Queensland region to which, Aboriginally, he now belongs, Peter Sutton feels a tingle when his armpit is rubbed and his hair blown through to introduce him to new country or to a new spiritual guardian.

The anthropologist Debbie Rose felt the connection one nightfall in the Victoria River district not far from the Daly. Sitting beside her in the ute was her mentor Jessie. Debbie was normally conscious of what she called Jessie's 'attentive acceptance' of the natural world, which that evening so affected her that Debbie experienced something of what, she believes, is an Aboriginal perception of country, 'channels of energy connecting everything to everything, every tree, every leaf, every blade of grass, every stone, the hills on the horizon'. She felt 'concentrated and connected, incredibly alive and incredibly valuable'.[2] Would Ian, the Westernised sceptic, feel anything of this close bonding of human and land?

Ian was not, as has often happened to other academics early in their fieldwork, formally taken round the country to be introduced to the sites, then quizzed on their names and significance. But intimacy followed intense experience. One early morning he sat up over some fishing nets with a Malak Malak speaker, Pincher Ginger, waiting for the tide to turn.

We sat there in the moonlight on the riverbank for about five or six hours, from four o'clock in the morning till about nine, we just sat there together. I had a bottle of Suntory whisky, and he spent the whole time telling me things that I would have taken months and months of questioning to find out about, customs along the river, and of bird calls, ways of cutting fish up.

Intimacy brought affinities and a sense of belonging, not to Aboriginal Australia but to those precise sites within Marrithiyel country, rights to visit and to be there, denied to others and acquired because the people who owned those sites and that country vouchsafed that right to him. Interviewing Ian in 1991 for the first time on his experiences, I asked, 'In what sense was that a right?' *Well, I feel like I belong there.* The first connection. As Debbie Rose puts it, 'Dream country is belonging. Every person has a place in the world in which they are needed, and in which they are "healthy".'[3] Explanations about language often involved Ian in site visits where conversations turned philosophical. In the wild country Ian felt his Western conceptions begin to shift uneasily.

One site which Bill Parry frequently spoke about was Watjen Gusrifumpu, 'where the dingo bubbles up', the birthplace of the Marrithiyel people. A good day's drive from Nambiyu, Watjen Gusrifumpu was described by Bill as a bubbling mineral spring where the mother dingo had given birth to the Marrithiyel people in the form of dingo pups who later transformed themselves into humans. Dingo gave the Marrithiyel (and other Aboriginals associated with the Dingo Dreaming) their characteristic shape, brain and culture.[4] Watjen Gusrifumpu, though not a dangerous ancestral site in Marrithiyel mythology, must certainly be respected. Bill was connected to the site through his mother's country. It was the point at which three closely related Daly River languages—Marrithiyel, Marringarr and Marramaninjdji— seemed to converge. Was it possible, Ian asked himself, that this mythological creation site could have been the actual site where the ancestral group which gave rise to these languages might have lived? Was the site of the confluence of language and 'where the dingo bubbles up' one and the same?

Marrithiyel people are Dingo people. The shooting and trapping of dingo to Marrithiyel people is totally forbidden. Dingo guards the people, dingo is the mother of the people, dingo is the people. Early in 1981 three teenage girls studying in Darwin were killed in a terrible traffic accident on the Stuart Highway. Four or five months later some of the community, still in fathomless grief, acutely aware that they were travelling in the deep dingo country, packed up supper and made their way slowly back to Nambiyu. Ian and five or six others were travelling in the back of the ute. Someone turned the spotlight behind the vehicle. Padding silently 30 metres behind were three dingoes ghostly pale in the gathering dusk. When the vehicle stopped, so did they. For some seconds they stared, then turned into the darkness. Profound terror seized the party.

More than two years after Ian arrived, Bill announced, as part of a mapping project requested by the Northern Land Council, that a visit would be made to Watjen Gusrifumpu where the dingo bubbles up. Bill had not visited the site for some years, never by vehicle, and would have to navigate by the 'footwalk' bearings of resting point and water-course. Many were the punctures in the four vehicles of the party, the false starts and stops for tea and johnny cakes; in the end the party came upon Watjen Gusrifumpu quite suddenly from an unexpected direction. Like many other Aboriginal mythological sites, Watjen Gusrifumpu was not visually stunning—blackish brown, set around with pandanus and paperbark, at this point in the dry season about 30 by 20 metres. Bill approached first, calling out in Marrithiyel, 'This is me, the Watjen Gusribek. We have come to look at the site, come to look after it.' He moved round the waterhole, touching certain pandanus trees, sometimes talking, sometimes in silence. The others approached the waterhole, a site both sacred and social. Bill allowed people to drink from it, take from it water to wash in—indeed, probably in the dry season it was the only reliable water for many miles. Now to intro-duce Ian to the mother dingo. Bill called out in Marrithiyel, 'I know this bloke, it's all right, his name's Ian, we've taught him to speak Marrithiyel, he's coming to say hello.' Bill asked him to shout back to the dingo spirit certain Marrithiyel responses. The party withdrew a little and camped for the night.

In the course of the mapping survey, Ian was formally intro-duced to twenty-five additional significant or sacred sites. Whenever he revisits them he finds himself, against his rational judgement, shouting to the creation ancestor, or whispering in his mind, the same formulas of respect and care. *Here I am, I've come to have a look to see if this place is all right. Is it all right if I come in?* I ask: Do you do this out of politeness? Ian replies that it's neither politeness nor habit. Would anything bad happen to you if you did not say the right words?

I think probably not. My Western self thinks not. But I don't know. I've never actually thought about it in terms of myself, and in fact no-one said, except in a few dangerous places where nobody goes at all, that harm would befall me. At the creation billabong, people have never said, 'if we don't do this there'll be trouble', it's just that things will be generally disrupted or out of kilter. I assume that's what they think. It's not out of fear that they perform the introduction rituals. You find yourself doing that. I don't know why. When you go there it's just so strong, they do it automatically and of necessity, it's unthinkable not to do it at important sites. You absorb these things. They rub off.

From his Aboriginal teachers Ian absorbed the sense of the law being incarnate in the land. *The people have such strong convictions about the land and everything connected to it. If you wander in ignorance you're in danger of disturbing*—what? Land and its meaning is such a fundamental part of Aboriginal life that Ian shied away from violation. He learned to respect the 'incredible amount of Aboriginal knowledge, so detailed and so all-embracing that it takes the best part of a lifetime to acquire'; as an outsider his understanding would always be limited. If Ian had read, he said, the entire anthropological literature he would still have put the significance of Aboriginal landscape at the 'myth' end of the spectrum, a bit of a fiction. Now deep in the bush with the elders, men with whom he had discussed deeply the grammatical and structural complexities of the language, the Aboriginal reality of a sacred, living inspirited landscape was the only reality. Perhaps, Ian reflected, that should be the case with any different set of beliefs. If he met the right Christian visionary it would be the same:

The men have such a powerful feeling for the life force, or spirits of certain rocks or trees, and it's just their conviction and their vision, and it's just so strong and so powerful that you can't remain sceptical. You can say, 'In our own scientific terms there's nothing there', but that's totally irrelevant to what's going on. Some of it rubs off. You find yourself being less overtly sceptical or dismissive of such things, less Anglo-centric, even if you don't believe it or sense it yourself, you start to see it as a possible belief, a possible world. You learn to feel it, you get a glimpse of the way Aboriginal people might feel and in some way you feel it yourself. I've not been religious, I've never felt Jesus or God was actually there, and nobody else has managed to convince me of their vision, nothing rubbed off. Full-on Christians seemed fanatics or psychotics. But the Aboriginal people really feel there's something there. People talk to rocks, you can feel it.

In deep Aboriginal land, Western conceptions of the reality of the world shimmer and distort. The country was made by spiritual ancestors, that, almost, is obvious; the spirit ancestors and those of the human departed, so intimately linked with this group of rocks and that waterhole must be respected because ... is it because they are really there? Enlightenment was the moment he realised that competing explanations do not need to be reconciled or made compatible. If there seem to be contradictions, let them co-exist.

The far ebb of Western certainty was the moment in which the older men not only spoke to the physical form of the spirit forces but saw them. When telling Ian creation stories the older men would point to distant landforms and see—in some sense literally—the physical landform and creative spirit simultaneously. It was no vision; not 'looked like', not Westerners seeing a hill in the shape of a horse or dingo. The elder saw at once both spirit and landform. The nearest parallel in Western thought was the vision of the mystic; but these were no random revelations, the older men saw them, and casually, every time they looked at the mountain. How could one explain it? *Being with Aboriginal people defeats all your attempts to intellectualise. Even if one clings to scientific rationalism, then the Westerner is forced to accept that there are many competing explanations for the world as it seems to be.* Realities co-exist. Explanations co-exist. The Marrithiyel showed him that there was no single truth, no simple or right way for human beings to think about the meaning of the landscape which had been so much the assumptions of his university education. To the Marrithiyel there was no problem of contradiction because there was no contradiction. We accept contradictions in our own society, Ian reminded me: consider the theoretical physicist who goes to church on Sunday.

In the western desert, where Ian worked as a linguist later in the 1980s, he once more felt his normal rationalism suspended. Trustworthy senior men whom he knew to be learned and wise reported to him seeing what they called devil-devils run across the plains towards the hills. Ian's own conviction did not carry to the belief that he would have seen them, but this did not altogether mean that they were not there. Devil-devils were there for those men. *You can't doubt it. You believe them. They were neither deluded or hypnotised, they really saw them. They're in their world, and here's your world, and you see things from both sides. It's not that one is 'true', they're just alternative ways of understanding and explaining the world.* In deep Aboriginal country the life force was so strong. Ian's experiences had been so powerful, so instructive that he felt almost obliged to write them down or somehow explain them. *But I don't know what sort of form to put them in. I don't think I've talked about this with anyone.*

Eight years later Ian, now working at Bachelor College some 200 kilometres from Daly River, and visiting Marrithiyel country once a month, reflected on his experiences. Those who had been the young layabouts smiling uncertainly about *menumemeri* are now the community leaders, but few reside permanently within Marrithiyel country. The generations there now are very fine people but have evolved a more contemporary Aboriginal culture. It seems to happen very rapidly. He misses the elders and the matchless moments when his Western self dissolved and the spirits and the landforms were one. Being without his old friends changed the sense of connection and mental image. Belonging to the Daly was now more internal, historical and personal.

In 1999 most of the outstations have been established; land is important as a retreat and a source of income as well as for its traditional ties. Europeanisation is rapid, ambitions and lifestyles have changed, many of the older people have died, and much of what seemed the antiquity of the traditions has gone. The culture is expressed in equally strong but different language; the young PhD students are not told quite the same stories.

I ask: Does the land know you better now after twenty years? *No. I don't think of it as a gradation, that's what I got strongly from Aboriginals: you know it or you don't. That used to intrigue me. People would always talk to me as though I knew every site and spot—because I knew the language.* In the north of Australia, language is country.

What was the meaning of his experiences? He felt that he belonged more closely to this part of Australia than anywhere else in the world; but his corresponding sense of belonging elsewhere was in proportion weakened; for the whole of Australia he felt hardly a sense of belonging at all. *I never felt I had a strong sense of belonging until I worked with Aboriginal people.* Down south in the bush, aware of alternative explanations, he was more confident about how the land and the waterways would have been used. Simultaneously he realised his ignorance. How valuable would have been an Aboriginal guide and interpreter without whom the land loses almost all its meaning! While visiting the sites of southern Australia to which he has not been introduced, he may feel limited and inhibited: he may unknowingly violate a creation ancestor or show disrespect. He reflects that country which has been grazed or built upon surely cannot carry the same spirituality as the deep traditional country. And yet the Daly River elders hold such conviction in the spirits, the rules and the configuration of the land that the mythology seems everlasting regardless of its custodians.

You feel that these details of the inner life of the country are always there, just waiting for the person with the right kind of vision to make them apparent to you.

Do the people respond to the forces in the country already—or it is humankind which sacralises the country?

I can't see you can have landscape independent of the human perception of it.

Seven years ago I interviewed a number of the nation's most eminent younger anthropologists, historians and geographers of Aboriginal Australia about what their experiences had meant to them, especially how they came to terms with the competing explanations of the dual universe.[5] Almost all, like Ian, had been profoundly changed. One believed that sickness will befall a person who deliberately flouts traditional knowledge, such as a woman entering a men's site. Another holds that country can sing of past bloodshed even to whitefellers, that the forces in the land do not last forever but dissipate without Aboriginal spiritual care, that culture is a package of which the observer cannot accept the mentally convenient parts, that there is no dividing line between 'truth' and other people's culture, that a deep relationship to country affords a sense of human connection to land never experienced before. One has been rescued, when lost, by spirit ancestors; one tries not to think about dual realities too much. Almost all regularly talk to country to which they have previously been introduced. They belong more strongly here, less strongly there. *I do believe some. I haven't unpacked all that because I know I can't.*

The three languages that bubbled up at Watjen Gusrifumpu will be extinct within twenty years: Ian may well be the last surviving speaker of Marrithiyel. A road now sweeps the knowing or unknowing visitor past Where the Dingo Bubbles Up, but Ian is not sure whether the site is visited more frequently. Whether it did in fact mark the source of the three languages will never now be known.

MY ART IS ABOUT MEN AND LANDSCAPES

Bill Insch has been my friend for nearly twenty years since he studied art in Canberra. He was born in Britain in 1950. In the late 1970s he volunteered to work in Papua New Guinea, where he met another volunteer, an Australian named Sylvie Mester. At the conclusion of their contracts they married and travelled to Australia, seeking an environment to which they could physically contribute, and would enable them to provide for their own needs.

Bill and Sylvie were looking for land in the south-eastern corner of New South Wales when they saw an advertisement for membership of a farming co-operative, Reedy Creek Farm, a former dairy and grazing property of some 400 hectares. They travelled through the open dry country of the tableland on the way from Melbourne, descended the steep mountain road known as Big Jack to encounter, set behind the coastal plain, the granite valley of the Towamba River, inland from Eden. *It was lush and, with the rivers flowing, a beautiful place, always very appealing; hilly or undulating, it had plenty of trees.* Most of the coastal grey and yellow box trees had been logged long ago by the farmers and timber-getters, but the gullies sheltered some remnant stands of lillypilly rainforest. On the steep slopes stood the dry sclerophyll bush, peppermints and stringybarks, understorey of dogwood, black wattle, the tea-trees ever encroaching.

Generations of non-Aborigines had used the land for free-selecting, grazing, soldier-settling, dairying, timber-getting and recreation. A derelict community hall and a butter factory spoke of the thronging population before World War I. Three kilometres from the co-op on the road to Wyndham a sign identified an almost deserted site as New Buildings, about which few structures now remained. Dairying and grazing lasted until the 1960s, before the collapse of the markets terminated them both.

The co-op members met and liked the Insches; they invited them to purchase a share. Their holding would be two hectares of cleared grazing land fronting the river. Apart from the dozen other home paddocks, the rest of the farm was theirs to roam as they liked. The Insches began a garden, worked on the co-op riverside flat. They learned the areas of the farm by a new generation of occupants: Lorraine's, Trappo's, Clint and Sue's, Steve's, Julie's, Shirl's. It seemed as though they would live here forever, first in the caravan, later in the mud-brick house they built with the help of the co-op community.

For several months in the late 1980s, Reedy Creek Farm became a staging post for the protesters who chained themselves to the trees, blockaded the forest tracks and traded insults with the loggers and officials of the Harris–Daishowa woodchip mill at Eden. Bill took an energetic part in the organisation and the protest; he was once arrested when his dog revealed his presence to the police by barking at him hiding behind a tree. The old-growth areas, newly logged, would recover only after centuries. *I was very deeply emotionally affected by what I saw, I wanted to make those images speak in an artistic context.*

Reedy Creek was not yet home, nor was Bill scarcely capable of making it home. Like Ian arriving on the Daly River, Bill did not yet know how to make mud bricks, run chooks, snig logs, drive tractors, build sheds or grow vegetables. Essentially Bill saw himself as far more of an artist than a farmer. *I'm a literal person who relies on the visual appreciation of what I see. And love it.* Bill's strengthening connections were to time as well as place:

But here I've gradually built up this place over twenty years: shed, house, studio. Those connections have taken a long time to build up. The sailing boats in the shed are connections with the coast, the camping gear is for camping out in the estuaries. It's been a very gradual process. And one of the richnesses is that it's still working, I'm still working in the studio, art work has been a very slow evolving process, and part of that process has been my involvement in the environment.

Security and knowledge remained close to home. Even today Bill is not entirely at ease in the whispering gorges of the Coolangubra Forest.

Shortly after the family home was complete Bill's marriage broke up, the girls left school and departed and Bill's relation to the land acquired new meanings. As a single person it was too difficult, as well as pointless, maintaining hens and a large herb and vegetable garden.

I think my role here is basically fairly passive. I spend most of my time here working off the place [teaching at Bega High School] or in the studio so it's around this place and the building. Now as a single person I have an open gate policy, which is not fix up fences when they collapse, because the 'roos keep down the grass, the trees are high enough to be secure from them. What I try to do is to keep the trees going. This is a fairly beautiful environment which I can keep with minimum intervention, all I do is to keep down the tea-tree and the wattles.

My knowledge of Aboriginal people in this area is very slim. I understand they went up this way to the Bogong moth feasts and would have lived in forests. But all our knowledge seems to be coastal. Bill has had only one direct experience of Aboriginals on the farm. The Native Title Act allowed a Koori family recognised by the Eden Land Council to claim some 40 hectares of the Crown land above the farm, ten minutes' walk up the steep slope from Bill's home. It was a poor block, dry and fire-prone, without water or access to water, and heavily logged. It would be a very difficult piece of land to settle. Their request was gazetted; the co-op did not object. At length the family arrived in a red Falcon, walked about, put up a boundary sign, boiled the billy, and planned where they would build their weekender. Bill was pleased. Whenever he saw the car he would go up for a chat and invite the family down for a cup of tea, but they never came. Sometimes the sons arrived to make plans, but the problem seemed to be the health of their mother, who would not be well enough to live there even on weekends. After the fourth visit the family did not return. Since then Bill has met the owner, who told him that he was now trying to sell the land—to non-Aboriginals. Bill hopes that it will be purchased by the National Park which holds most of the land round it.

On the hottest day in mid-January, our formal interview complete, I rise with the dogs before dawn and imagine myself approaching the home paddock for the first time, this land now settled and conceived without Aboriginality. The house in the distance: tall but at the same time squat (mud-brick construction imposes a number of architectural constraints) standing on the lower ground between two saddles. I approach. Bill describes his home as the outcome of values of low environmental impact and artistic integrity. *It's a privileged position to have some land and to build a family home with your own labour using your own resources which you manipulate.* The timber is not only local but natural. Uprights carry knots; roof and ceiling poles are undressed and barky; the lattice of the verandah posts is curled, bent or knobbly. By the front door is a wheelbarrow load of stringybark stove wood; above it a row of horseshoes is set into the mud walls above the door; inset beside the door is a cast iron image of a lighthouse. I think of the old Latin proverb which translates as 'It is no false fire which I have followed here'. The mud walls inside carry small sculptures of life's connections: a sailing boat, birds. Paintings on the walls, on the staircase, three-dimensional pieces in clay or shell. The main bedroom: huge windows, handmade furniture, candles, art books, light and space; in the kitchen-living area: an aerial photograph of the farm, solar-power lights, wood fittings, cream Rayburn woodstove, paintings, an astrology chart. In the bathroom: a round, stained-glass window pierces the wall; beside it hangs a charcoal drawing of a dog, viewed from the back, staring over a logged and destroyed hillside. Its emotions cannot be deciphered. From the upstairs verandah the gaze soars over fruit trees, the empty chook yard, the advancing tea-tree and wattles, across the Towamba dark in the shadows of first light, leaping the hills dazzling in the rising mist to vanish into the granite hills of the uncleared and illimitable bush.

I move to the studio, huge and airy, stone-flagged, reminiscent of French provincial farmhouses, high clerestory windows, light and space, shelves with small sculptures of animals and birds, hundreds of representations of nature, charcoal, gouache, oil, pastel on butcher's

Three paintings by Bill Insch, from the series of man in the landscape.

paper, art paper, canvas, wood. Closer now, to disclose a disturbing theme: unlike the real view to the north-east, these paintings depict the blackened stumps of bare and naked hillsides. Elongated birds, mostly black, mourn rather than ascend the wasted hills. In recent work the landscape is less severe; but now each painting holds a solitary man. It may be his head and torso, sometimes in profile, or grim and unsmiling as he stares at the viewer unseeing. Trees grow on and in his shoulders or are rooted in his chest. Here a profile head growing from a tree stump inclines from a fragile standing forest towards a blasted land. In this oil, the central image is repeated, but now the head is surrounded by black stumps burning. Two trees grasp this man's cheeks like fingers while other male faces hover ghostly above him. This man is half a tree, his fingers grasp the soil like roots; he wears a crown without authority or joy for his kingdom is barren. This man stands naked, his arms raised like branches, supporting wild birds on his upper body as if he were a tree; but the landscape is destroyed. Each face in this impromptu exhibition is male, each face is solitary, each face is melancholy, or worse; every landscape is fragile, windrowed, clear-felled, threatened, barren or destroyed; every shape is tormented.

CONNECTING

Following the collapse of his domestic life Bill Insch began to face more rigorously the dilemmas of masculinity in the natural world. Brutalised by his English boarding-school, for much of his life he had distrusted —no, had almost hated—the concept of masculinity. While woman supported life, man went hunting, man drove the dozer, he logged, he shore and dipped the sheep, he mustered the cattle. Once in a sassafras forest Bill had seen how men, evidently out of the sheer joy of destruction, had chain-sawed the forest giants simply to watch them topple over the escarpment, sometimes to split from end to end on the rocky floor far below. Men were portrayed, portrayed themselves, and in fact were principally the destroyer of forests, gobbling the resource till it was gone. Art which united man and nature he saw as constructive: *It's like feminists, their awareness of their own femininity, and a lot of their art is women's art because it's that search within their gender. So I've had that search within my gender, and that's been a shift.*

Bill's art sought to reassert man as healer and nurturer in images of what ought to be his true role in the forests. The bird represented life.

I have this little silver necklace I bought off a friend, a flying bird, the alive bird, this is the one I take out with me when I go around the world, I can feel it under my shirt. If I get into situations which are a bit anxious, I can feel this alive bird.

Another symbol is the solitary head which to the artist is archetypal, symbolic, in pursuit of the lost, or vanishing, garden of nature.

I want man the king to be a more sustaining character, not just taking the resources but also giving back, being more heroic; man as man, male, gender-centred. As a young man I didn't respect men enough. Fighting for the forests showed me my male friends more sustaining and nurturing. Working with some of the scientists was a real privilege.

How could this self-made destroyer belong in the bush? How could Bill make himself belong? By 1995 Bill was trying to locate man-as-healer in the forests:

Man as leader, man as king, man the modern archetype, the greenie, a little wimpy, but he's there in a heroic way, a protester, a jester or a poet, but his face is sombre.

Sombre?

Because he's losing. The environment is still being destroyed.

To me the paintings carry a more personal despair. I ask—does the sadness stem from the failure of man—of you—to belong to the natural world as easily and as naturally as a tree? Is Bill in the paintings, as well as Man, trying to belong? Bill concedes:

In terms of yearning, that's personal, it's almost like a prayer, I'm trying to validate my feelings about masculinity, to show men in a positive light, listening to the earth, the archetype. If we were really listening, we men would not carry on like this.

Should we men, then, be bonded to a local place? *Yes, definitely. The experience of being in a natural environment is a very strong one.*

The Marrithiyel men are natural healers and carers; to destroy bush wantonly (though it can happen when young men hoon off in the

Toyota) is without sense or meaning, indeed man the healer/destroyer is an unreal and an un-Aboriginal dichotomy. The bush speaks and sings whenever its spiritual guardians are present; but without an Aboriginal guide Ian knows and can feel only a fraction of its story. Can the Aboriginal life-forces help Bill in what is essentially, for him, a solitary exploration? He reminds me that he is an artist, he observes and is affected by the land and all that is above it, but not whatever forces may lie below. His land, like Les Murray's, is exterior. The kangaroos and the birds know when he returns, not the land. *Metaphysical stuff I'm ignorant about.* The past was immanent, but factually and physically: Bill notes the hollows in the ground where once stood the huge red and yellow box trees, ringbarked by the farmers before burning the stumps.

FOUR GUMS

The Yuin had and have their powerful sites. There is no reason to think that the Towamba valley did not—and still does?—have its equivalent or exact analogy to Watjen Gusrifumpu. Two hundred metres to the west of the house is Four Gums, a high point which commands a view down the valley to the coast. On it stand four huge coastal grey box trees not cleared by the earlier farmers. Flints have been found on the track from the river. An older Yuin Aboriginal named Des, visiting the site for the first time, covered his eyes at the sight of carvings which one of the other members of the co-op had sculpted, and refused to visit the site again. In Dingo country in the Northern Territory the elders assert: *You see that hill over there? Blackfellow Law like that hill. It never changes.*[6]

Four Gums is an important site for all the co-op members. Waking, Bill can see the magnificent boxes from his bedroom. *They just feel special where you've got old-growth trees and there's four of them; and for two years there was a kingfisher nesting in one. It is a lovely place.* I ask if he responded to it as the Yuin had done. *Quite possibly.* Four Gums has always felt good; he can wander up waiting for the Rayburn to warm up, to check out the evening.

You think about what the next day's going to be weather wise, you go under there: the canopy is fantastic. It's not a thick canopy, but there's branches that just go up and up and then at the top of them it's like a little tuft of leaves. I think of wedgetail eagles landing in there blowing in the wind, and you see the currawongs, all the life there in the canopy, 'cause it's big, wide, it's expansive.

Four Gums to Bill is a powerful site, but not because of its Aboriginal connections.

My knowledge of Aboriginal customs is very very weak. I've never felt any vibes but I can understand someone who has.

Had Des sensed something at the site?

Definitely, I'm not at all surprised.

Four Gums is special in more complex ways. Five years ago Bill's father died and it was at Four Gums that Bill enacted the rite of his passing. Over several weeks he built three large fires. At one, a man whom he had met at a men's camp played the didgeridoo:

He stands behind you with the didge and starts at the bottom of your spine and just works it up to your neck and then goes over the top, so you are basically doing the Chakra from the back. You get the vibration of the didge going up your spine. He did that for me and he hung in all night, and I said things about my dad and he did that for me. My dad died on the other side of the world, so it was me getting in touch. I wasn't at his funeral but I had my own ceremonies for my dad. It was lovely.

Above the charcoal Bill constructed a cairn and concentric stone circles out of the granite rocks of the valley. In the centre of this strengthening man's place he placed some bones and feathers of a wedge-tailed eagle, the graceful and powerful, the strongest bird. The outer stone ring formed an opening to the north-west, facing Europe. *So my entry points towards home where I was born.* A smaller rock follows the path of the seasons around the eagle heel-stone which Bill moves on the last day of each season to conjoin the rising sun and to re-orient himself, living, with the living environment. *It's a tribute to my dad as being a man, a very caring man. So that's my man's site.* On the hillock on the other side of the saddle Bill has built another stone arrangement for his mother, not yet complete while she lives. It too bears the cardinal points and indicates the north-west.

What was the purpose of this intuitive configuration of realities on the same earth, amidst the same trees and rocks in which the Yuin order their own universe?

I'm trying to integrate my masculine and my feminine, for myself, like I have my masculine site up there and my dad's site, and I have my feminine site up there which is also my mum's site. To have those two in balance in one's life is a challenge and a very healthy awareness to aim for. I'm roughly in the middle so when I'm away I can visualise that and I've always got it with me. So it's like a symbolic way of trying to integrate those two things in my life.

Only once has Bill been 'vibed out' from a place by what he takes to be Aboriginal forces. Camping by himself in the Croajingalong National Park in what was obviously, to him, an Aboriginal camping ground, he was driven away by mosquitoes. *After three times I'd fixed it up, the mozzies were inside the tent and there was no logical reason why they could be inside. And I gave up, got in the boat and rowed across to this sand island where I spent the rest of the night.*

Does Bill belong to the land? As a man, is he entitled to belong to it? He believes he relates at a surface level, first as country to be shared.

It's a beautiful place and I really love being able to go wandering up the creeks and down to the river when the acacias are out in the springtime, all that yellow reflected in the water, the mist in the hills when the moisture's around, I mean it is a beautiful place to love.

To share country is not necessarily to be worthy of it, not because of the Yuin dispossessed but because the land has been destroyed, not nurtured. From attending meetings of his men's group, Bill has grown more optimistic. *Now I feel more respect about being a man and the men that I know and the strong possibilities of forming close relationships with men which are nurturing, and a lot of my art is more about men and landscapes.*

Bill affixed his signature as nominee for the status of the Coolangubra Forest as part of the National Estate. That was a step to belonging. At Easter 1999 he visited the Coolangubra, now a National Park, with his friends the Artists for the South-Eastern Forests.

We found one of the tree-sitting trees still standing, used to block the Wog Way construction. We walked up a logged hill and sat on the edge of a scarp looking into the upper catchment. One coupe was completed and a track snaked down into the valley and stopped down below us. The rest of the catchment was pristine and with the late afternoon sun slanting down it all looked magnificent. And that's where the Forestry [Department] were stopped. It was a wonderful moment to share with my friends. Very healing after those years of campaigning. I left feeling that I could return and paint all those wonderful places in years to come.[7]

Bill will be buried, he says, not on the farm, where his presence will be too strong for his daughters who may return, but certainly in the valley, in the consecrated ground at Rocky Hall. Aboriginality? That cannot help him; the past is almost unknown, the people are gone from the valley, and the only attempt to repeople it was a fiasco. Yes, there may be Yowies remaining in the wildest country where nobody goes; and Four Gums still speaks to Des. But modern Man, deprived of Aboriginalities, must make the best way he can. Stone arrangements speak, they point to England. Organic relics speak: of the great wedge-tailed eagle and the life of a caring father. Trees speak: they seize the morning mist and the first light of dawn. Birds speak: the flying bird gives succour in times of anxiety. Animals speak: they understand in Bill a parallel universe, they know but never touch. Men's sites speak: they connect a man born in England to his parents. Hills speak, coupes speak, tree stumps speak. Man speaks, but mostly in an alien tongue, Man the destroyer, the solitary, the wistful, the observer of the real and the tangible in sites of fantastic beauty and brutal destruction. Bill seeks to belong in the natural world with an artist's, not an Aboriginal, sensibility, 'at a surface level'.

FIRST THE ABORIGINALS RESPONDED, AND NOW THE OTHERS
To Chas Read, the landmass Australia shares a world soul but expresses its own moiety through a distinct language of expanse and clarity and light. *Australia is a primordial spirit, that's why it seems a strange place. It's timeless. That's what we tap into when the veils are torn away, into ageless time. Normal time doesn't apply.* Other landscapes are as old, but spirits discrete and specific, and prior to humankind, reside here and affect the consciousness of all Australians. These spirits, Chas believes, have been

there from the beginning, antedating the Aboriginals who perceived and interpreted them as and within their own culture. *Some earth spirits are uninterested in humans and may even be hostile.* In India, which Chas has visited several times, the people have been so numerous, and for so long, that the spirits have been drawn and condensed into the temples, but in relatively empty Australia they still remain in the landscape. There's an all-encompassing Australian energy, independent of humans, to which first the Aboriginals responded, and now the others.

> The wind makes a remote sighing sound,
> everything is quiet and still.
> Boundaries seem to slip away
> and the mythic spirit world enters my mind again
> like an evening mist.[8]

We are still in Yuin country, in the south of New South Wales, inland from Bateman's Bay. My brother Chas has lived on the river on a 18-hectare farm since 1990. Fifteen kilometres downstream is Moruya, 60 kilometres upstream is Araluen. I've been here many times.

The Deua River is stony, not deep but always cool in summer. On one side the slope rises abruptly for hundreds of metres into the Deua National Park; on the settled side the land gently slopes for half a kilometre before it too rises into the bush of the State Forest. The *feng shui* principles of Chinese geomancers approve a home by a river and enclosed by mountains. Hindu principles concur. *You are able to get in touch with your psychic level here relatively easily.* Here in the Deua valley, then, the mythic world is very close to the surface. The principal spirit of the Deua to Chas is one which he identifies as the female spirit or archetype of Maiden Goddess. She is youthful, creative and joyful, a wild energy: perhaps for millions of years a wild river. Perhaps because the area is unspoiled, spirits residing for such aeons have not been destroyed or interfered with by the Westerners. *Most men don't even realise that they are affected.*

Chas can tap into the reality of the river-spirit, he thinks, by allowing and encouraging certain experiences to occur. But beware. The drift of the valley is introspective; in time personalities slow and turn inward. The valley grows progressively harder to leave. Since the maiden-spirit is pre-sexual, she is uninterested in men. Such female spirits even may be a problem for men.

> Within these quiet, green spaces of wilderness
> I have entered other realms
> and felt the gentle touch of the Green Goddess.

The presence of this earth spirit first manifested itself, Chas believes, in his unconscious:

You feel something going on, but how are you going to give it expression? You feel a presence, and look for ways to encourage it. I went through a period when I practised a lot of ritual, trying to get into contact with that spirit. I can't say it's been 100 per cent successful.

To realise the energy, Chas constructed a stone circle enclosing the four quarters of space and their spiritual guardians.

So you follow the circle, following the patterns and seasons of the year through the solstice points, a yearly cycle occurring within the circle too. You try constructing rituals around the places where the symbols mean certain things for you or maybe to a group. You're endeavouring to get closer through chanting. You can build on different influences to get a deeper contact somehow with whatever the spirit is, and try to understand it.

But why, I ask, why through Hindu principles, why Chinese, why not Aboriginal? Chas replies that there appears to be no-one to teach him, he relies on his own intuition. Besides, in India spirits are known as Devas, 'shining beings', which take no particular form. Different cultures will imagine and project them in different ways. Chas interprets the shining being of the river as Maiden Goddess. Others will see, or have seen, different forms. Different cultures may represent them as—devil-devils? One must have a language, Chas explains, to form and shape the emotional and psychic reality.

Things happen, we must recognise them for what they symbolise. The mist closes over the valley. You can almost feel the presences around. Part of my experience in the river was rediscovering in a pretty dramatic and radical

*way, getting in touch with my own female side, my inner psychic side, the
whole meaning of mother-religion or goddess-religion. Not only on a personal
level but as a force which won't be denied. It can erupt in your consciousness
whether you like it or not, totally out of your control, it's quite capable of
transforming your life.*

GULAGA

Stronger still is the spiritual presence of Mt Dromedary, known to the
Yuin and to the other people of the valley as Gulaga. Unlike the Maiden,
Gulaga cares about people. At this mythical level God is present as the
transcendental rain-forest nature spirit.

> How high and alone
> does Mother Gulaga stand!
> Up on the windy ridges,
> stringybarks, like frozen people
> showing various gestures,
> overlook the hazy, blue abyss.
> Giant boulders are dealt with like marbles,
> the wise are dealt with like children.
> Thus does Gulaga teach.

But Gulaga is a sacred Aboriginal mountain, primarily a series of
women's sites. Debbie Rose, who has worked with the Yuin as well as
in the Northern Territory, found that Gulaga is recognised by the Yuin
as a place of 'supreme significance', as place of origin, as a continuous
living presence, as the abode of local ancestors, as a teaching site for
women and men, and as the home of a variety of living beings called by
Europeans 'supernatural'. The huge boulders which ring Gulaga are
known as Guardians. Part of its power lies in the fact that it is largely
unaltered by human activity. It is the uncleared nature which allows the
Dulagal spirit beings, associated with ancestral spirits, to survive.
Gulaga contains men's and women's sites, the most significant of which
for men is the granite outcrop known as the Tors. Traditionally men
approach Gulaga from the east. When the women ascend the mountain
they wear red headbands as symbol both of their powerful business
and the danger with which they were thus associated.[9] Gulaga was the

mythical birthplace of the Yuin in a manner closely analogous to Where the Dingo Bubbles Up.

Wary of 'stomping on someone else's sacred ground', Chas waited for a sign that his own relationship to Gulaga was appropriate and welcome:

I went to Tilba Creek and did some chanting, and tied a scarf round a branch, and came back several months later and it was on a branch somewhere else, with a knot in it, so there were three bits of the scarf, going in three directions; I'd seen the three rocks on Gulaga, and three is an ancient number of the Goddess; since I was a devotee, I knew it was okay to go up and keep interacting. I took it as a positive sign.

He joined a tourist party led by a Yuin elder, Mervyn Penrith, who introduced them to the mountain. Penrith spoke of Gulaga's mythology and daubed ochre on the faces of the group. He explained that Gulaga, the sleeping woman wrapped in a possum-skin rug, sometimes covers herself with her misty cloak if she does not desire contact with humans. Penrith can see the spirit in the landscape, in the bush. To Chas the claim was not surprising: the place has spirit. People also have spirits which, if they allow, interact on a psychic or mythic level below our normal rational consciousness. *It's there all the time, you can access it. The less disturbed the bush, the easier it is to make connection.* Mervyn asked the party to think of a living creature:

I thought of a king parrot. Others of the group said a snake, a crab, a dolphin and Mervyn said that that was our animal spirit which we were not allowed to harm and that we should look after them. And after that time, the king parrots started hanging around the house. Now we feed them.

Chas took the episode as an initiation. *That's the way it works in India. It doesn't matter who the guy is, you respect where he's come from and that's the only way you're going to get it.*

Intense experiences followed. If the Maiden, the first phase of the goddess in Hindu philosophy, lived on the Deua, the final phase, that of Grandmother, traditionally with her head in a dark scarf, resided in Gulaga. On later trips up the mountain Chas took lavender for the Grandmother spirit before beginning chanting. Once he forgot to take it—and found lavender before him, apparently left on the path. Surely this was a sign that Gulaga welcomed his response. Peter Sutton had said: 'It's the connecting sensibility, and that's what Aborigines are doing talking about the dreaming and land.' Chas drew the lesson that if Gulaga wants a person to make contact, she will allow it.

> The cold darkness of the earth is growing steadily,
> Solstice is not far off.
> As evening deepens
> a thin line of fog appears and hugs the ground,
> mysteriously penetrating the air.
> The hills are nothing but a black silhouette
> against deep blue.
> Now is the time of the Dark Grandmother,
> to me, she has made herself known.

I ask: Can or should a non-Aboriginal make contact independently of the Yuin? Chas replies that in truth he was more worried about his establishing a good relationship with Gulaga than with the Kooris. Gulaga is quite capable of making you aware of her disapproval! Now that his relationship with Gulaga has developed strongly, he does not need Aboriginal help. Landscape is more powerful than person: it was not disrespectful to relate to the mountain directly. *I believe that Gulaga, and perhaps other sacred sites, cause a subtle shift in our normal state of mind. Different aspects of consciousness present themselves to us and we attempt to interpret them using logical, linguistic thinking. We Westerners would be better served in allowing our intuition full play.* I observe that there are nevertheless Aboriginal elders who have a great deal of knowledge. Chas replies yes, but his feeling is that Gulaga wants to interact at some level with anyone willing and receptive. *Gulaga is a teacher, but this depends on my being open, being led.* Gulaga has answered many difficult problems in sudden flashes of insight.

This is the point at which Chas has now arrived. Gulaga is no mere nature spirit, but transcendental. She bears many times and generations simultaneously.

I persist that the Yuin possess local understandings, perhaps a collective unconsciousness gained over many generations.

Yes, they have a collective unconscious, archetypal ideas, universal meanings, and they'll be a key to greater understandings. We can't say what Gulaga is. It's a mystery. We can only use some symbolic language, myth and symbol. It's reality but not an everyday reality, there's more than one.

Perhaps your spiritual journeys proceed alone because you lack an Aboriginal guide?

Perhaps, but I think it is possible to interact with the non-physical, living landscape directly, using the psychic mythic material as it emerges. The ultimate goal is self-understanding through the local and specific qualities of our Australian landscape—and that includes the stars and the planets. I think that's how we could have an Australian cultural identity.

I wake during the night
and step outside into the freezing air,
it is the time of the new moon.
The heavens are dusted with powdered glass
the earth vibrates with stillness,
amazingly alive.
Deep, deep is the dreamless sleep,
that Peace
from which all things grow.

Ian, Bill and Chas are in their forties. Chas is not surprised that each has become more reflective. Men in this period of their lives, he believes, try to get in touch with the female side of their spirit. They become more integrated, more sensitive, more psychic, less macho.

Back on the Daly a man in his prime, at the same age as Ian and Bill and Chas, will carry full responsibilities to his country which he will continue to visit, speak to, keep 'clean' by burning and at which he will perform ceremony and ritual. He will have perhaps six children from two or three marriages, with commitments to the local Aboriginal council in roads and housing developments, responsibilities to the Northern Land Council, and to many groups and individuals in resource development, 'Canberra business', language maintenance, school attendance, academic and other visitors and, not least, 'the ceremonial business', as Ian puts it, 'that goes on under the surface constantly'. He will worry over his outstation and the normal family businesses of who is entitled to drive the cars and who rolled the Toyota. The law's connection to the land is strong. It does not disappear because it cannot; but the father will worry about his children achieving the right balance of Aboriginal and Western education. It is in the collective wisdom and security of the group as much as in the ancient traditions that confidence seems to reside.

Let's connect. Bill and Chas seek to join to forces greater than themselves by means of the landscape. To Ian and Chas the greater force is the uncleared landscape. Bill and Chas connect with the spirit forces as solitary individuals. Each reinforces that connection with the land through ritual. Ian speaks to Dingo, Bill constructs a stone circle, Chas finds transcendental nature in the sharp atmosphere of a starry night. Ian needs his Aboriginal guide, Bill's valley does not hold him, Chas is guided by nature. To each man the landscape speaks not to him who is ready to listen, but to him who knows the language, which may not be merely verbal. Language interprets and knows country; language almost is country. All three may agree that Devas the shining ones ever inhabit the earth, focused in a billabong, in a stone circle, on a high ridge, or on the Gulaga Tors. Landscape is knowledge and communication, language and form. Men seek to connect themselves to the spirit forces by means of the landscape.

The Yuin believe that the power of the mountain may extend to non-Aboriginals who have been born and raised near the mountain, or who have been drawn to the area.[10] If 'the greatest gift of Aboriginal society to multi-cultural Australia is a spiritual concept of place',[11] all three men may be the beneficiaries of this great wisdom. To hold the Towamba and the Deua valley and Gulaga as spiritual places without the direct intervention of Aboriginality may be part of that gift.

| SINGING THE
NATIVE-BORN

Can you sing the blues, can you sing the sad songs
Can you tell the stories of our land?
... Do you think you really understand?[1]

Anyone and everyone who walks on this land needs to know the
history, Aboriginal history, to fully appreciate their home.[2]

Old bandsmen never die. As a former high-harmony singer and retired
player of the viola da gamba and electric bass, I'm interested in every
type of music. One form that I like but do not know well, as I begin this
chapter, is Australian country music. It is here that I expect to find
brawny resistance to any sense of second-class belonging. Now after a
buying spree I have five hundred songs, written mostly in the last
fifteen years, and mostly country, to enjoy. I will explore how this
immensely popular form of Australian musical culture is, or is not,
meeting the challenge of contested senses of belonging.

I begin with the double album *Country Music in Australia,
1936–1959* which contains seventy-five songs.[3] Heavily influenced by
American singers who established themselves in Australia before our
artists had a chance to express their own voices, the collection soon
reveals that this was not our finest musical hour. Titles like 'Hillbilly
Valley' and 'The Hobo's Meditation' give an indication of un-Australian
cultural antecedents; even 'Mustering the Woollies' and 'When it's
Springtime in Victoria' are of historical rather than musical interest.
Evidently other parts of the Australian conversation of the 1930s never

penetrated the country musical halls and recording studies. The poem 'Belong', published in the famous Aboriginal newsletter *Abo Call*, was written at almost the same time as Tex Morton produced 'The Happy Yodeller' in 1936. I can find no trace of its fierce negatives in any popular song written in the period.

> They're trying to convince you you don't belong
> when the wireless drowns your corroborree song.
> They're trying to kick you out of the city
> They talk of your whole dark race as a 'pity'.
>
> They seem to forget that all is yours
> as long as their 'home' land drags and draws.
> That white old Europe is the whole of their song.
> Dammit, Jackie, they don't belong.[4]

Perhaps, though, these evidently unwelcome sentiments of the 1930s were revived among later singers. How do modern Australian songwriters feel that they belong?

The obvious place to start is to search for Aboriginals or Aboriginality in the songs of our own time, but I can now report that there is little to relate. Most country songwriters seem to be unable or unwilling to wrestle with shared, still less contested, forms of belonging as the poets have done. The most common musical strategy in country and western song has been to ignore the Aboriginal presence altogether, even though—or perhaps because—Aboriginals are likely to form at least a sizeable minority in many smaller rural regions. Another strategy is to hint at a somewhat obscure affinity with Aboriginality:

> Hoist up the kangaroo, red ochre, Uluru,
> Golden wattle and blue gum green,
> Under a blue sky, surrounded by oceans
> Where rain in the inland is gold.[5]

The strongest statement favouring shared land is John Williamson's rather less than effusive 'Shivering':

> I hope you get your land
> If land is what it takes

> If land will bring back self esteem.
> The new world brings you grog
> Sees you stumbling in the park
> Children shivering in the dark.[6]

Slim Dusty's 'I've been, seen and done that' lists some impressive Australian achievements, but whose only reference to Indigenality is the innocuous:

> The click of singing sticks and didgeridoo
> as dancers tell the legends old and new.[7]

A third strategy is to mute the presence of actual Aboriginals into 'spirit voices'. John Williamson, one of the commendable few who join issue at all, invokes harm to the environment rather than to the Indigenous people. It is not Aboriginality which is ill at ease, but Uluru; Uluru is no spirit of Aboriginality but of Australia:

> The message came from Uluru, a spirit ill at ease,
> The ancient voices sounding out a warning.
> You've taken all you wanted, I heard the anguished cry—
> Time has come to say 'enough' before the well runs dry.
> This is Australia calling.[8]

Williamson, perhaps aware that not all his many admirers support shared belonging, has nevertheless often allowed himself to be photographed with his Aboriginal friends of Central Australia. He has travelled further than most.

Slim Dusty's 'Song of the West', summoning the joys of touring Western Australia, invokes a past-tense 'dreamtime', not present-time Aboriginals:

> Where the salmon gums grow free
> A peaceful beauty there that seldom can be found ...
> A dreamtime kind of beauty there that's so hard to explain
> When you've tasted their reception you'll be going back again.[9]

Michael O'Sullivan implies that trees, rather than Aboriginals, embody the dreamtime:

Cork wood, old acacia
looks at me and smiles.
He knows this tribal valley, he keeps its secrets well.
A thousand dreamtime stories how I wish that he could tell …
Blue outback skies again, white gums on river bends.[10]

Deep belonging, in this John Williamson number about an escaped convict, may be deceptively easy to acquire:

And the native blacks are friendly, even though a bit suspicious
   Of anyone with a redcoat or a gun.
If I could learn their lingo and listen to their dreamtime
   The bush and me and the animals would be one.[11]

Grant Luhrs' song 'Men without Shoes', like Bob Brissenden's poem 'South Coast Midden', suggests a succession of occupation from Black to White, even though, unlike Brissenden, Luhrs acknowledges that the successors have an active role in the dispossession.

What will we do with these men without shoes
Dancin' on ground they were born to lose …

Where are their churches and where are their towns?
They must learn about our sacred grounds
… And their dreamtime will soon be over.[12]

Ted Egan argues for a resolution:

What do you say about Tjandamara?
What's your opinion of Che Guevara?
Were they justified? Have they really died?
What did you think about Robin Hood,
Could you really call Ned Kelly good?
Are you satisfied when you speak with pride?
Were they freedom fighters or agitators,
Bloody killers or liberators …
It's the people who make the legends
So let it be cut and dried
What's the verdict on Tjandamara
The people will decide.[13]

Ted Egan is a second eminent exception to the mainstream White country and western thesis that—even in traditional country—Aboriginality is finished. Brian Young's 'Kakadu' is quite explicit:

What about your people of 40 000 years
To the tribal lands diminishing through sad eyes filled with tears.
When they listen carefully they can hear the big land die,
The passing of their culture through promises and lies.

And your dreaming has vanished as though it's never been,
Gone with all your culture like the passing of the wind.[14]

The position, as pessimistic as it is wrong, is little different from Eric Bogle's 'Hard Hard Times':

His dreamtime people ran wild and free,
Pitjantjatjara and Gurindji,
But the dreamtime's finished and so is he.[15]

It is clear that a search for 'Aboriginality' in country music will yield us little. At the end of an initial survey I feel a little disappointed, because in other contexts country songwriters do address serious issues. John Williamson earned himself few thanks from mainstream rural music for his courageous 'Rip Rip Woodchip':

Rip rip woodchip, turn it into paper,
Throw it in the bin, don't understand.
Nightmare dreaming,
Can't you hear the screaming,
Stirs my blood, gonna make a stand.[16]

Lee Kernaghan's famous number about the Birdsville old-timer intimately unites man and land:

He sat by the door of the grand old Birdsville pub.
His swag and gear was guarded by a faithful heeler dog.
He wore a shirt that would blind you and a rumpled ringer's hat.
This old man was country—he left no doubt of that …

His pride for his country rang true in every song,
And I wondered if the chips were down would I be this strong.

Graeme Connors' 'Sicilian Born' is a powerful affirmation of warring senses of belonging. It's about a Sicilian migrant who, having spent sixty years of his life in Australia, abruptly returns to a land and the village which gave him something more precious than his own birth.

> And he never talked in his native tongue
> And he never talked about going home
> And he told me once the reason why.
> He said home's not where you're born;
> Home is where a man's prepared to die.[17]

Our great Australian country songwriters indeed tackle difficult issues, but shared belonging is very seldom one of them.

Yet the very meat and drink of country songs is expression of attachment to place, to the outback, the bush or the nation. Every male country singer has three or four musical affirmations. Slim Dusty:

> A day of toil ... sing while the billy boils ...
> It's a life I was born to, and here I belong
> In a wild rugged land that I love.[18]

Lee Kernaghan:

> He's a member of the Outback Club,
> He don't back down and he don't give up.
> He's livin' in the land he loves.
> Born and raised, he's a member of the Outback Club.[19]

Graeme Connors:

> Songs from the homeland, songs from the blood,
> Songs to remind me of the country I love.
> There's beauty no doubt beneath foreign skies
> But songs from the homeland bring tears to my eyes.[20]

Hundreds of singers in thousands of songs attest their love for a place more precise than 'the outback', a town, a river or the family farm. But since the genre of the loved place is at least as old as the first Australian recordings of the 1930s, precise musical belonging is now so well-worn that it's hard to distinguish serious attachment from formalised cliché. Lee Kernaghan's 'High Country' is one of the minority which, to me, achieves much more than rhetoric:

> In the drought of 1882
> The Maddisons brought the cattle through
> From Mountain Creek to the Staircase Spur.
> We'll follow the tracks where they picked up the herd
> To the high country.
> … you can see forever across this land.[21]

It is interesting that the songwriters seldom make actual claim to these places; the attachment, and the right to uncontested attachment, to the loved country is simply assumed. Yet I can sense amongst some artists a need for more than self-assertion, perhaps to demonstrate that some kind of justification of occupation may indeed be offered— if ever it were needed! In these songs the physical presence of the writer is subtly justified, first through the achievements of British Australians:

> I've stood where our forebears stood in chains—
> They'd never know their prison from today.
> And wherever and however I may go
> My country is implanted in my soul.
> I've been, I've seen and I've loved that.[22]

Physical beauty:

> Even so I fell in love,
> To meet her beauty was enough.
> And forever we will roam
> Forever always by my side,
> And with her I still reside.
> She is the land I call home.[23]

Deep personal attachment:

> Have you ever spoken to a gum tree?
> What am I trying to say to you,
> Love this place half as much as I do,
> Then you're a true blue too.[24]

Some real strength of feeling is beginning to emerge. But just as the moral necessity for land rights seems much more obvious to Australians in the cities than in the bush, so, perhaps, the weakness of the non-Aboriginal moral claim to the land is more obvious to those who see (but may not speak with) Aboriginal people in the bush every day. My feeling is growing that the once implied and now explicit Aboriginal moral claim to the land perhaps is being answered, not by contentious or aggressive assertion, but by a statement of countering values. We have already met this in the verse of Les Murray, not opposed to Aboriginality, but deeply affirming Anglo-Australian history:

> Abandoned fruit trees, moss-tufted, spotted with dim
>   lichen paints; the fruit trees of the Grandmothers,
> they stand along the creekbanks, in the old home
>   paddocks, where the houses were …[25]

The moral justification is evolving through a three-way relationship between a man, his work and the land. Consider the meaning of rural labour in, say the nineteenth-century classic 'Flash Jack from Gundagai'. The song seems to relate work, men and place:

> I've shore at Burrabogie and I've shore at Moulamein,
> I've shore at Big Willandra and out on the Coleraine,
> But before the shearin' was over I've wished meself back again
> Shearin' for old Tom Patterson on the One Tree Plain.[26]

The places are important, but in the end, I think, of less moment than the celebration of a relationship not to the land but to *other men*. Work is but the medium through which relationships with fellow workers are transacted.

Listen now to some contemporary bush ballads invoking physical labour. Fellow workers are unimportant, even irrelevant in the Flying Emus' song 'It's a Sunburnt Country':

> Two feet on the ground
> Both hands in the dirt.[27]

James Blundell and James Reyne:

'Cause it's tough out here, livin' and a-workin' on the land.
What a change it's been from workin' at nine to five,
How strange it's been when I get the feeling that I'm really alive.[28]

Slim Dusty:

You gotta muster three thousand head in a day,
Move 'em to the yards and water them at the end of day.
That's not the sort of job you'd take if you're looking for a soft one
'Cause you take a kind of pride in saying
I'm a ringer from the Top End.[29]

Attachment is being born out of labour; the harder the labour, the greater is the implied right of attachment. Lee Kernaghan:

> Works a twelve-hour day from sun-up to sundown.
> He's doin what he can to make the wheels go round.
> In a shed down the track, knows how to bend his back,
> Salt of the earth, he's got a heart of gold.[30]

More explicit is another Kernaghan number:

> We work the land through fire and flood,
> It's in our heart and it's in our blood.[31]

While most nineteenth-century bush ballads derived from Anglo-Celtic sources denigrate authority or celebrate adventure, male workmates and alcohol, very few express any overt attachment to the land.[32] In contemporary country and western songs, the right to work confers, or generates, the right to belong, a right which was of little interest to nineteenth-century songmen because physical—and moral— possession of the land was to them obvious and permanent.

Work, when denied, renders the labourer purposeless and uprooted. Whether the cause is men in 'steel grey suits', publicans, squatters or migrants,[33] without labour the working man begins to relinquish his right to belong:

> They're bringin' in new people to fill up the land,
> Take away a job maybe meant for him.
> There's a few months now since he's seen any work.[34]

He loses his right to bequeath it:

> And every second home hangs its head in shame
> 'Cause poppa can't support his family.
> And all he says he needs is an honest day's work
> With his hard-earned pay at the end,
> So he can offer his son the chance just like the one given him
> When this was his father's land.[35]

By the 1980s the focus of deep relationship was changing in rural songs. Simple assertion, contemplation, historic achievement, wandering, admiration or simply being at the site—once sufficient to confer true belonging—all these were now challenged. The rural man today finds a renewed right to be in and to belong to the land through his labour. The Aussie bushman checks on the boundaries, drills for oil, loads a truck, fixes fences, hauls in the strays. John Williamson:

> It's good to be me ...
> Workin' hard in my own country
> With the Southern Cross and Saucepan shining really bright.[36]

'Big Red':

> She's a tough country, but ah, she's my home.
> She's a hard and cruel land.
> You can make a living if you only make a stand.[37]

Sometimes the bush will beat the man who loves it (it is almost always a man). But the hard-won relationship with the land will endure:

Every heart's a gambler's heart who ever loved this land.
At the start of every season, with the odds set short of even,
It takes skill and luck to make it pay when God's betting either way.[38]

Most suggestive are the songs of belonging through sacrifice. Work is sacrifice, sacrifice is blood. The 'Ringer from the Top End' achievement is the equivalent of Bob Brissenden's 'Blood,/Semen, sweat, dung, tears' which conferred the right of belonging-as-successor at Durras Beach. The continued Aboriginal presence is rather too obvious to maintain that thesis in the outback, but the spilling of the working blood of the 'ringer from the Top End' bears an implication quite as serious:

> Out on the fence line swallowin' dust,
> Blood on my hands from the barbs ...[39]

Settlement ideally is difficult: Nineteenth-century horses:

> Carried dreams of brave explorers
> And carried hopes of battling settlers.[40]

Work is parallel belonging, a response to spiritual possession. Its reiteration may be a rejoinder to prior occupation. Country songwriters, therefore, do not grant themselves the right to attachment to the land without thought or without responsibility. Yet in the end they do grant themselves—unlike the poets—the right of unquestioned belonging. Work runs as a not-quite-explicit masculine parallel to Aboriginal spiritual belonging.

Loving the country implies responsibility which many songwriters are willing to acknowledge. The country and western songwriters who unite bush themes with environmentalism put this most clearly. John Williamson:

> I believe in the ancient spirit of the Great South Land.
> Her health is my responsibility,
> And her fruits will be mine only in return for my caring.[41]

From physical obligation, green movement songwriters of the 1990s shade into the role of what, in the 1970s, was more often taken to be an Aboriginal prerogative: the songwriter as spiritual guardian. Eileen Ryan's bush and people almost are one:

> Dr Brown still held a captive
> Man's fear of all its darkness campfires at night …
> To rescue the deep rainforest, some chained up to the gate.
> So silent the deep rainforest, all its wilderness outgrown,
> Protected by its people has a heritage all its own.[42]

Eileen Ryan is the first female songwriter whom I have cited, and Ryan is well outside the country and western tradition. Few women country songwriters seem to choose themes of relationships other than with men; in fact the country woman is sung about by male vocalists much more commonly than she sings about herself. Yet one of her principal *raisons d'être* is work:

> Never have I met anyone
> Who works herself harder.
> She raised up three young kids alone
> Battled with the banks and bosses …[43]

She laughs away hard times:

> Up in the backblocks to the west of Moree
> Where the hard times grow hard like the ears on the wheat,
> There's a green-eyed girl with a heart concealed
> Under laughter like a shield.[44]

She doesn't make decisions:

Her husband's a good man though times have been tough
And had made some decisions that turned out rough.[45]

She respects the right of her man to travel:

> Knows of her man that stayin home ain't his style.
> When the money dries up and the creek's overflowing
> It's time to go drovin' again.[46]

She sometimes travels with him:

> She was a drover's wife,
> Lived in a caravan.
> She could match the work of any man,
> In the morning haze be gone.[47]

When men sing about her, they connect her to themselves in a battler's world:

> And it takes a special kind of girl
> To stay out here in this rugged world,
> Keep her dignity when the oaths are hurled,
> I pay my respects to you.[48]

Even when she is better at the job than they:

> She's a match for any man alive when she works them all
> Before the job is done, there's another just begun.
> She's the kind of woman that any man'd be proud of.
> She's a member of the Outback Club …[49]

I have the sense in these songs that women are neither acquiring, nor being granted, their own right to belong to the land. The most remarkably explicit denial of female attachment I found in a song a little outside the country and western mainstream. It involves Old Sydney Town, the first of the Australian historical theme parks, and the Bank of New South Wales. As a major sponsor of the project, the bank in 1967 produced an LP record entitled *January the Twenty-Sixth*. The only song on the record which appears to be about rural women, like many others similar, turns out to be about men. Woman's love for land must be channelled through her man. Lana Cantrell sings:

> Out there is somewhere. A woman forgets
> The smoothness of linen, the perfume of roses.
> Out there is somewhere. A woman belongs
> With a man who's wed to the land. His land.

The lyricist does not allow the land to belong to her; rather she belongs to it:

> Home is a hut made of wattle and clay,
> Hard-beaten earth makes a floor and a carpet.
> Woman forgets about spinets and dances,
> For now she belongs to the land. His land.[50]

Six months later I still admit to a little disappointment. I love the big chords, the vocal quality and the instrumentation of our great country artists. I'm discouraged, though, by their unwillingness to confront the issues that deserve more serious musical attention than powerfully and poetically expressed belonging-in-parallel. This itself is indeed a step forward: but it is not shared belonging. We need to try harder. Is it the genre, the place or the market which produces this verse by the usually thoughtful and passionate John Williamson? In 'Back to the Isa', he sings of the rodeo ball:

> Where out in the parks some black people sprawl
> And spend their money on flagons.
> There's so much more to be understood
> Before coming up here like Robin Hood.
> The do-gooders do more harm than good
> Without really knowing the Isa.[51]

White country and western songwriters rejoice, and belong, in the bush through their appreciation of its beauty, their pride in achievement after years of battling. Attachments grow from their tragedies, their intense experiences, long residence, the almost mystical bond between land and hard labour. With such emotional armour and a rhetoric often slightly strained, they defend themselves against Aboriginal belonging premised on ancient spirituality. The constant use of the first-person pronoun in the sometimes semi-spiritual journey which the Australian country songwriter takes to affirm his belonging sets him apart from the famous affirmation of 1950s American un-challenged belonging:

> We know we belong to the land
> And the land we belong to is grand.[52]

And the pronoun sets him apart from Aboriginal singers, to whom the personal 'I' is almost never used in song, and to whom the spiritual journey is communal:

> Without the land you could not eat
> You could not eat, you cannot sleep or breathe or live.
> We sing our home, our home, our home,
> We dance our land, our land,
> Where we stand together.[53]

INDIGENOUS BELONGING IN SONG

Let's listen to some Aboriginal country songwriters. They too can dwell in the American-style nostalgia of 'the home place I will return to'.

> I can see that Fitzroy River in my mind
> And I remember just how sad I was when I had to leave,
> But I know I'll be back again some time.[54]

The New South Wales singer Ceddy McGrady draws upon rural regret—not for the family farm, but for Toomelah mission:

> Going back to the mission where I came from
> See all my people, clapping hands and having fun …
> I remember your mission lorry going to town
> Bringing flour for the johnny cakes
> That we all used to share around.[55]

Archie Roach takes the moral high ground:

> We are young, we are old …
> Oh, but what we have can't be bought or sold.[56]

Peter Yamada McKenzie takes the political high ground: the Mabo judgement shows:

> That you can stand up and help yourself
> If someone comes to rob.[57]

Kev Carmody celebrates the defeat of power and privilege in the struggle of the Gurindgi people to regain their land at Wattie Creek:

> Gather round people I'll tell you a story … of power and pride
> Opposite people on opposite sides …
> Vincent Lingiari was little, dirt was his floor …
> This is the story of something much more:
> That power and privilege cannot move a people
> [Who] know where they stand and they stand in their lore.[58]

In some contemporary Aboriginal country songs, I can hear the anxiety of the oppressed even when the dispossessor is not named. Bobby McLeod cautions against Aboriginal people being indoctrinated into thinking, as Oodgeroo once did, that 'we are going'. Children need to be reminded that Aboriginality is now:

Teach the children, let them know the beauty of their land,
That the culture is their own time, the strength that helps them stand.[59]

To Yothu Yindi, the non-Indigenous are a relentless and permanent threat:

> Oh you children of the land
> Don't be fooled by the Balanda [White] way.[60]

They can share the overstated rhetoric of some White Australian songwriters:

How it used to be then
When all the time our people smile.
A black man's crying
A black man's trying
To make you see this belongs to me.[61]

Yet the Aboriginal sense of loved place is generally quite precise:

Walk around the hill side
Like any kid would do,
Throwing stones at the gum trees at the crows and cockatoos.
It was just one big playground,
Big mountain, you mean so much to me …
The old Adnymathana people told me stories about you,
That's why I always feel so glad when I see you so misty blue.[62]

And so are their own remembered experiences at precise locations:

Side by side we'd walk along to the end of Gertrude Street
And we'd tarpaulin muster for a quart of wine …
We'd cross over Smith Street to the end of the line
Have a sip and roll some smokes,
We'd smoke tailor-mades if we could …[63]

Aboriginal songwriters, of course, reject the phenomenon of 'the last of his tribe', beloved by nineteenth-century Anglo-Celtic poets. But much Indigenous belonging in song is self-inclusive and closed. Australian values, in principle shared by all Australians, can be offered to fellow Aboriginals alone. Ceddy McGrady:

Bright lights in the city
Aren't so damn pretty
When you're black, or broke,
But you know I love you, sister.[64]

Aboriginal women are much more positive in their sense of being female. This is a Tiddas number:

We're women we fight for freedom …
We've been hiding in the background for too long.[65]

Classic southern country artists like Jimmy Little utilise a grammar of belonging quite unlike their White contemporaries:

> As I walk through this great and ancient land …
> My father taught me all the things I needed
> Like identity and dignity with love.[66]

To Archie Roach, the non-Indigenous aliens do not belong at all:

Ah but change appeared and through the years
They introduced some foreign plants.
Familiar things are strange while strangers played upon the shore.[67]

One only has to listen to half a dozen representative Aboriginal country and western songs to realise that the discourse of Aboriginal belonging in song is a pointedly articulated spiritual attachment, against which, I suggest, the non-Aboriginal songwriters' theme of painful or difficult work is presented as a belonging-in-parallel.

It is hard to sing a riposte to either moral or spiritual expressions of Indigenous belonging. The Central Australian band Amunda asserts that the Whites are robbers:

> Where's this flag gonna stop and let the people alone,
> And where's this flag gonna stop,
> When's the white man goin away?
> They rip up this land to satisfy their greed.
> Black man only takes what he eats
> Because this land here belongs to all men.[68]

> Let's stand up, let's stand up.
> Never mind the white man …
> Fight for the sacred right
> Give me back white Australia, it has a blackfeller history.
> Let's stand up for the land rights...
> Give me back my Arnhem Land, give me back my Australia.[69]

It is difficult to answer the unaffected simplicity of the Warumpi Band in this song:

> As I travelled through the sandhills I couldn't find
>   anything to eat.
> I was in my grandfather's country
> But the land was strange to me.
> And I dreamed, old people
> Coming to see me.
> Old people they rub their sweat on me,
> Singing and dancing, old people.
> When I woke up, I was changed
> The land had recognised me again,
> And I knew I'd find my food that day
> 'Cause old people are looking for me.[70]

A sense of spiritualised place is almost unassailable:

> The night is dark
> And not a light in sight.
> Ancestors wailing 'cause we're back again …
> We'll stay as long as we want.[71]

The threatening violence of the Wedgetail Eagles would not be tolerated in a mainstream band:

> I stand up for my people
> I won't ever let them die.
> So look out you white boys
> The word has got around
> 'Cause the Wedgetail Eagles
> Are gonna hit this town.[72]

Do Aboriginal singers concede that the land can be shared? Interestingly, it is the far northern bands which most commonly accept or advance reconciliation:

> I can't remember your name.
> What country did your people come from?
> We'll take you in just the same
> And share our land you called Australia.[73]

A recent double CD album produced by the Central Australian Aboriginal Media Association begins, 'This CD is for all Australians who live in this land'.[74] 'Reconciliation' by the band Blekbala Mujic takes the listener as far from the White country and western mainstream position as it is possible to be:

> Forgive the wrongs of white man
> They're our brothers and our sisters.
> Let's join hands together
> Share one earth forever
> Teach the young our culture
> Be happy and be peaceful.
> This land's for you
> This land's for me.
>
> Take pride in it—it is ours.[75]

The Indigenous offer seems, however, a little less enthusiastic than first appears. Top End singers propose a shared nation—but an Indigenous Arnhem Land! It is generally some other Aboriginal people's land that the strangers are to share. Yothu Yindi:

> Living in the mainstream, but under one dream.
> Cloud formation in the west today,
> Thunder and rain reckon here tonight.
> Listen to the music of the sea grass drying
> Along the rivers and the valleys in the Yulngu land.
> Reflection in the water I see
> Yulngu and Balanda living, we're living together now,
> Sharing the dreams of the red, black and gold,
> We're living now in the Yulngu way.[76]

The only Aboriginal and genuinely country songwriter to advance reconciliation is Troy Cassar-Daley. An example is his song 'Dream out Loud', which he sang to the vast, emotional audience of the Australian Reconciliation Conference dinner in Melbourne, May 1997:

> There's two people in love, one black and one white,
> Who's to say who's wrong and who's right.

Both standing tall, both standing proud, both not afraid
To dream out loud.

Dream out loud, it's up to me and you,
Dream out loud, it's not too hard to do.
So if you see your brother/sister falling on the ground
Don't be afraid to dream out loud.[77]

Troy's song is about reconciliation amongst people. They share love and pity and health: not land. But wait. Maybe that's what reconciliation, amongst our own generations, will mean.

BEYOND COUNTRY AND WESTERN

In folk music one finds more sympathetic understanding of Aboriginals, not least in the Irish tradition of singing the suffering of the downtrodden and its implied moral distance from the perpetrator. Alistair Hulett goes beyond this now familiar depiction of the shared suffering of Aboriginals, the Irish, convicts and the working class, to acknowledge that Aboriginal pain was inflicted by Irish settlers displaced elsewhere:

Driven like dogs from your own native home
Hardship and poverty caused you to roam
Over the bracken and over the foam.
Blood stained the soil of Australia.

Then in the fever for fortune and fame
You caused the poor blacks to suffer the same
Imprisoned on missions or hunted for game.
Blood stained the soil of Australia. …

Koori and white, old Australian and new,
Brothers and sisters of every hue,
The future is ours, take the wealth from the few
And raise the red flag in Australia.[78]

Hulett's harmonious future may not be attained so easily. Though some Aboriginals applaud the song, I'm not sure it's so easy to raise any kind of united flag. We'll need to look further.

At the end of the 1980s Midnight Oil united environmental and ethnic destruction; they put 'shared history' more problematically and Australia's predicament more poetically:

> So we came and conquered …
> River runs red
> Black rain falls
> Dust in my hand.
> River runs red
> Black rain falls
> On my bleeding land.
>
> One ocean
> One people
> One landmass
> We are defenceless
> We have a lifeline.
> One ocean
> One policy …
> One movement
> One instant
> One difference
> One lifetime …[79]

But the Oil's *Diesel and Dust* revealed a touching uncertainty between self-assertion and self-abnegation:

> This is the brown land
> This is not our land …
> The law is carved on granite,
> It's been shaped by wind and rain.
> White law could be wrong,
> Black law must be strong …
> Diesel and dust is what we breathe.
> This land don't change and we don't leave.[80]

Some of the strongest numbers are sung by those non-Indigenous who have lived and worked closely with Aboriginals. Paul Kelly:

> My land was once a river.
> I hate to see it bleeding dry.[81]

In the six verses of his powerful song 'Special Treatment', Kelly registers forced removals, imprisonment, unequal pay, legal restrictions, separated children and forced deculturation as the themes of Aboriginal life for two centuries:

> I never spoke my mother's tongue
> I never knew my name,
> I never learnt the song she sung
> I was raised in shame.[82]

These lyrics on behalf of the stolen generations to me are poetically stronger than the song of the Aboriginal group Tiddas about Malcolm Smith, who died in custody after being removed from his family:

> Was the system that took his life.
> How did he die?
> Did he hear the mopoke cry?
> No guilt no shame
> Just got locked up again.
> Deaths in gaol became an issue:
> Wipe your tears, here use my tissue.
> I'm hurtin' so bad,
> I knew Malcolm, Malcolm's dead.[83]

Yet by the beginning of the 1990s, speaking and singing on behalf of Aboriginals had become more problematic. Aboriginal artists assumed the right to sing of their own histories. By the end of the decade thoughtful non-Aboriginal singers seemed to accept this. There's a difference between the strong and poetic 'Special Treatment' which speaks as an Aboriginal, and Goanna's 1998 song 'Sorry', which speaks *to* an Aboriginal stolen woman, Margaret Tucker:[84]

I'm sorry they took you away,
Away from your mother to a strange place

Where they made you a slave and they slapped your sweet black face …
Sorry, so sorry. I'm sorry they took you away.[85]

While the country songwriters seemed almost imprisoned by the
rhetoric of the genre, some of the urban bands constantly reassessed
and enlarged their thinking. Consider the tone of Goanna's 1982
'Children of the Southern Land'. Many early 1980s bands hammered at
environmental destruction, but hesitated to link care for the environment with indigeneity. For their time Goanna's lyrics were courageous
and innovative.

> Look across the western plains,
> See the danger there.
> They'll take your land, they'll take your soul
> And leave you with despair.
> (Who's gonna care?)[86]

'Black Mary', by Penny Davies and Roger Ilott, whose self-critical
analysis seemed appropriate in the 1980s, paralleled some of the
thoughtful poets of the same period: 'Betrayed by her white bushranger
lover, [Black Mary] is symbolic of the relationship between black
and white Australians since the colony began.'[87] Goanna again, another
voice of the progressive 1980s:

> They were standin' on the shore one day,
>   Saw the white sails in the sun.
> Wasn't long before they felt the sting—
>   White man—white law—white gun.
> Don't tell me that it's justified.
> Someone lied,
> Someone died,
> Genocide.[88]

In 1998 Goanna did not sing 'I'm sorry we took you away', but
'I'm sorry they took you away'. Not all-of-us Whites committed an act
of infamy, only *those* Whites; and we, who merely inherit this history,
regret it deeply. The band has led listeners away from the now dis-
tracting incubus of assumed personal or collective guilt. Some level of

sharing is possible. Goanna's 1998 album *Spirit Returns* took its epigraph from the words of the Aboriginal writer Lionel Fogarty: 'the spirits are all still there in the rain the wind the bush walkin' talkin' singin' dancin' in the land'.

Part of the advance of the 1990s to me is less intellectual than personal and emotional. Paul Kelly often works with Aboriginal artists. On *Spirit Returns* Anglo-Australians and Aboriginal singers harmonise with each other. The album draws on events in Aboriginal history in Victoria, New South Wales, Queensland and the 'special thanks' on the sleeve notes contain almost as many Aboriginal names as others. Real, personal sharing of the earth takes place not among spirits but ordinary people. Goanna's friends are less tense than Geoff Page's Bandjalang negotiators, perhaps because they do not negotiate sharing land but a common, and respectful, humanity:

> We sat down upon the earth,
> Talked of reason and of fear,
> Sang our songs into the night.
> Stars rained down on black and white.[89]

That's the 'Dream out Loud' shared human harmony (not shared human land) of Troy Cassar-Daley.

Much harder to resolve is shared land, but arguing shared space is a fine and important step beyond belonging-in-parallel. These four lines from Goanna's 'Poor Fella My Country' are heard at the very end of the album, the last lyrics evidently a quotation from a song by the Aboriginal songwriter Jimmy Chi:

There's a place they call Mt Warning where the first light of the sun
Should remind the hardest hearted that the land and man are one.
Until we write our makarrata and carve it in that stone
Though you've been here two hundred years you'll never be at home.[90]

'Dammit, Jackie, they don't belong.' The sentiments of that 1930s poem offer no release. We have advanced to 'You'll never be at home. Until …'

In 1942 Ian Mudie's 'until …' was a 'vision resurgent' of the nation.[91] Eileen Ryan's 'until …' was saving the trees:

> The greenies are protesting to keep our country free,
> Stand behind the barricades, fight to save the trees.[92]

In 1994 the Reconciliation Council's 'until …' was viewing the land 'through the eyes of the Indigenous owners'.[93] To Goanna in 1998, 'until …' is the union of non-Indigenous and land, expressed in a Makarrata, or formal peace treaty between Aboriginals and other Australians. These are the furthest points we have reached so far.

Neil Murray is a white man who grew up in Victoria's western district, but which he also identifies as 'Tjapwurrung Country'. Neil has wandered through his own deep sandstone gorges pondering the silence:

> But why does this place seem so empty
> Home of my spirit but pain in my heart?[94]

He answers that question in prose: 'Sadly, by the end of the nineteenth-century, the Tjapwurrung had all but disappeared. It remains a profound and terrible loss to me that this occurred. A people and cultural heritage I could have shared in have gone.'[95]

> I sing to be healed in Tjapwurrung country.
> I'll keep on singing till my people come.

Who are Neil's people? He means not only the returning Tjapwurrung, but all those who revere and care for the country in the way that the Indigenous people of his own born-country did, and may do again. Their spirits invest the land, Neil Murray's land, their land, our land. Neil concludes the note, 'You'll hear a voice singing an answer in the chorus. That's him. Archie Roach, singing for his mother's people.'

NATIVE-BORN
In an autobiographical novel about his life in Central Australia, during which Neil Murray helped to found the otherwise all-Aboriginal Warumpi Band, he recounts returning with a Pintupi elder to an

ancestral creation site. At this sacred place the old man points to the lines of ochre and blood on the cave wall:

> 'You see this, nagyuku [mine]—this is me', he said proudly.
>
> I nodded humbly. I wish I had a place I could say that about. But there was not a one. Not in the entire continent. Not a stone or a claypan or a bush that I could attest to being me. I could make my own perhaps. There were plenty of places in the bush that were dear to me. But who would recognise it or give it veneration? Who in the minds of men would remember it and pass it on? Who would know the story?[96]

Who is native born? Murray's friend, the Gunditjmara Koori singer Archie Roach, in the very first song of his first album, holds that all the living world of Australia is native born: except for the invaders and they were aliens:

> But no one knows and no one hears the way we used
> to sing and dance,
> And how the gum trees stood and stretched to meet
> the golden morn,
> And motherland still sheds her tears for lives that
> never stood a chance,
> And Albert Namatjira cries, as we all cry—
> The native born.[97]

The contrary position of the Warumpi Band song unites land and people:

> It doesn't matter about your colour
> As long as you a true fella,
> All the people of different races
> With different lives in different places,
> It doesn't matter what your name is
> We have got lots of changes,
> We need more brothers
> If we're to make it,
> We need more sisters
> If we're to save it,
> Blackfella, whitefella, yellafella, anyfella.[98]

Add the theme of environmental care. Warumpi sang:

> I believe the time will come when everyone will join in
> And understand our way of life and know we care for this land.[99]

Murray counters Roach by asserting that he too is native born, but not by turning his head from the chilling history of the empty Tjapwurrung land. He knows well enough, like Geoff Page, that the voices in the river will never be silenced. He has won his own right to native birth out of his own profound experiences with Aboriginal people in and out of the central desert. Belonging is not never, not in the future, not unobtainable; belonging is possible, belonging is now. Belonging is now because Murray's sense of belonging, intimately tied to the future of the sacred earth, has been earned.

> Australia, where are your caretakers gone?
> I am just one who has been battered
> By the damage within your shores.
> Australia I would not sell you for a price,
> I would not strip you of your forests
> Or pollute your clear blue skies,
> I would not desecrate your sacred lands
> I would not plunder on your shores
> I would not foul your precious waters
> For I am your native born.[100]

Neil Murray's experiences cannot easily be generalised. Some may admire, but we cannot easily emulate his hard-won sense of belonging.

Singing the loved place and the working land, our country songwriters have alerted us to our own achievements and the depth of our attachments. They've brought us no closer, though, to our shared history. The singers who are friends and work professionally with Aboriginal musicians give us best a sense of real individuals with whom we share more than belonging-in-parallel.

WOMEN'S BUSINESS

AUSTRALIA IS HOME. BUT MY PEOPLE ARE CUBANS.
Marivic Wyndham belongs to Australia because she can take part in its conversation and because she believes in its virtues. Her spirituality resides in the aether, not the land.

Marivic was nine years old when Castro seized power in Cuba. One of her clearest memories is visiting Jibacoa, the seaside mansion of her uncle who had already fled with her father to the Dominican Republic on the first day after the revolution. It was less than a month later. Her aunt knocked; a former maid appeared to stare at the former owner. '*Señora, esta no es su casa*' (Madam, this is not your house.) And she slammed the door. Marivic's mother and three daughters, of whom Marivic was the youngest, left Cuba two years later to join her father, by now in the United States.

Later Marivic married an Australian diplomat, and she arrived in Australia for the first time in December 1974. She found a country as foreign as Ian Green had found the Daly River. Australia seemed a land of insecurities. Her well-established parents-in-law explained to her that Prime Minister Whitlam's rampant state socialism was threatening the best of Australian society. The country was still deeply divided over its attitude towards the war in Vietnam. The nurses had helped themselves to her perfume while she was in a Canberra hospital. That never ever would have happened in Havana! Eleven months later she wrote to tell her father, exiled in Miami, that Whitlam had been defeated. Thank God, he replied, the people had rejected the red menace. *So this placid land came to me packaged in terrible and dangerous*

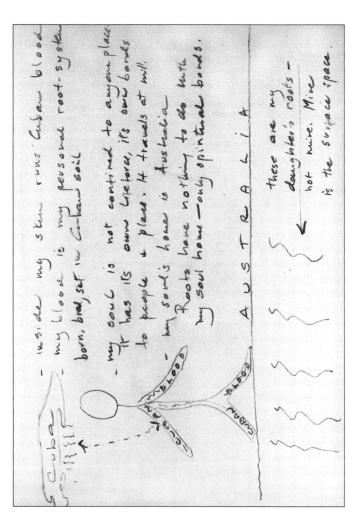

Marivic Wyndham's belonging: 'Inside my skin runs Cuban blood / my blood is my personal root-system, born, bred, set in Cuban soil. / My soul is not confined to any one place. It has its own lifeforce, its own bonds to people and place. It travels at will. / My soul's home is Australia. / Roots have nothing to do with my soul home—only spiritual bonds. / [Below the soil] these are my daughter's roots—not mine.'

terms. Aboriginals too offered potential, though minor division. Some friends of her husband's family spoke of Aboriginal bones found not far from their property in Cooma. Marivic remembers the chilly unease which greeted the news. It was obvious that this was a real nuisance. It was ominous. To Marivic herself, Aboriginals seemed far away and disembodied, just bones. She never imagined herself actually meeting one.

Bonding with Australia came very slowly. Marivic lived in Canberra with her husband for five years before a three-year posting in Germany. She returned to Canberra in 1984, at first without him. Alone with her young daughter, she found herself, as she puts it, renegotiating her contract with Australia. It was the first place in her life to which she could return. *This was the place I wanted to be, these were the people I trusted; now, naturally, without meaning to, without trying, I felt connected to this place.* Connected to what? Unlike Bill Insch and Chas Read, her sense of belonging had not much to do with gum trees, light or space. Her belonging, in part, was specifically female. Men sweat, women shed blood. The act of the life cycle, of giving to the earth a living child, the placenta and the blood, are as close as a woman comes to claiming that bit of earth as hers, not because she protected it in battle but because here was where her body met this place. *We have the juices of life too.* At this site at Woden Valley Hospital Jessica her child was received by the arms of earth, growing and living, forever Australian. *I'll never have that belonging, to live in the land of my ancestors.*

The act of giving birth, to Marivic, is distinct from the implications of one's own birth. *Cubans speak the language of my blood and I don't believe I'm in the blood of Australia. But my soul lives here.* Cuba holds her and claims her because earth had received her there in a Havana hospital. *Speak to me, you saw my birth, you are my parent, you owe me.* But the contract which metaphorically she signed with Australia as an adult she believes binds her equally permanently. *My family, my mother and father, fashioned themselves in Cuba. I did it here.* Nor is physical death or site of burial her ultimate question. *Australia set out for me a deal, and I bought it.* Marivic gave to Australia her Jessica, she gave it her trust, she returned here deliberately to embrace the land and the nation to close a working relationship. Australia, this place. I ask: What do you demand in return? *Australia owes me refuge, the ultimate betrayal would be to spit me out.* The deal struck as an adult, she explained—for she believes no

Anglo-Celtic Australian understands this—is to accept her as an Australian with an equal right to participate. Approaching the end of the millennium, she is upset by watching the apparent procession of Anglo-Celts fill the television screen rejoicing in their history and nostalgia for their own twentieth century. She finds herself constantly looking into the mirror of Australia and not seeing herself reflected. Where were the non-Anglo-Celts? *I rage into the night when I think I'm being spat out by the Anglo-Celtic thing. I take it profoundly personally. I don't want to be exiled once more!*

For belonging as a migrant Marivic sees as achieving a right to be part of the society, *that after so long to have a right to say 'it's mine', to be part of the conversation, a ticket to be more than an observer in someone else's conversation, that's how I felt.* People knew her, she was returning as one of them. *Maybe that's the definition of home—a place you leave and return to.* In 1996 she returned again to Cuba. The Cubans, she thought, understood her language, her pain, sorrow and needs. Curiously, she now also felt the better bonded to Australia. Something had been settled but in a new relationship. *Australia is home. But my people are Cubans.*

To Marivic Wyndham soul opposes blood. It is in Australia, she reasons, that her soul dances, but only on the surface which, unlike her daughter, she cannot penetrate. *I can't go beneath that, I have nothing to do there, I wasn't put there.* Beneath that surface flows the blood, coursing almost independently of the beings it forms. Cubans says, '*La sangre llama*' (Blood beckons):

that kinship of connections that you almost didn't want to make but you had to because they're part of who you are. We carry our roots in our blood—we have to, those of us with no fixed homeland. Otherwise we would be truly exiles, forever elsewhere, forever rootless. The root-system of belonging as Australians of several generations might understand it in the blood system of belonging of Cubans like me.

If belonging embraces security, then Marivic brought her own spiritual shields. Cuba gave her the spiritual protectors both of the Spaniards and of the Africans, the Catholic Virgen de la Caridad del Cobre and the West African Chango. '*Because these spirits can move around is what makes them so powerful.*' Both the Virgin and Chango had already migrated to Cuba, Marivic explained; they don't mind travelling with me, they already have their passports! *Chango and La Virgen know all about exile, and they know all about return too, they're always there with us to ensure our passage to the next world. They've travelled, they're the diasporas of the spirits.*

Central in Marivic's life is Chango, who she believes entered her life, uninvited, when she visited the centre of West African influence on Cuban culture, Trinidad de Cuba, in 1996. Chango is a woman's fierce protector, a spirit-man, and sensuous. Traditionally he wears a skirt to deceive the unsuspecting husband that he is a female friend come to visit his wife. *I needed a strong male, a protector and a spirit that I could take wherever I went.* Chango guards against evil, he deflects ill-will. Very many Cuban women adopt him as their personal protector in defiance of the wishes of the Catholic Church. Chango himself doesn't mind. He accepts Santa Barbara as his *alter ego* in Catholic iconography and says to Cuban women—and to this Cuban-Australian woman—'put your saints wherever you like, but I'm your protector'.

He's a male godlike force. He understands me because I'm a Cuban. I can't give him to anyone, he comes where I come from, he's part of my cultural baggage. As a woman, if you are negotiating a relationship with a new land, or a homeland in your own terms without husband or family, or father or a son, then you need to lay down these other presences in that life, you need to trust it with presences for protection. I doubt if he looks after men, I don't know. I don't think he would want to get into that. He wants me to think of him and me. Chango travels everywhere, not in the earth, he's in the aether but with immense earthly power.

Chango conjoins a specifically Australian belonging. In a craft shop Marivic found staring at her a wooden Aboriginal snake. *It really beckoned me and I touched it and I could feel this thing go through my skin, my blood, more than just an icon, it wanted to penetrate me.* Marivic placed it on the dresser in her bedroom in the hope that it would forge a relationship with Chango, whose portrait hangs above the bed. *It's the first thing to come out of the Australian earth that wanted to get inside my skin.* The snake, which represents the female, stares upwards towards Chango. Chango the male spirit stares down, serious, impish, from the wall, across the bed, into the eyes of the female snake. To Marivic, the snake now forms part of the Chango empire united in her protection. She sleeps between them. Like Bill Insch, Marivic has created belonging and security in a new country in direct relation to the old, betwixt male and female, mother and father, abiding and peregrine, a spiritualised belonging that owes nothing to the physical earth.

In 1997 Marivic finished her PhD in Australian cultural history and while teaching Australian history at the University of Canberra, began tutoring an Aboriginal student, Ida.[1] At first it was not clear whether Ida would accept Marivic as her teacher, for she had rejected others. She was very fair, she had a long scar on her neck, she had few teeth; when a young woman, as Marivic learned later, she had been gang-raped. *I'd never been so close to someone whom life had dealt with so savagely; those physical scars drew me to her, though in a way they were a problem. They made a barrier we might not get over.*

There was so much to learn that no-one at university had ever explained. She had not expected Ida, nor any of the other Aboriginal students she met, to be so streetwise. Some, enrolled as teachers, had no intention of continuing; they felt they might as well join the public service and earn easier money.

They were still struggling to join the system at any cost, they seemed backward in that way. I wanted them, I guess, to remain where they were, an aggrieved culture, maintaining their cultural integrity. I imagined they would not want to join us. Ida puts tea cosies on the teapot and wants to go to England. I don't understand how you can want to do this, given where you've come from, and who's dealt you the bad hands. I've never seen a people so keen to survive, so keen to make it to tomorrow. Hang the gestures, hang the symbolism, hang the anger, hang the memories.

Hang the memories? Marivic the historian and Marivic the Cuban, to whom revenge is an act of personal honour, was mystified by the position of Ida and her husband Alan. Ida was quite adamant that her appalling life scars of Redfern and the north coast of New South Wales would die with her, or the next generation would not be able psychologically to survive. Seeking an explanation, Marivic reflected that perhaps that is how human beings best live, best survive, best love, best do anything! Aboriginals replace hatred with a deliberate instinct not to hate. The art of survival was to forget.

I have never ever encountered a people with so much dignity, with so much fire and yet with so much understanding that silence is their biggest weapon of survival, silence, looking the other way, forgetting. I understand it but culturally I will never relate to that.

I ask: Is the experience of Aboriginal people worse than you thought? Marivic replies no, but that she thought that such atrocities were in the past. Ida has a child in jail for murder, one has been raped, one is a drug addict. She lives the tragedy and the threat which society still presents to her for being Aboriginal. *I had no idea that this was daily life, nor that my neighbours in Canberra could be perpetrating those things.* What things? They involve Ida's youngest child, Claire—Claire of the 'softest, lightest most exquisite white skin', Claire the 'militant Aboriginal who wears the colours everywhere', Claire at whom the neighbours shout out when she leaves the house, 'There goes the black slut.' *It never crossed my mind that these friendly bland footy-loving Australians could turn round and call any little girl a black slut.* It was ominous for Ida, who, like other Aboriginals living in a predominantly non-Aboriginal suburb, has little alternative but to internalise the deadly insults. In Cuba, there'd be a street gang war. *Students have been shot on the steps of University of Havana.* Changes, to Marivic, flow from the real, the radical, the physical! And to Marivic herself such events were just as ominous. She had not known that such anger existed in this sunny, uncomplicated land with which she had sealed a solemn pact.

It put the Australia I thought I knew much further apart from me. I felt icy that these people exist that I had no inkling about. The Australia that does this is much more alien, I don't really belong to this. I couldn't give it a face, I couldn't imagine anyone I knew that could do such a thing, I didn't think we harboured that kind of thing in Australia.

Conversely her Australia becomes more human by such dishonour. *There but for the grace of God walks an Aussie instead of a German.*

A year after meeting Ida, Marivic, like Ian in the north, felt that she was being drawn to the very heart of the Aboriginal civilisation of southern Australia. Her admiration of Aboriginal culture was intense: the amazing delicacy with which Aboriginals related to the land and to each other, the elegance with which they negotiate what in any other culture would be coarse.

They've perfected the art of survival, it makes us all look like savages, it's so civilised and intricate and elegant and subtle. I am a Cuban American Australian and you, Ida, are an Aboriginal Australian. I crossed into a world which we both understood was composed of age-old rituals of showing how you love and care for each other. This was the language of my own family, except my family never got it right. The gifts she brought me, the hugs she gave me, the looks she threw me, everything about Ida rings such instant familiar bells. That was what drew me in and draws me in. They are the essence of my tribal world.

The women touch in their respect for the spirits of the recent dead. They speculate that Ida's mother and Marivic's father may be co-operating in the care of their living children. *I connect with that immediately, they become your agents in the afterlife.*

But no further. There are cultural areas which Marivic will not embrace. Alan told her that when he introduced her to his Arrernte kinfolk in the central desert, she would have to lower her eyes. *I'm not prepared to do that. I love you dearly but that's too far. My cultural pride.*

The most serious cultural divide concerned the spiritual nature of the land. Those protected by La Virgen del Cobre and Chango alike know that the family dead communicate with their family living, and that to this communication the land is irrelevant. The two women unite their spiritual heritages, they hold much in common which they call sacred, but they part at the independent spiritual life of the land. *I can't follow it and that's my problem. I lose Ida at that point.* In Cuba, Marivic explains, one spills one's blood for the land, wrestles with it, buries one's dead in this very active and central part of your life. *You would die for your land. But you don't make it sacred.*

There is a site on a headland on the south coast of New South Wales, wherein many of Marivic's most ecstatic memories have been invested for more than twenty years. Both north and south of the peninsula are touched by the sea, and in the distance the surf is singing. To Geoff Page the voices in the river sing of old wickedness and urgent requital. The chipped nails of 'Koonya a black girl' abrade forever beneath the shells of Cape Barren Island. The sea to Chas is the mythic embracing mother of all creation. I ask Marivic if at this lovely place anything remains of her own spirit, or her experiences, or those of her friends, or those of the Aboriginal dead. *I've no idea, I don't feel it.*

I ask if that makes a rift between her and her Aboriginal friends. No, no. The women accept their differences calmly. No-one, she replies, who isn't born to it can understand the way in which British Australians regard Aboriginals. For Marivic there is nothing different about Ida; she sees in her many members of her own family. She is not a different sort of Australian, only a nicer sort.

I don't see her as a separate race: if anything I belong to her race.

Are Aboriginals the same as other Australians then?

No, they are utterly special. Special because they come from a much longer line of thinkers, philosophers and dreamers, the tribe that arrived before us, who learned to live with the land upon which we have made so many stupid mistakes because we regarded them as idiots.

Special because they are missing from the equation, but it is the rest of Australian culture which was being deprived of their wisdom. Aboriginal culture has never been sold in Australia as our legacy. *That's a real shame. They are our elders.*

'But that doesn't mean,' Marivic adds quickly,

that I'm prepared to say 'I'm very sorry for what's happened to you, now how much land do you want back?' Bloodshed, literal or figurative, holds a power of redemption. Soft love of the land will hand it back. Hard love says, we both love this place to death, that's where warriors ought to meet. Don't think of it in dollars! No, it takes away the heat of love of the land which we have been tilling for four generations. You say to Aboriginals, 'Yes. I'm paying homage to my great-great-great-great grandfather, it's mine as much as yours. You have a better political case than I do, but I'm not just giving it up, because if I don't love it as much as you, then I should just give it to you.' There has to be hard negotiating. I gave birth to a little girl on this soil. Part of it now is mine. I'm not going to do the martyr thing, just hand over the microphone and the knife and say you do with it whatever you want. The hard love, that's when we start talking real business. We non-Aborigines have never shed blood in Australia for anything that matters. That's the hard politics of reconciliation.

Marivic is contemptuous of recent migrants who may claim that the past is the problem of the Anglo-Celtic Australians. *It's like a road that has to be fixed before any of us can go on. Anyone who wants to sign up for today's Australia has to get that through.* Do we owe them more? *As a race, yes.* She continues to find the Aboriginal connection of lives and landscape too passive. *I can't understand it. If it is that cherished and that sacred, how have you allowed people to desecrate it?* How, she asks, can it be so important and yet you Aboriginals are so unwilling to do anything about wresting it back again? *I don't understand it. I don't understand it.*

Indeed Australia is multi-centred and Aboriginality is one of those centres. Like Ian Green she feels enormously privileged to have been invited to share it. *It's not everyone's heritage yet, there's still too much to negotiate.* Land rights? Sure. The problem is there's not enough talking to what it means to you and to me. Connect the little lines first. Negotiate in your daily life:

I want my relationship with Ida and Alan repeated ten million times. The conversation matters, and how it ends matters, and how we get to the next point matters. The right of reconciliation has been taken away from the people, it only occurs politically, not face to face, and it's set up along adversarial lines. In Cuba, the big steps are taken by the individual Cubans, not by governments.

If Aboriginality is one of the centres, to which, in the end, does Marivic belong? She is drawn to what has been mixed and contested, not to the icons of gum leaves and koalas but to the blues, the rusts and the greens of the dusty landscape. Australia's colours live within each other, they are truly blended, rust, and blue, and green. But in the end, Marivic's Australia is neither land nor people nor colours, but an abstraction of goodness. Here, she concludes, is the last place you can trust when there is nowhere else to go.

Australia the most bewitching, the most endearing, the most fragile, strongest in an innocence still unviolated. You can't appreciate it unless you see the horrors of the rest of the world. In this land there remains a goodness still unsullied. Australia is the last decent society. I rage against what still happens to Claire. But we can confront it together.

REALITY IS IN BETWEEN

Manik Datar belongs through all her senses to many places and many times of her life, but none relate to a spiritualised landscape. Land is not much more than stage. She arrives at a new place, finds a little of herself and departs, leaving a little of herself. The ultimate question of a migrant's belonging is not where or how one belongs in a new country, but the relationship between the old and the new.

Manik is an accomplished writer of short stories. One concerns a woman like herself, Indian-born but living in Australia. Her sister, who has always lived in India, arrives for a holiday and expects life to be the same as in the village. The two sisters, she supposes, will share every domestic activity. They argue whether pumpkin should be cooked with—in addition to turmeric, asafoetida and coriander—mustard seed or fenugreek. The older woman pities the younger Australian–Indian sister, surrounded by machines 'for washing this and cooking that', for she has no-one to talk to in her domestic life. They hang the clothes out together at the Hills hoist, 'that symbol', says the sister, 'of Australian woman's solitary efforts and loneliness'. The Australian–Indian finds her sister's opinions patronising as well as wrong. She finds herself seeking her own space. Radio programs set them arguing, their humour 'cannot bring us together any more'. On 'sister's day', the fifth day of Diwali, the two women are cooking a special vegetarian meal as they imagine that their mother would have cooked it, but now in a domestic Australian bungalow. Their brother arrives, and gives each sister a gift. They honour him with little lamps and with auspicious red rice grains, which they sprinkle on his head. He bows and touches the elder sister's feet; she blesses him. 'It is the custom.' The youngest sibling, the Australian-Indian, is supposed to do the same to him. She refuses. 'He tweaks my nose and I punch his arm. This is not the custom.' In this sharply observed story, more sardonic than melancholy, the sisters remain divided.

> My sister, who has always lived in the country of our ancestors, in a town where she belongs as a native, believes fervently that outsiders from other provinces in India should recognise they are guests and not

demand equal rights as the local people. I who am an emigrant in a country already taken from its local people, point out the particular irony in her way of thinking.[2]

Manik Datar was born, she writes to me, in Calcutta, the Land of Enchantment, within walking distance of the National Library, brought up in the Brahmanical traditions of respect for learning and strict vegetarianism, tempered with Gandhian principles of community service and tolerance. She grew up aware of Calcutta's splendour, history and incredible poverty. She played in an old estate of gravestones, statues, palace ramparts, tree buttresses and ponds, surrounded by banyan, tamarind, jamun, frangipani, sundari, bakul, mango, hollyhock, canna, dahlia, bougainvillea and lotus.

Calcutta was a strongly Bengali city. Belonging meant speaking like the Bengalis, whose highest compliment was 'Oh, but you speak like us, I thought you were one of us'. Manik reflects that she belonged in the city by blending with the locals, 'speaking Bengali in the desired accent', she writes, 'preferably that of the higher echelons'. Like Ian Green, she found that fluency in the local language brought access to the high culture, the privilege of being simultaneously an outsider and an insider. Her mother in particular insisted that one should not discriminate in friendship between people of low and high status. *Belonging came from feeling comfortable with living in the place.* Her heart map of Calcutta surrounds herself and her friends with protecting trees. In the encircling grove and amongst her friends are gathered the institutions of high culture, the Ramakrishna mission, the Vedanta Centre, the Indian Museum. Like most educated Indians, Manik learnt several languages: her mother-tongue Marathi, the language of western India; Bengali, the regional language of Calcutta; Hindi, the national, and English, the international, language.

After a secure, loving and culturally rich childhood, at fifteen years of age Manik travelled with her family to London, where her father worked as a librarian at the Indian High Commission. Intellectually she gained confidence, which she lists as the first of the four ways of belonging to a place. This was the land of the Imperial Ruler. Her anxiety about not belonging, or at any rate, not fitting in, was tempered by the knowledge that their stay would be a short one. She took the trouble, she writes, to learn about the English 'natives': art,

Manik Datar's London. The places she identifies include her own home, Harrods, the Tate Gallery, Westminster Abbey, Highgate Cemetery and the Tower of London.

religion, classics, history, geology and biology. She found that she could belong: 'One can make friends with just about anybody anywhere. There's always some common ground if you loosen up.' Perhaps she remained more on the edge of British society than she now realises. Though deeply aware of the history which connects her birthland and Britain, her heart map of London positions herself and her family on the edge. Within inner London she identifies fifteen places of high culture.

Her father's three-year term expired. Where next? The White Australia policy had only recently ended; Australia was not an important part of the Indian diaspora; the general impression was that Australia did not welcome Indians. But Manik's mother in 1952 had visited Canberra under the Colombo Plan and found the people likeable. Her mother's qualifications in advanced librarianship won for the family the right to migrate.

In Melbourne, their first Australian home, belonging as an Indian and belonging as an Australian were different paths. Manik's own sense of belonging was, and is, partly rooted in the intricate kin network. Returning to India for holidays, it was not unusual for Manik to stay with her mother's father's brother's daughter, a relationship which in Anglo-Saxon Australian families might be that of strangers. As the eldest child, she is expected to look out for her younger siblings, and to maintain the family connections in a manner that would be considered by Anglo-Saxons intrusive.

Brahmans are the priestly class of the Hindu caste system, and her father has for thirty years carried out voluntary community service in the role of a *pujari* or priest. Manik too is a priest in training, taught by her father, though her senior tuition would need to be completed in India. Mindful of how Chas Read has been influenced by Hindi beliefs concerning country, I ask Manik about the relationship between priest and land. Yes, she can carry out the *puja* or household ceremony, intended to bring peace, well-being and happiness, if requested by her Indian friends. The priest is responsible for the mantras which, if recited properly, should have efficacy and power. Is the priest, conducting a *puja*, a conduit for forces in the earth? Manik considers.

No, the priest is a conduit to God the transcendental. The earth is significant, though, as mother: even classical Indian dance requires that acknowledgement and reverence be shown to the earth.

Are there special sites, or do you mean the whole earth?

It's more the whole earth, earth as mother.

Are all sites equal in their power to absorb human mantras or prayers?

I don't think sites absorb mantras or prayers, but you see, Peter, the teaching is not based on a book or prophet. Sites can be shrines.

Are they object and spirit at the same moment?

Yes, God is everywhere, and therefore when praying one can ask God to be present in the nominated object, it might be a rock, a pebble, an idol or an image. That rock can become consecrated. The teaching can be very sophisticated.

I propose that a temple is built on a certain site because the builders perceive some energies or forces. *I don't know. I've not been involved. I'm not especially interested in that.*

In truth Manik is not particularly interested in the questions which engross Chas, Ian and Bill. She allows for spiritual experiences, and concedes that the earth may or may not be a series of connected sites. Indeed people can have mystical experiences in a cathedral, but for Manik spirituality is not connected with specific place. Nor is she much perplexed about the origin of such experiences. *I'm not at all inclined towards the mystical, though it's fine for some people, I'm willing to accept that.* She concedes that some Australians build stone circles in order to relate themselves to the earth, or the cosmos, or the dead. These are personal rituals, a privilege for those with time and space. *Sure, it gives meaning to life, an ordering. To me it doesn't matter, it doesn't turn me on at all.*

Much more critical to Manik is her concept of *dharma*, her moral, religious and customary role as person and woman. I ask: Do you belong, then, more to people than to place? *Oh yes, I'm a social person.* One can belong by intellectual engagement, through affinity, through one's acceptance by the place, by the local people; and one can belong through contribution to the place. What will she leave behind? Manik accepts the Indian philosophy of birth and rebirth which stems from the notions of *karma* and *dharma*. She accepts, in a Western-modified form, the concept of woman as hearth. *It's a very powerful position.*

Woman-as-hearth, a source of ultimate belonging for others, is not a tedium. It's a privilege to hold together a group of people, and the obvious place to start from is the home. For there are four stages of life: student, householder, *sunyasin*, and renunciation. These are coupled to the four pursuits: *dharma*, earning a livelihood, enjoying the pleasures of life, and spiritual attainment. Manik considers herself to be at present in the stage of householder and contributor to the community. Home is where burns the flame of the hearth, that larger metaphorical sense of bringing people together. Woman, she thinks, does it best. Men may try to create a hearth at work, but they mostly rely on others to provide. More often they are onlookers at the hearth: they warm their hands and depart. Belonging is hearth, belonging is community, in Calcutta, London, Canberra or Alice Springs.

Alice Springs? Yes, and Darwin. After two years in Darwin, Manik, the only Marathi speaker between Darwin and Adelaide, moved with her family to the multilayered town of Alice Springs. It is clear from her heart maps that neither experience was altogether happy. She draws the Darwin community perched on a high and remote cliff above an unquiet sea. Alice Springs she depicts bisected. A heavy black line, geographically negotiating Heavitree Gap, metaphorically denotes division, separation, isolation. Six people, four cars signify transience. In the notes to her map she writes of Alice Springs as 'a town defined by definitions where people were habitually slotted into categories'. Here Manik worked for the Central Land Council and the Tangentyere Town Council for three years.

Working with Aboriginal people in a community that allowed no neutrality made for disconnection. Dichotomies were everywhere: insider/outsider, blackfeller/whitefeller, bush/town, urban Aboriginal/ bush Aboriginal, old timers/newly arrived, man/woman, defendant/ prosecutor, pro/anti the Pine Gap defence base, Top End/Centre, partners who worked out bush or partners who stayed warming the hearth. Whitefellers, she now reflects, belonged by staking a claim on some aspect of knowledge, usually Indigenous—making it (archaeologists, writers), minding it (public servants, anthropologists), or using it (doctors, diesel mechanics). Though Manik had studied anthropology, linguistics and archaeology, she was not professionally engaged in them and was therefore excluded. Worse than excluded, worse than marginalised, Manik was always categorised. Everyone, it

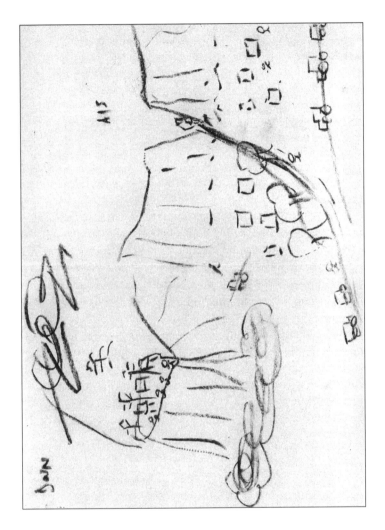

Left: Manik's Darwin. Perched on a high and remote cliff above an unquiet sea. Right: Manik's Alice Springs. She writes of it as 'a town defined by definitions where people were habitually slotted into categories ... Multiculture, subtleties, multiple axes of belonging had no place in this *zeitgeist*.'

seemed, occupied one and only one classification. Even her colleagues saw her in terms of honorary Black or honorary White. Sometimes she was mistaken for an Aboriginal woman by Aboriginal men who made a pass at her, and then apologised when they heard her non-Aboriginal accent.

Divisions and definitions are deeply foreign to Manik. *If you ignore political correctness, you can be an insider and an outsider at the same time, they're like parallel realities.* She is unsure if she would respect a prohibition to enter a male Aboriginal sacred area. Certainly it would bother her if she transgressed as a tourist, but if she were there as a professional a decision would be more difficult. *Is my gender more important, or Aboriginal feelings, or my profession? It would depend why I was there. I'm not sure which one would win.* Aboriginal identity itself naturally can be deeply divided and confused. Much of what she experienced at work she found distressing; she was critical of certain Aboriginal individuals. *They're ordinary people like anybody else but I don't want to be specific on tape.* In the 1980s Australians, accepting that Aboriginals had suffered deeply, strove to compensate, *but sometimes my friends in Canberra want only a sanitised view of living in the Territory. Reality is in between.*

Despite working for Aboriginal organisations, Manik remained somewhat distant from all but the urban culture of Alice Springs. She began learning the Arrernte language but found the bush community rather inaccessible. She often went camping, but not with the Aboriginal custodians who might have given her personal insights into Arrernte and Pitjantjatjara spiritual relationships to land. She understands that Aboriginals are engaged more deeply with the desert, which, like a cathedral, may summon a state of serenity and spirituality. She comprehends emotional bonding, less so mystical bonding. *We tend to do things and rationalise afterwards.* Is the land aware that you are here? Manik, like Marivic, does not think so, though she accepts that, as an embodiment of an intellectual engagement, such questions are creative and useful. I discuss the way in which some Aboriginal men have seen devil-devils. *I'd need more proof or personal experience before I believe in them myself.* Are the different philosophies of Central Australia, then, equally valid? Yes of course. Spiritual country neither contradicts nor complements her own beliefs, it merely runs parallel.

Manik left Alice Springs without much regret, further curiosity or intellectual engagement. She concludes, 'Multiculture, subtleties, multiple axes of belonging had no place in this *Zeitgeist.*'

Multiple axes and an absence of arbitrary definitions are central to Manik Datar's sense of belonging and of being. Yes, Aboriginals can know more about the land, they add the richness and complexity of their culture; but no, she believes they have no deeper insights unless learned in the law and lore. She believes in land rights for the Indigenous but is worried by ultimately privileging any group on the basis of ethnicity. The decisive question is: are some people special? Manik answers her own question. As far as history is concerned, yes. Aboriginals have not occupied, and do not now occupy, a level playing field, but the world is much too complex for separateness. We all share multiple identities. Obviously the pendulum has to be righted, but to claim to be 'blue-blooded' is mere rhetoric. She can understand the need for separate cultural identification, but who can authenticate descent, and under whose criteria? Genetics soon becomes politics. 'We can't undo our genetic make-up. I don't like the concept of pure and authentic.' In answer to my proposal of the Aboriginal house in which other Australians are tenants, she replies that, though it is clearly wrong that tenants can oust the owners, the analogy itself is false. *The world is full of cultural mixes. We all have to live somewhere. India has been invaded by Greeks, Persians, Moghuls as well as many Europeans including the British, wave after wave of different ethnicities and religions all superimposed on each other.* Despite the divisive caste system, India has accepted communities persecuted elsewhere: the early Christians, the Jewish diaspora, Parsees, Baha'i. To establish who was indigenous to India would not only be meaningless but deeply divisive. *We can't untwist history.* In Canberra Manik feels that she belongs in many ways, including as Indian, ethnic, woman, Hindu, Australian, mother and suburban dweller. Like Marivic, she holds that belonging in part turns on acceptance by those around one, from participating and contributing, raising children, paying taxes, being a good citizen. She belongs on axes of time and place, culture and culture, smells, taste, memory. She is not sentimental about India; funds permitting, she returns every four or five years.

My reading of her short stories is that the sharpest issues of belonging are intercultural and international. An Indian expatriate can be portrayed as unpatriotic in leaving India and dishonourable for not returning. 'Go, but you will not come back to the land of your birth' is more hurtful a jibe than 'You do not yet belong in the country in which you have chosen to live'.

In a powerful short story called 'Point of No Return'[3] an awkward youth, newly arrived in Australia, waits for the moment to return to India to marry his Rita and to bring her to Australia. Still culture-shocked, and while paddling a boat on Lake Burley Griffin in Canberra, the young man experiences a kind of double vision. He has an urge to name the world in the language he knows best, for in the naming of them in Bangla he can testify their reality. He recognises a black swan as the emblem of the goddess Saraswati herself. People pull at oars as seriously as any fisherman at Mazerhart, the fisherman's mart in Calcutta. Women tramp in the sun for fuel and water is already reticulated to their homes. The young man's admiration of the National Library of Australia is 'spiked with a shot of pain' as he sees in his mind the National Library of Belvedere. Are Australian youths, he asks rhetorically, told by their families to forsake one land for another? At a cultural function he hears voices speaking of India as a holiday destination, one amongst many. The songs he hears are 'feeble enactments of Sundays long past'. The young man realises that belonging 'comes with incremental dues paid over years'.

Manik belongs on axes both geographical and temporal. The sight of a tamarind tree will remind her of her birth country, while the scent of a eucalyptus in India summons a longing for Australia. In India: A birthplace may be significant, but not necessarily a place one wishes to visit. The home of her ancestors is not necessarily the land where she would wish to be cremated. In Australia: Manik belongs for many reasons: because she has consciously grafted herself here; because she likes the look of the land; because it gives her space as a non-Anglo-Celtic Australian; because she feels accepted by its people; because she holds a commitment to its democracy; because of her memories; and because occasionally, she tells me, she now feels an ache for the land. In Canberra: because it has the critical mass which allows for people of many beliefs to flourish, because she has lived there for many years and has many friends. Of the suburb of Downer, she reflects:

It's nice enough, but belonging is far more diffused than contained in a suburb; the images are fragmented. Yes, there are several significant spots and that's symptomatic of the multiple-identity living which one does. We place too much emphasis on these place memories as if they were religious icons. More important is the web of social connections.

Australia must be multi-centred, she believes, for if there is only one way to be Australian, there will be many who will not fit. Manik's heart map in the end is of people.

Manik is undecided who should bear the burden of Aboriginal dispossession. She concedes that the descendants of Anglo-Celts or others, who might or might not have committed atrocities, may have to carry that burden. I ask if responsibility should be shared also by post-war migrants. *Interesting. I don't know. Some may see themselves as global nomads.* She knows Indians who say they are only Australian in certain circumstances: *I don't agree with that, I won't accept that.* Affirmative action is necessary; the problems of prejudice and unequal distribution will not work out by themselves. Post-war migrants should share responsibility for reconciliation because they share everything else. But in the long run, we should accept that unity is more important than difference. Belonging is diffuse, formed of many elements. Belonging must in the end be equal.

SECOND SETTLERS DO HAVE SOME OF THAT SAME CONNECTEDNESS

To Mandy Martin, the degradation of the environment is a far more fearsome apprehension than Aboriginal land claims.

Mandy, the landscape artist, visually understands the western division of New South Wales. Part of her heart's country is Wapweelah station in the far north-west, which she describes as '150 square miles of red sandhill and black soil flood country'. There is much to concern her and the other pastoral lessees—'coping with Wik and Aboriginal Native Title', the myriad acts of the Western Lands Board, 'fighting the cotton lobby and the Queensland government who between them seem intent on damming and irrigating from the last unregulated river system in Australia',[4] and the fruits of 140 years of deadly degradation.

The historian Charles Bean travelled to the 'red country' in 1909 and wrote of it:

out here you have reached the core of Australia, the real red Australia of the ages ...

Sketch by Mandy Martin, 'Winroe, 11 July, dusk'.

This is the real Australia, and it is as delicate as its own grasses. In parts the sand, which covers it and contains the whole calendar of priceless seeds that have taken a few million years (at a low estimate) to evolve, is not more than one foot thick; so thin and light and delicate a skin that only the delicate Western scrub holds it in place at all.[5]

Ninety years later Mandy says of it: 'I feel best in a very open and fairly treeless environment, the most complete sense of well-being in a landscape and it comes with a sense of gratitude or recognition.' Many of her landscape paintings of the north-west contain text that represents the human presence. She uses found pigment to represent 'place' in landscape, which she describes as 'culturally integrated and many-voiced'.

Of the many voices, the clearest is her own. In the 1990s, while art became international and globalised in themes of dislocation and alienation, Mandy Martin describes herself as having become doggedly regional, progressively specific. This journey of much soul-searching and analysis, she explains, was not easy, but left her feeling much more centred.

You can't get much more local than this particular tree on this kind of soil at this time of day in this kind of weather. This is where I want to be, this is my landscape, this is what I want to say about it, this is why I'm saying it, and to me that fits together with a whole picture to do with the environment.

Recent paintings pinpoint a precise time, date, site, environment and climate: 'Dust Storm over the Bottom Ten Mile', 'Flood below the Shearing Shed', 'Home Paddock, forty-four degrees, 3 p.m., 18 January', 'Irarra Creek near Billie's Pig Trap', 'After a Little Rain in Seven Mile, 29 January 1997'. Even paintings without a written location may take geographic markers. A dotted line connects the viewer to the viewed place and the unseen country beyond: 'Due West', 'Pooncarie', 'Mt Deception'. They document an ongoing sequence. *There's an inherent truth in that.*

This country of the far north-west of New South Wales environmentally is wounded, and not only by those of no spiritual connection to the land. Even in Bean's time, almost a century ago, people both loved the country and ruined it. He met an old man who told him of the

1870s, 'When first I rode my horse on to this red country, it was all beautifully grassed open land away to the hills—not a pine tree on it. And the soil was so loose that my horse sank up to his fetlocks at every step and the sheep drove their feet deep into it as they walked.'[6] The grass died and was replaced, in the southern part of the western lands, by pine trees. Bean continued, 'And where the earth was once grass-covered we found great piebald patches of shiny bare clay, which, if the sheep went on with their work and trampled it to powder, might possibly bear grass and saltbush again some day—or might not.'[7] And it did not. The end of firestick farming, rabbits, greed, pigs, goats, overstocking, drought and legislative failures produced an imbalance between edible and inedible shrubs and trees; the latter multiplied, choking grasses and accelerating erosion. In 1885, the western division supported 17 million sheep: they number today perhaps one-third of that.[8] Stations which once employed one hundred people now employ three.[9] The native game competes with three to five million feral pigs; perhaps 20 million hectares are affected by the almost impenetrable woody weeds growing two metres tall.

'Woody weeds' is the convenient name for a variety of dense timber-like shrubs that began to recolonise country severely grazed from the 1880s, and for whose later expansion everything was blamed —cattle, sheep, lack of regular ground fires, and myxomatosis. Woody weeds are dark and dense. They change the look of the country; they obscure familiar places; they extinguish tracks seldom used. They alone seem able to subsist despite flood, dust storm and drought. Removal by deep ploughing and burning is expensive; and the weeds always return. Eventually they may render the country quite useless for production. Ironically, woody weeds are native to the region; ironically, they render the land useless for the grazing which has ruined it.

Though parts of the country may well be useless as pasture for centuries, Mandy Martin's vision is not desolate desert but closely observed cultural landscape. A Wapweelah painting is entitled 'Woody Weeds and Coolibah Fringing a Claypan, 1996'. Woody weeds and coolibahs are natural vegetation. The scalded claypan upon which the solitary indigenous coolibah stands once was abundant with native grasses so tall that mothers tied scarlet cloths on their children's heads to locate them.

The art curator Peter Haynes wrote that to her detailed observation and historical rendering of landscape, Mandy Martin has added land, by which he meant the cultures of humankind in relation to country. To the 'normless continuity of country' she subjoined 'the normless discontinuity of culture, and the land seemed on the brink of extinction'.[10] Paul Sinclair, who was her collaborator in a project of words and pictures of the Darling Basin designed to imbue the observer with the spiritual presence of the country, wrote, 'Profound relationships, stretching deep into time, have always existed between human beings and this land … arid ecosystems have longer memories than we do.'[11] Mandy paints no ruined homesteads, no broken windmills, no fences, no deserted roads: no evidence, apart from the specific locations written on the paintings themselves, that humans have ever been there. Yet I agree with Peter Haynes that Mandy's landscapes are always acculturated. Somewhere they touch my—our—memory of centuries of painted European landscapes, the cleared and abundant foreground, the darker forest or hills enclosing the prosperous humanised settlement. Here the eye is drawn to dust storm, solitary tree, roaring wind, towering cloudscape, exposed root, dead stump, scalded claypan: and the ever present dark line of woody weeds. Yet in this astringent universe I don't perceive a judgement on our ancestors. Whites cared about this land, even if they did not care for it. In 'Woody Weeds and Coolibah Fringing a Claypan', the shrubs stand clumped in the distance; they do not lower or menace, they exist. The oppositions expressed in her Wapweelah paintings to me are light to dark, single to many, foreground to background, empty to crowded; not exotic to native, not evil to good, not belonging to alienation, not before to after, not loved to hated. The painted landscape is beautiful because Mandy Martin responds to the natural beauty which it possesses.

Possesses? Mandy is too subtle an artist for explicit information. The lustrous gold of a whirling sky may be a natural hue; or may be stained by the last vestiges of eroded topsoil. The people who perceived this beauty, and wrought this destruction, may be temporarily absent, but Mandy enters no judgement on their loneliness, carelessness, dislocation or failed enterprise. Her mental landscapes are peopled and cultured, engrossed and absorbed. She believes that the aesthetic and the cultural must have a place in the evaluation of future landscapes;[12] because land is cultural, it is peopled, it is changed, in the end it is contested. Mandy distils the theme of this book as she tells me: 'I feel I belong here, though I know the dilemma of being a second settler with a legacy of genocide and dispossession and cultural dislocation, and also to reconcile one's own sense that this is where you belong.'

Where you belong. And yet to this powerful country where we belong the destruction is immense and catastrophic. Denudation of the cane grass flats: *You can't talk about what's beautiful without speaking of destruction. But I can only do this by mediating the unthinkable with transcendent beauty.*[13] What is unthinkable? That the eroded land is not, can never now be, beautiful? That the land we love and belong to has been desecrated by those who loved it? That the land, already unrecognisable to the nineteenth-century Gurnu, will soon become unrecognisable to us all? Mandy's landscape paintings are filled with light, too sombre for joy, too vibrant for despair, too closely observed for optimism, too ecstatic for sorrow. Her colours are blended because the land, as Marivic puts it, is blended with the human culture of the first and second settlers.

Mandy Martin knows Aboriginality. En route to Uluru, she travelled through remote south Australia as a young teenager and painted Aboriginals in the desert for years afterwards. In her first year in art school in 1972 she joined in South Australia's first land rights demonstration; later in the decade in Canberra she donated paintings to aid the cause of the Aboriginal Treaty Committee. *Although I didn't actually know many Aboriginal people, I could see it was a process that we had to go through in Australia.* She has worked at Ipolera in the Northern Territory among the Arrernte, watching in awe as an older woman painted a breathtaking landscape entirely from memory. She accepts that Aboriginal sacred landforms must be approached respectfully: elders must be consulted; recognisable landforms in the western desert or Lake Mungo she paints in the far distance, without detail. She recognises *places where I simply wouldn't work, where I've been a little bit spooked and you kind of know you shouldn't work there.* At the Lake Mungo lunette: *I'm hardly able to walk on it, let alone depict it.* She respects that the former head stockman of Wapweelah steers her away from certain places, and will not divulge his knowledge of the scarred trees. She feels the lack of a spiritual guide on Wapweelah: 'There are so many un-explained questions.' She has examined the scatters of stone tools in claypans and beside creek beds and marvelled at their depth and incredible antiquity. Not conventionally religious or spiritual, and with no intention to become 'feral or a quasi spiritualist', like Manik she has not considered whether her own country knows her when she returns. *Maybe if you get down to it you can find a scientific or a phenomenological explanation for everything; but Aboriginal people have pointed the way really well to have both spiritual and pragmatic information involved in almost everything.* But of course, she reassures me, she respects other people's cultural practices. *Coming from a scientific father I tend to always tend to look for more rational and scientific explanations.*

Out in the west 'there's no denying there is real racism and there are real problems'. Travelling to Uluru for the 1984 ceremony in which it was handed back to its Indigenous custodians, she heard of Aboriginal visitors who, having travelled thousands of kilometres, were denied diesel by the last garage proprietors. *I've seen the extremes.* How did one cope in South Africa? How does one cope in the nearest town Enngonia? *We just don't go to the pub. We drive straight through and don't stop. The Enngonia pub alternates from being Whites-only to Blacks-only. There is no middle ground.* She has witnessed the drunken Aboriginal riots in Bourke, the fire-bombed cars, the barricaded shops, her friends having their handbags snatched, and being smashed over the head. *I've seen the hate, the division on both sides, I've seen all those.* She listened in her studio to the Wik debate,

that inappropriate English system trying to grapple with something which in real life is being grappled with in much more sophisticated ways that haven't been described or even thought of by politics and legalese, it gave me a lot of hope. Minds were leaping light-years ahead of the political system.

Following the Native Title Act came the land claims.

Three or four overlapping claims may in future be brought against Wapweelah. Two claims already exist, the first by New South Wales Aboriginals, the second a huge tear drop-shaped claim beginning in Queensland and stretching down to Wapweelah, lodged by 'a mob in Toowoomba', of whom she and the Enngonia Aboriginal community know nothing. One of the claims is for everything above the ground, below the ground, all the artesian water, all the air space above. Bourke, she points out, has a tragic history, of 'missions and people having been moved out of their country and sent into Bourke'. She asks herself,

'Who are the claimants? Why at least don't they come and see the country they are claiming and talk to its occupants?'

There is much in what Mandy says of the tragic history of dispossession and dispersal. A large number of Aboriginals were killed at Hospital Creek near Brewarrina before 1850. Bean wrote of the last quarter of the nineteenth century, 'It did not matter who was shot. Every blackfellow that was killed was considered a pest.'[14] Yet after the initial dispossession, and unlike further east, work was available on the enormous stations especially for the growing number of part-descent Aboriginals. By 1915 part-descent people were one-third of the enumerated Aboriginal population.[15]

It was amongst this generation that the intimate knowledge of culture, language and knowledge began to slip. Jeremy Beckett, an anthropologist, writes that the generation born after the turn of the century were itinerants; they were no longer attached to any one station, but formed part of the mobile labour force which extended into South Australia and Queensland. Probably his remarks apply more to men than to women, but Beckett was right in his estimation that the people of 1910 were the last full generation to be initiated, to know all the stories of all the sites intimately, to respect and to follow up the dreamings, as Bill Parry put it, Where the Dingo Bubbles Up.

The issues are important for Mandy because even the Aboriginal women of the following generation, born in the 1920s, knew the station surrounds better than the bush. Knowledge of the recent Aboriginal history of the region in part comes from a book by Evelyn Crawford, *Over My Tracks*. Following the female descent line, Evelyn, born in about 1920, was Barkindji. She was an eagle-hawk woman. Some time in the 1920s her father, a Wankummurrah from Queensland, received a message from his kinfolk inviting him to Yantabulla station, which adjoined Wapweelah. In forty pages of her book she describes her adolescence and early womanhood at Yantabulla, spent mainly at the camp near the station homestead. The Depression changed her life abruptly by terminating paid employment. Evelyn recalled:

'Where's everybody, Charlie?' Dad asked Charles Zooch.

'Some've gone to the Government Mission at Brewarrina. They reckon you get food for your kids, and a house to live in.'

'Who said you can?'

'Some government fellers came while you were away, told us all about it. Made it sound real good.'

The family left Yantabulla for Brewarrina, where soon occurred the first confrontation with the manager:

'Right, you'll have to sign a paper to say that you'll stay here.'
    'What d'you mean, "stay here"?
    'That you stay here and don't leave. You stay here till you die.'
    'I'll see 'ow we like it here first, see if we want to stay. If we don't like it, we'll move on.'
    'Well you can and your wife, but the kids'll have to stay.'[16]

All over the north-west the old Aboriginal communities were moving, some voluntarily, most by force, from Tibooburra, Angledool and the great sheep walks of the Darling. By 1935 Brewarrina contained some 400 desperately miserable Aboriginal people, without work, out of their country, in dreadful conditions. Many children taken to the Aboriginal institutions were never seen again by their families. The effects, as the historian Heather Goodall writes, were devastating.[17]

Families began leaving the hated Brewarrina settlement as work became available during World War II. They returned to their country, but not to the old ways already half forgotten; they went back as itinerants, back to the fringes of towns, back to Bourke itself, where they camped by the railway line or the rubbish tip. In 1948 the Aboriginal population of Bourke was fifty-five, some of whom almost certainly would have lived at Yantabulla and Wapweelah previously.[18] Though Evelyn passed through Yantabulla station many more times during her life, she never returned to live permanently in her ancestral country. Nor has anyone else. It is not possible to take up permanent residence on the old living areas unless the land has been bought by an Aboriginal corporation. Nor has any descendant of the traditional owners returned permanently to Wapweelah.

Between what she calls the ignorant and evasive diatribes of the White stakeholders and the non-appearance of the Aboriginal claimants, Mandy finds it difficult to know what to expect from the legal process. I ask: Isn't the land supposed to be shared under the Native Title Act, prioritising pastoralism? *Yes, Aboriginals already have hunting rights, as they do on all the pastoral leases, but Wapweelah is a little far from town for this right to be utilised. So actually, now, it's really interesting to be the same person who's been involved in all of that and believed all of that to be also one of the people who are under Native Title claim.* It is no gentle reflection that in parts of South Africa the working norm among the rural guerillas was 'one settler, one bullet'. Mandy has little sympathy with the vitriolic outpourings of those opposed to land claims. *I don't feel I'm one of those settlers.* Yet she has no obvious connection with the Aboriginal women of Enngonia.

It's difficult for a sophisticated middle-class second settler White woman to actually reconcile herself on an equal level with Aboriginal women [here], and most of my Aboriginal friends are just as I am, they've been to the same art schools or exhibited in the same galleries, and are feminists.

Mandy knows Wapweelah intimately; she cares for it deeply. While she would love Evelyn Crawford to return to explain Aboriginal meaning and connection, its Aboriginal meaning is no essential element in her own sense of belonging. It may be, as she puts it, that 'One of the most crucial problems presently bothering second settlers in Australia [she means anyone non-Aboriginal] is that same moral and spiritual connection with landscape.'[19] But any lack of connection is not that of the poet Coral Hull who, visiting Brewarrina, felt herself alienated because she stood outside Murawari culture:

> the concentric circles & Gunderbooka totems remain guarded, fragmented & aloof as an elder with sealed lips, sun ripe and wind blown it's as though some secret of the land is locked inside them, its big silence drawing me into its deep time, judging whether I am ready, to be on the in, i am fearful with this desire to belong, fearful that in the end i will be cast out along the ruined land, beneath a white full moon, half living, half knowing nothing, in Murawari country.[20]

Mandy considers herself to be neither half living, nor half knowing nothing. Nor, she believes, do many of the other Whites of the red country; it is the shooters in their four-wheel-drive vehicles from outside the region who don't care and will never belong. She writes:

two hundred years later, second settlers do have some of that same connectedness [i.e. spiritual connection to the landscape]. One only has to stop at the Hungerford pub, and talk to Maxi, the dog-fence grader driver, or Stan, the stockman who has worked on all the stations in the region, to discover that they are far from blind to it.[21]

Is this loved country to be shared, or given up? I put to her Marivic's conception of hard love:

You say to Aboriginals, 'Yes. I'm paying homage to my great-great-great-great grandfather, it's mine as much as yours. You have a better political case than I do, but I'm not just giving it up, because if I don't love it as much as you, then I should just give it to you.'

Mandy replies that she wouldn't put it like that,

but I suppose the first thing that flashed through my mind when we first heard of the first native title claim lodged with the Tribunal was the brolgas. I know six were shot on Danny's property last year, and he has his suspicions who shot them. Echidnas, the going rate is ninety dollars, eggs are twenty-five. I don't mind if they take the odd sheep, but it's quite difficult because my husband has turned that property round from a place that was really overgrazed and abused into something that's good enough to become a national park. If it was people like Harry Boney [believed to be the last man with traditional knowledge of the country] going in there, with traditional respect for various trees and plants, I'd be delighted; but I don't see a lot of difference between a bunch of white shooters and a bunch of black shooters fundamentally. They're my real worries. If it was women and kids going out there doing the bush tucker thing and sitting round under a tree enjoying the place like I do with my kids ... but I suspect it'd be more to do with pushing the white shooters out of the place. They're big issues.

A shared belonging at Wapweelah, an Aboriginal homeland centre like Ipolera in which people painted, sat down with their children and re-embraced their own traditional land—and Mandy's cherished red country—would be ideal.

It's fantastic to go back to Ipolera again, to see an Aboriginal outstation which is run so impeccably and the boys are involved in cattle work and women in

*community arts and a mild degree of tourism and there's a little caravan park
there and a nice school and you feel terrific about it.*

At Wapweelah she suspects that Aboriginal land claimants might
suddenly arrive to hunt the threatened wildlife. *I'm appalled at the prospect.* Successful claimants might open gates or leave bottles about, cut
their feet and sue the white leaseholders. *It would be interesting to know
who the people are and walk through your landscape with them.* I ask whether
in a perfect world jointly sharing Wapweelah would be possible.
Mandy replies that it would be 'really terrific in one sense', that she
'does not see why not'; yet she remains apprehensive because of the
'fairly large issues like access, hunting and public liability'. *It's an issue
that we're bang in the middle of, and one which we live with in a real and daily
sense. Which is why it's important to find out about the land and what it
means, our efforts to get Evelyn out here.*

Mandy has two strong reservations about reoccupation. First is
the landscape she wants to protect from further degradation, and its
wildlife which she and her husband have nursed back to good health.
The only future for Wapweelah is its long-term sustainable use. *We don't
want grazing; it's really marginal.* The other uncertainty is philosophical.
A party of art students, led by Mandy, were about to set out for the
rock art site at Namadgi National Park near Canberra. One asked her
whether there were gender restrictions at the site. Mandy was shocked.
*It hadn't occurred to me that a site which is pre-current Aboriginal occupation
might be subject to the same laws, particularly when there's no connected
history.*

Though there may be rather more remembered or transmitted
Indigenous association with Wapweelah than might appear, and despite the clear moral case which to Mandy sustains the land rights
legislation, the issues of actual Aboriginal reoccupation of deserted
sites remain intractable. She may be right in her estimation that the
recollected associations of Aboriginal people with Wapweelah are not
as full as those of the second settlers. *That's a real problem. Aboriginal
people have lived in the north-west for thirty thousand years—up to 1930;
then the ancient association was broken. I think it's coming back to a place
where no-one can tell you what it means.* Mandy drew an analogy to
returning to her mother's home in Liverpool, UK: it was meaningful when accompanied by her mother, but without her it was 'just

a really depressing brown brick house in a street'. Then she qualifies the position:

But having said that, a lot of my Aboriginal friends are just as middle class and move in the same gallery and academic circles that I do, and some have been successfully reintroduced and rediscovered country, under the wing of Aboriginal elders, not necessarily the country they were born in because they don't know where it was. I believe that an Aboriginal person who's got a recent history of being from the land will feel that when they go back, whether it's the right country for them. That may be a bit quasi-mystical but I believe that's true. So it's more than likely that people from Bourke or Enngonia or Brewarrina taking them into that land, they will find some sort of reading there which, even if they can't immediately understand, they will make a connection [to], given the right information and a bit of guidance. Yes, they can share, all of the problems can be resolved through negotiation.

We must talk to each other as individuals. Among Geoff Page's Bandjalang:

> *And once more in a final silence,*
> *before the scraping back of chairs,*
> *before the wary net of handshakes,*
> *they hear the rapids in the darkness,*
> *the voices in the river.*[22]

In the words of Marivic Wyndham:

I want my relationship with Ida and Alan repeated ten million times. The conversation matters, and how it ends matters, and how we get to the next point matters. The right of reconciliation has been taken away from the people, it only occurs politically, not face to face, and it's set up along adversarial lines.

Now Mandy repeats the theme:

On a human level, finding the face and being introduced to it is the trouble; we would do much better in reconciliation now if we had face-to-face negotiations. Not only poor Blacks but poor Whites are very distrustful of promises. I think the only thing to work is one-to-one.

In 1996, after an absence of thirty-six years, Marivic Wyndham returned to Jibacoa, the mansion where her aunt was scolded by a former maid, '*Señora, esta no es su casa.*' She had already spent a few days in Havana returning to the houses where she had lived as a child, and wrote of the experience, 'My visit prompted a sense of disorientation, mourning, loss.' Jibacoa, though, represented her family's stolen lands, demanding not mere return but symbolic reclamation. No longer a picturesque estate, Jibacoa had become a rest and recreation area for junior military officers.

As the day approached I realised that strange forces were impelling me. The weight of the family grief and the family honour sat squarely on my shoulders. … I was the family at that moment, and trustee of its unfinished business. … I went there to defy fate and those who'd usurped control and possession over this, our sacred family ground. … As I approached the place I realised I had business to transact there.

Marivic entered unobserved from the rear of the building to find the place shabby and decrepit, the walls ripped, the old dining room filled with notice boards, a bomb shelter in the garden, billiard tables in the lounge, the interior swimming pool filthy and half empty.

This was family country. Occupied family country. Here was aggravation, hostility … striding in, unannounced and uninvited. A man with a mission. I repossessed the place at a glance—the sheer fact that I was there had conferred ownership of it. In Havana I was the little girl returning to visit the country of my childhood. While in Jibacoa I was the son repossessing my family's stolen lands.[23]

Manik might argue that in time Jibacoa, like Australia, will be shared, must be shared, by all the descendants of invaders, rebels, usurpers, revolutionaries and counter-claimants, whose first concern will be to the people who share their stage rather than the stage itself. Mandy, mindful of the incongruities of history, may restrict the right to share it to those who revere and cherish it. Marivic symbolically has reclaimed her country, but urges all her fellow Australians who revere this land, first settlers, second settlers, migrants and exiles, all to assert their claim to it with a hard love.

CHAPTER 7

FOUR HISTORIANS

I DON'T FEEL UNWELCOME THERE

What was it, Heather Goodall asks in the introduction to her history of New South Wales Aboriginals, *Invasion to Embassy*, that white Australians like herself found attractive or compelling in the land rights movements? Land rights privileged Indigenous over egalitarian principles, which needed a stronger rationale than historical disadvantage. So was she, she asks, seeking to cement her own relationships with Aboriginal people by endorsing unquestioningly their priorities for the land? Or was she seeking Aboriginals to clarify or strengthen her own tenuous, even imaginary, relationship? And if the starting point was complex, what fruitful synthesis would emerge between White and Black? Heather asks what has she and others standing beside her learned from this engagement with Aboriginal people and the land?[1] These intriguing questions are not answered in her book.

Heather grew up, she tells me, in the Sydney suburb of Padstow. She describes the area as 'such a disaster', 'petty bourgeois post-war fibro', with broken glass on the ovals, bitumen and heavy pollution in the creek. How little she knew about it, she now reflects; how great was her detachment from the urban environment. In the 1980s she met a local Gundangara woman, Robin Williams, who revealed to her some of her grandmother's stories of southern Sydney, the stratum of Aboriginal memory and experience in the same area of her youth. *There's some hand-stencil sites in an overhanging rock shelter almost directly opposite Picnic Point, very close to Padstow where I grew up.* Flashed upon her a sense of the human relationships and the land they crossed which she had never suspected. *It was an extraordinary experience to see the place I thought I knew so well suddenly have a whole very much more interesting and deeper dimension to it.* But the revelation of rich overlay brought no deeper affection. Discovery allowed her to re-evaluate her growing-up place now criss-crossed with multiple sets of meanings; but discovery brought her emotionally no closer to it.

I invite Heather to tell me about the relationship between herself, her own country and the Aboriginal lands of the far north-west of New South Wales. The connections, it seems, have deepened.[2] She tells me that her pulse quickens after Dubbo, where roads straighten and memories thicken of twenty-five years of profound engagement with Aboriginals. She recalls fishing, exploring, sleeping under the stars, telling and retelling events till daybreak; familiar dwellings, campsites washed or blown away, and out on the wide plains the great arc of the Darling River: sunlight, steep banks, gigantic trees, the flow of the water, the quality of sand or mud. *That freshwater country. An extremely beautiful moving place.* Heather's country, of which she writes and speaks so strongly, is in part the same far north-west absorbed in the imagination of Mandy Martin.

Like Mandy, Heather Goodall has no strong sense of the unconscious. She has no experience of intuiting violence or old magic from an unknown site, and finds it difficult to rationalise how people have strong dreams of events in places which are later revealed to have actually occurred there. The land remains dynamic, fragile, entwined with a sense of enormous breadth and scale, the huge overarching sky; but though meaning piles upon meaning, Heather's north-western New South Wales landscape is not enchanted. The spiritualised and mythologised land of her Aboriginal friends is not her land. She feels herself untouched by spirit forces. *I've felt enough of the power of memory of places not to feel a need for it.* The creation stories belong to the communities and are closed to the outsider. Nor is it necessary for outsiders to comprehend the non-human and the psychic. *I appreciate but do not understand. I don't understand what that story means to them in its details or its cultural meaning, but I have an understanding of its emotional force. There's no one single set of meanings. All of our understandings of the land are cultural.*

The power of her own north-west is its history. For this historian, the deepest emotion flows out of human agency, those events that people whom she loves experienced on the land, things that happened and continue to happen, the sense of how people from choice or the burden of invasive governmental intervention have continued to traverse the network of association, land and place. Her own connection endures and strengthens, not because she shares the moral force or insights that the stories impart, but through the emotional strength that these stories hold for the women that she has known and worked with for so long. The rolling plains between Collarenebri and Brewarrina meant little beyond their physical beauty until she glimpsed her friends' feelings for this solemnly historicised and ritualised landscape. Initially through them, but finally independent, the land became her own actor and stage, meaningful and historical, connecting through and to a knowledge of oral and written traditions, the cultural and social body of knowledge. Neither feeling nor not feeling the presence of the spirit ancestors, Heather rejoices in a sense ever deepening of the subtleties by which people construct meaning and the land acquires multiple significance. *I'll probably go to my grave not knowing how to explain it.*

Land becomes stage. Central to her own feelings about the landscape are the experiences she has shared with the Eualayi and Barkindji peoples. Looking for human remains along Hospital Creek, the site of an infamous nineteenth-century massacre, she sensed nothing subliminal. Rather,

I can remember it now. People were quivering with the intensity of the current meaning. That's been important in contributing to my sense of feeling for the place. The beginning of an appreciation of how the people I cared about felt about events. It is a significant part of interactions and inter-relationships on every level in my memories and feelings about the west.

Land becomes actor. In the 1980s her Eualayi friend Noelene Walford died suddenly and unexpectedly. The funeral was moving and terrible. Afterwards the mourners went down to the Darling River to fish: a way of coping, Heather explains, with the tragic and painful event. The enormous dusty banks sweeping down to the low water level, the exposed roots of the big river gums, the barbecue, the taste of proper river fish, the quiet sunlit afternoon, subdued talking, silence.

It was quite a complicated event, but it was about getting something, it was about drawing something from the land, from the places which people knew, it was a way of relating to each other which used the land in a really productive way to soften the blow and allow them to relate to each other and restore a sense of calmness. There's a sense of the land being an active participant in what you're doing.

The primary dimension of belonging is the memory that continues to make manifest Aboriginal relations to the land as partner. History persists. The sense of containment in this 'frighteningly frontier, racist society' intensifies. Abusive or threatening signs, shots fired overhead, padlocked gates. *There's a really strong sense of Whites holding on to the land as private property, with barricades against Murris up there.* At such denial Heather is outraged: this land is the life experience of the people, this is their country, they used to speak their language here, they buried their dead here. Their life stories are imbued with a day-to-day understanding of how to interpret the land in the context of living and working on a pastoral property. While only the quiet river projects a sense of unfenced freedom, memory endures in an Aboriginality most familiar: tenacity, the vast network of extended kinfolk, their sense of injustice, the ironic humour, simultaneously holding themselves in the dimensions of past and present, a relationship to one person acknowledged by another a thousand kilometres away. Her friends' connection to the land derives as much from their presence and actions after the invasion as from their ancestors before it.

This is the point at which we meet the principle that impels *Invasion to Embassy*. The historian's task which emerges from her book is to interpret the intimate association of post-settlement land and people. Work sites, camp sites, mission stations, stock routes, came to be revered as strongly as, though differently from, the sites of creation and renewal of the spirit ancestors. At the biggest stations the people formed large camps of laughter and pain and work and achievement, learned skills and natural talent. The 'protection' that effectively imprisoned the majority of Aboriginal people in managed reserves was little more than a surrender to the demands of white townspeople; the attempts to avoid coming under the control of the Protection Board led to such 'desperate flight'. The revocation of reserves was 'morally indefensible'.[3]

Such are the theme and substance of *Invasion to Embassy*. We outsiders need know no more than that the land is powerfully myth-ologised. The experiences of Aboriginals on the land *since* the invasion have overlaid upon the spiritual landscape new associations equally strong and important:

> So the richness of daily life was experienced there repeatedly over those decades, and the memories of the everyday events, as well as the know-ledge of the past meanings of the land, and the hopes for the future, were also embedded within the boundaries of the reserve lands. Thus an intense new web of significance and meaning was being laid down on these lands through this period of colonisation, adding to the traditional meanings for land.[4]

I ask about the Whites who shared with Aboriginals the lands of the north-west. Heather is unimpressed. *They're not there. Aboriginals carry that sense of endurance, the Whites didn't stick with it.* They lived on their own little patches, talked about shearing and their relations, knew where their fathers had come from or where their grandmothers were buried. Though many undoubtedly loved the land they worked, they tended to locate it as peripheral to their fundamental sense of what ordered their lives. *Maybe their stories aren't so powerful. They have strong stories, yes, but not on the same scale.* I think how association transfigures the imagination in the way that the Orley School girls talk about their own fathers. Mandy Martin too believes some of the western Whites to be much underestimated, and wonders to what extent an unjust dispossession, last century or this, privileges the Indigenous over others who love the land and fight fiercely for its preservation. Heather, associating mostly with Aboriginals, believes it does.

For the north-west, she writes, was different. Much larger num-bers of Aboriginals were employed here than in the east of the state. They formed 30 per cent of the labour force. They gathered on the largest stations in groups large enough to allow the preservation of collective rituals and lifeways. Most pastoralists did not try to destroy customary law.[5] Ceremonies were still performed in the 1920s.[6]

Now I begin to grasp the relation between the theme of the book and Heather's own experiences. *Invasion to Embassy* describes the re-formulation of new relations on old land, on mission stations, pastoral camps, in the schoolhouse, the church, the stockyard and the kitchen garden. We readers do not need to fully comprehend—as Heather does not—the mythic significance of country. We do need to understand—as Heather does—the new and emotional relationships that Aboriginals have formed with their land since, and because of, the pastoral settlement. After invasion, warfare and settlement, Aboriginals reconfigured their relationship with their own land that fashioned new entitlements. Soon there were new, experiential layers of meaning overlying the old. Aboriginals cleared the bush, farmed the land, built huts, fenced boundaries, bore children, nursed the sick, buried the dead on the reserves and stations. Old and new relationships as a consequence now unite in an Indigenous culture no longer traditional, equally valid. Thus Heather describes, in the very last passage of her 400-page book, how Aboriginals at La Perouse greeted the dawn of invasion day, 26 January 1988:

> All through that night, the dance fires burned. Young and old, men and women defiantly, joyously, danced the stories for the country.
>
> At sunrise, exhausted but elated, the dancers ceased, and Aboriginal people from Sydney and the south-east spoke to us about what had happened on that land and what it meant to them. Then, quietly, Aboriginal leaders from across the country shepherding people into lines to walk through the smoke of smouldering green branches, a ritual of cleansing and protection which can be used for many purposes.
>
> Most saw that dawn through tears, Aboriginal and non-Aboriginal people there both profoundly moved by the power of the night and the ritual of care and protection.
>
> The custodianship of the land had been made again a public thing.[7]

Heather now feels a connection ever increasing to the Darling Plains formed out of a physical beauty at first elusive, a sense of its power, the emotional bonds to her friends, and a 'fairly substantial' knowledge of the past. What has not emerged is that 'this is my country'—a presumptuous claim, she reminds me, given how well she knows its Aboriginal owners. She has no wish to usurp their deeper knowledge and commitment. Her strongest emotion is an intensely felt custodianship, set against erosion, blue-green algae, the chemicals of the cotton industry upstream, a close sense of responsibility for its future.

My hard-won sense of not being unwelcome is to me a real shift and a major component of 'belonging'. The aim is not to attain ownership but a sense of being at ease with the land and its owners. Reading the draft of this chapter, Heather writes that her experiences with Aboriginal landowners have metamorphosed her sense of belonging to an equally intense commitment to the welfare of land and people. *I now feel a bond to that land, I don't feel unwelcome there.*[8]

TRUE BELONGING NURTURES THE FUTURE

If Tom Griffiths the environmental historian belongs anywhere, he feels that it is to the ravaged lands of the central Victorian goldfields. His heart's country is where his ancestors settled in the 1850s, first shown to him by his parents, and where his great-grandfather is commemorated as one district's discoverer of gold. Though its recuperative powers were stronger, this is country that was, perhaps, as sorely ravaged as the Darling Basin. Ravaged or not, it is beautiful! To Tom the worked-over quality of the landscape, the eroded gullies, the unexpected depressions, the mullock heaps, the old mine chimneys, the messy buildings of the functional towns add to, rather than detract from, his sense of attachment. Though their impact was environmentally disastrous, the gold miners cannot be extracted from the equations of environmental history. Humans belong in this landscape, their part in its creation cannot be ignored or forgotten.

Part of Tom's awareness of being Australian, he tells me, is this consciousness of human presence, beneficial or harmful, the ephemerality of much European settlement, the successive advance and retreat of generations each leaving its imprint on the landscape. In the gold country[9] the Aboriginals were dispossessed, the diggers scarified and disfigured the country; but neither the broken land nor the decaying evidence of human habitation detract from Tom's attachments:

Awareness of environmental change and Aboriginality add to my sense of place. I disagree with wilderness enthusiasts wanting to eradicate human history, the mountain huts for example. They're an extra layer to treasure. Though Aboriginality in the gold country is hard to find, human interaction complicates the landscape positively. Aborigines and the environment: these are the two great historical revolutions of our generation. Writing both into

Australian history allows you to reach back beyond the moment of invasion and draw you into deep time as part of our own inheritance. We should discover the continuities.

In May 1999 Tom visited the north-west of New South Wales with Mandy Martin to collaborate in an exhibition of paintings and words about the environment of the western rivers. As a historian he thought it his role to absorb the regional talk, observe the landscape and offer historical perspective. A few properties in the region were managed with long-term environmental values in mind. Low stock numbers, water retention banks and fenced-off regeneration areas of land once productive offered hope that the relentless degradation of land was not only reversible, but had been reversed.

Many of the other properties which he visited displayed the social and historical forces still driving the pastoralists to mine rather than work the land: *Utterly, depressingly miserably degraded, the grasses gone and the feral animals everywhere.* The morale of property owners, he found, could often be gauged, before he met them, by how they kept their country. Broken fences and overgrazed paddocks suggested desolated proprietors, trapped in degradation or debt, human communities and land dying together, *immensely depressed and depressing.* Like Heather, Tom felt oppressed by the violence of the lowering frontier. The huge skies, the subtleties of dawn and dusk, the freedom and space contrasted with the lives of landholders constrained by distant political regulation, capricious markets, regulation, erosion, woody weeds, land claims and their neighbours. 'This is a spacious landscape full of secrets', he wrote for Mandy Martin's exhibition, 'a country which is both vast and claustrophobic'.[10] Some nights the land resounded with distant firing, spotlights swung about the plain in search of feral pigs; it was not unknown for shooters to arrive unannounced with injuries to be bandaged before reporting and departing on what seemed like an endless guerilla war just over the horizon. I ask Tom for the strongest visual image carried from his trip. *A rooting snorting set of boars heading across the sandy waste.*

In spite of the long-standing heritage they evoke, Tom writes, the western grazing families are often characterised by their transience. The West is more peripheral now than ever. Pastoralism is no longer central to the national economy. In the outside country there are overgrown tennis courts and cricket pitches, fewer sports meetings, diminishing populations and shrinking family units. Only very recently have settlers begun to act upon the understanding not only of deep ecological time, but of their own historical role in violating it.[11]

Like pastoralists elsewhere about whom Tom has written, some of those on the Darling hang on by little more than hope and history. Their heroic, defensive and conservative world view which helped them through many a hard stage has left many of them temporarily stranded, emotionally opposed to changing valuations of the rangelands away from pastoralism and towards tourism, recreation, the preservation of biodiversity, or traditional and contemporary Aboriginality.[12] But change depends on transforming national politics as well as personal sentiment: the pastoral leases still stipulate that the land must be used for grazing.

Don't mention the Aboriginals! Never before in Australia had Tom seen such a dense residue of Aboriginal civilisation: stone tools, ritual arrangements, the remains of ancient cooking fires. Could its rich diversity relate to the frequent injunction he receives to raise in conversation neither dispossession nor the killings? While the Eualayi tremble with emotion at the sites of the massacre of their ancestors, Tom is told nothing, or he learns surreptitiously, or he is advised not to ask. Fear and guilt, he explains in the introduction to his prize-winning *Hunters and Collectors*, were part of the colonists' moral puzzle from the beginning. Denial, the narrative of avoidance, was part of a genuine attempt to foster emotional possession of the land. Tom writes that the pastoralists and squatters sought to take hold of the land emotionally and spiritually, but they could not help but deny, displace and sometimes accommodate Aboriginal perceptions of place.[13] In the contours of such silence, the modern north-west of New South Wales Tom finds to be eerily contiguous to nineteenth-century Victoria. *There are still people in the region today who know the hidden waters and the paths between them, the signs to be read on the trees and in the stones.* Learning that it is perhaps unwise at stop at the Enngonia pub, he drives though the town. Aboriginals alone sit in the streets or stare without expression. In Bourke the shops are protected by steel barriers, homes by security dogs. Tom feels depressed and alienated by the cultural barriers, angry at the national political leadership's reluctance to open negotiation with either ravaged people or their abused country. *When I meet*

Aboriginal people in that situation, part of the discomfort comes because you feel as trapped by your skin colour as they are. His deep unease is not far from the Judith Wright quotation with which he begins *Hunters and Collectors*.

> The two strands—the love of land and the guilt of the invasion—have become part of me. It is a haunted country.

In Tom's vision of a morally and environmentally integrated Australia, some of the settler landholders and developers seem to belong to no time other than their own. One of the strongest themes of his recent writing is that of Australians connecting to deep time, that symbiotic relationship between human and environment which recognises no formal point of beginning. The chain of intervention of pastoralist, miner and Aboriginal upon the land is an essential element not only of time recent but of past immemorial. Land and all the humans who ever inhabited Australia are, or ought to be, at one with its history. They share its past and provide for its future.

The concepts thicken. Belonging to deep Australian time, whether on the goldfields or the Darling, surely means embracing Aboriginal history as part of our own history as Australians. Tom concedes that, perhaps, while Aboriginals remain dispossessed and gather unemployed outside the Enngonia pub, while governments seek continually to retreat from the Mabo judgement and complicate or obstruct Native Title claims, no non-Indigenous Australian can belong legitimately to deep Australian time.

To this landscape, then—not this one alone, and not only because it is degraded—the Aboriginals must be physically restored. The disparity of power, the history of dispossession and the unequal exercise of force demand restitution. An essential sharing of the country must begin with the non-Indigenous demonstration of goodwill. *I want to right the historical wrong.* Indigenous owners leasing the land to others—not necessarily pastoralists—might be part of the solution. Tom is prepared to trust the Aboriginal owners to negotiate occupancy and usage after the land is returned to them. He trusts that reconciliation will be as important to them as restitution. Much of his historical work springs from a respect for that emotional investment, directed towards teasing out and articulating settler senses of place and belonging so that they might become part of a cross-cultural negotiation.

I'm reminded again by that strength of attachment expressed by the Orley School girls towards their properties on the Darling or in other areas of the state almost as ravaged.

Does the country know you've come back? A thoughtful pause. *Well, no. My dogs know. A tree can't know you. A tree gets hurt if you drive over a branch.* Everyone laughs. I tell them how Aboriginal people introduce strangers to country. Another quizzical silence. They find it interesting rather than odd. *Well, when you bring people to the country you explain every single thing, why the tree looks like that and why the grass grows like that, but not introducing you directly to the country.* Less certainty now; fewer jokes among the considered silences. *I see it more as a rediscovery, I don't see it as a greeting.* Another opinion: *There's a degree of endearment that's …* *I won't say normal. You can, … I can comprehend why they do that.* Dads more than mums figure in memory and story, usually as the source of hard work, the ultimate expression of land and depth of feeling. *If my dad's been away for a while he walks along and he'll say hello to everything. That's just him.* But would he actually use the word 'hello'? *Sometimes if he's in a strange mood—but you can sort of tell that's what he's thinking.*

I remind Tom of the Victorian mountain cattlemen and women, of whom he has argued that although the environmental damage caused by their stock is now well established, outsiders have not been able to answer their deep attachment to the landscape.[14] May not environmentalists, appalled by the degradation beginning in the range-lands 150 years ago and continuing to the present, also underestimate the strength of the pastoralists' attachment to the Darling river basin? *Yes, I want to reward 'stickability'.* In a perfect world the Aboriginals will again possess the land. *Because they've had the tenacity to hang on there.* And they will share it. For a second important principle is that those who live in the outside country should want to be there. The red country of the north-west should not be for those who can't escape, only those who see it as home. Society has to assist them, free them, empower them—both Black and White—for the sake of the land as well as themselves.

Belonging to deep past implies nurturing deep future. Suppose that Aboriginals, repossessing the Darling properties, but constrained by a difficult economy, fail to follow the recommended environmental practices which should now be followed by all who share and cherish the land? Tom agrees that the concept of moral belonging needs disentangling. Central Australian Aboriginals regard rabbits and feral cats as part of the natural, and sometimes the mythological, environment, and see no need to eradicate them. *It's romantic and silly and stereotypical to imagine they all will, they are human beings under pressure.* It would be deeply patronising to Aboriginals resuming the land to assume that they would not make judgements that would surprise us, nor that, constrained by a terminal pastoralist economy, they might not be forced into the same destructive errors as their White predecessors. Tom believes that the ethical paralysis over Native Title has delayed the crucial debates about cross-cultural land management. The implications of the deep future insist that ultimately the environment precedes its custodians. *Whoever is managing out there is managing on behalf of the nation.* No racist argument this, nor act of environmental fascism. Tom is prepared to convince anyone unwilling to see that the land is capable of recovery. Degradation must not be allowed to proceed further. Nor should those who hold the red country as home be asked to carry the nation's guilt or the cost of the regeneration of the rangelands. They should be encouraged to talk of the land in terms of their attachments to it.

We arrive at the sticking point. To Tom there can be no legitimate affection for the land without care, and no lasting belonging without responsibility for its deep future. If all Australians are to rejoice in the deep past, then we must ask the non-Aboriginals to share responsibility for its mistakes. If all Australians are to rejoice in the deep future, then we must ask the Aboriginals to share in its responsibility. *I want an Australia which embraces Aboriginality and an Aboriginality which embraces Australia.*

But Tom, isn't this something of a presumption that Aboriginals should conform to a national interest? Tom replies that sharing deep time is a presumption, but one that he will continue to pursue because the current alternative, the mere expropriation of past and future, is worse. He reflects that perhaps we don't as yet have the right morally to share deep time, despite the 'incredibly generous' offer which has been made by some Aboriginals. *But I'd like to take it up. I want to celebrate the fantastic achievements of Australian humanity in the long term.* We need to accept responsibility for past as well as future. *Not shared country alone but shared history.*

True belonging for Tom Griffiths, then, demands acknowledging the past, reconciling the present and nurturing the future. *I just yearn for political and ethical clarity in Australia today, and this is the role that government should be able to play. When the government stuffs up at the federal level, it affects how we proceed with local negotiations.* Out on the wide plains acknowledging the past means taking responsibility for the destruction of a rooting snorting set of boars heading across the sandy waste. Reconciling the present means allowing the Aboriginals to return to their country and being able to yarn as equals in the Enngonia pub. Nurturing the future means a shared responsibility for its welfare by everyone who claims to belong to this land.

WE ALL HAVE THE RIGHT TO BELONG TO THE NEW COUNTRY

In *The Other Side of the Frontier*, Henry Reynolds sets out the perimeters of all his later work. He aims his histories primarily at White Australians, hoping they will appreciate the Aboriginal part in the history of the continent. His work is 'not conceived, researched or written in a mood of detached scholarship'; rather, it is 'inescapably political', dealing as it must with issues that have aroused deep passions. 'Many will find it', he predicts, 'an uncomfortable book.'[15] So they did.

Henry explains in an introduction to his readers that he grew up in Tasmania, where conventional historiography could not explain the violence and hatred, which often 'grew as lush as guinea grass', in North Queensland where he wrote the book. He found disturbing the more subtle manifestations of hatred, the expressions, phrases, jokes, gestures, glances, even the silences which sprang up out of local historical experiences of which he knew little. Children hid when he came to interview their parents. One little girl stared at him 'with a fear that was not personal at all but historical and communal and unforgettable'. I had similar experiences in the Northern Territory in the 1970s, but Henry went further to ask: 'Where did one go, what did one read in 1967 to understand that sort of experience?'[16]

The questions, more general and less personal than Heather's, were fundamental to the historiography of the recent past. Almost all historians of Aboriginal Australia have sought to answer them. Were the Aboriginals the true owners of Australia? What compensation should they have received? Was it legitimate—or even lawful—to annex Australia and expropriate their land? Was colonisation itself morally justified? Why was it that, like other historians, he failed to notice the intense racism hidden within many periods of celebration of White Australian achievement?[17] It was in the written records of the invaders that he first found understanding, for the systematic oral history of the Aboriginal experience had scarcely begun. This most magisterial of the historians of Aboriginal Australia was led by logical exposition of the colonists' own chronicles to conclusions which set the template of a generation: The British were 'people who talked of British justice and yet unleashed a reign of terror and behaved like an ill-disciplined army of occupation once the invasion was effected'; the Aboriginal response has been much more 'positive, creative and complex than white historians have hitherto suggested'; 20 000 Aboriginals may have been killed in the frontier wars.[18] In conversation he is more sympathetic to the Whites than Heather or Tom. He can comprehend the Queensland pastoralists who are angry at being forced to share with Aboriginals land where their kids grew up and granny is buried. They always thought it was theirs. The black-armband school of historians? Henry realises that pioneering was crucial to the national ethos: *If historians maintain that it was totally destructive, that doesn't leave us much.* He concedes that certain pastoralists may indeed have a longer memory of the land than the Aboriginals who claim it. But he reminds me that it is not a valid comparison. While feelings are important, it is the law upon which our society is based. The rights of inheritance do not turn upon physical presence. In conversation he compares Aboriginal claims with a hypothetical Tasmanian who in, say, 1933 left his holdings and went to Hong Kong, with the result that most of the inheritors of the land, that is, its legal owners, would be Cantonese-speaking Chinese. But they still own it. *It's not their culture but our system which says if you had legal rights then you still have them.*

In 1995 Henry published a major study of Tasmanian Aboriginals, entitled *Fate of a Free People*,[19] which considered the legal position of Aboriginals deported from mainland Tasmania to Flinders Island in

1833. He maintains that they expected their departure to be temporary. The few survivors returned to Oyster Cove in 1847, apparently doomed to extinction. That some part-descent Tasmanians survived is now well known. Apply the same logic. Henry argues that either the government promised the Aboriginals regular return visits to the mainland, in which case native title to their former homelands was not extinguished; or else it was extinguished, and therefore Flinders and other small islands were a reserve in compensation.[20] Therefore the descendants of Oyster Cove hold both a legal and a moral right to compensation. In never forgetting the deception, Henry writes, Tasmanian Aboriginals have maintained one of the longest political memories in Australian history. Concluding this work he sets again the famous question of *The Other Side of the Frontier*—'How shall we deal with the Aboriginal dead?' It is, he argues, an issue ever more pressing than when first asked thirteen years before, because national reconciliation demands reconciled historical narratives. The feeling of injustice survives among the Tasmanian Aboriginals to the present.[21]

In his childhood Henry sensed that Aboriginals had shared the island in which he was born. He learned their history; he was aware of middens and stone tools. His great-grandmother told him she remembered the famous Aboriginal Tasmanian Truganini; his father showed him the site of a battle between Aboriginals and settlers on the road to Launceston. Yet in the early 1960s, like most others, Henry imagined there was little new to be said about Tasmanian Aboriginals.[22] At that time he recalls that no-one publicly claimed Aboriginality. But the 'garrulous, opinionated student' found himself lost for words when a history lecturer announced, 'It's a bloody sad place. You can still hear the Aborigines crying in the wind.'

Thirty-five years later, his sense of Tasmanian belonging stems more from the people he has known, less from his knowledge of the Aboriginal past. Never has the island been more important to him than now. In Hobart he feels closer to his deceased parents. *I can sense them because I've walked with them there. No, it's a place-belonging which underpins any political nationalism I have. Regional and local belonging are two quite different things.* Ultimately belonging is physical and personal:

the light, the shadows and the sky, the way the sun is in the sky, I have epiphanies, so far from latitude 43, it's like being in a different country, certainly environmentally, you feel there are parts far beyond consciousness which feel at home. One day I realised the sun was where it should be, where it really belonged. I think I realised then the old saying being under your own sky. This is my country because it's the country I knew when I was very young and had tens of thousands of impressions which I connect with and can't if I go outside that environment. ... Tasmania is an island, that makes it different. There's something about the southern latitudes and the wind and the sky and the light, day and night, which is quite distinctive. It's clearly got to do with your earliest experiences—that's an old idea, the patria; and when I return across Bass Strait and Tasmania comes up, I'm excited. This is going home.

Henry recognises only a few special places, for the macrocosmic force is the call of the entire island:

I can hear the wind blow and the wind sounds right, the way the clouds are, the shadows and the sun's in the right place and the shadows are the right length, all those things feel right, the wind in the trees, I must have been aware of them when I was little, everything is in its place. [This is] the sense that I have of being, in the foundation of my psyche.

I ask if the country knows when he returns. No, but its indifference does not diminish his sense of intimate belonging, not *in your head, it's a sense of ease, relaxed and easy when I'm at home which I don't feel anywhere else in the world. It's not intellectual, but quite distinctive.* Like Heather, he does not feel a need to have come out of the land. *It is just that I was there at the beginning. I grew in the land.* He does not speak to the country like a Marrithiyel or a Eualayi. *I go and look around and take it in with my eyes, walk and drive. Something inside relaxes, that's as near as I can put it.* Now, he tells me, he is hungry to go back. *I need to go back, I have a sense of growing urgency.* Returning is part of the human life cycle. He does not wish to die, eventually, in the alien soil of north Queensland. Tasmania seems to be the place.

Belonging in Tasmania, Henry believes, is less problematic for descendants of convicts and settlers than elsewhere. He proposes that convicts can hardly be seen as dispossessors because they were themselves exiles and prisoners. Settlers began to say that they belonged on the island from the 1830s. Eight generations of settler society, Henry reminds me, form a not inconsequential stability. There is much less sense of the Tasmanian Whites as dispossessors. Hardly anyone has migrated here this century; the population is established and permanent. He concedes that perhaps it was easier writing from a Tasmanian viewpoint: the 'bushman' image has never taken root here; whatever he has written threatened only abstract ideas about Australia. *I never ever felt once that I didn't belong.* Perhaps, he reflects, he has never felt shame about the brutal colonisation because he did not share a strong enough sense of identification with the British colonists.[23] 'Sunlight in Montacute', the poem in which a settler descendant reflects upon his murderous Tasmanian predecessors, seems as apt for Henry as it did for Jamie Grant the poet. The past is finished and the living must make their own way:

> Believing in self-defence, they'd picture God
>
> bearded like Darwin, smiling Natural
> Selection. I can't inherit the guilt
> of such innocent men, as guilt's an abstract
> like blood, replaced throughout the body,
> changing in shape all the time; those human skulls
>
> were mashed years back, reduced to bracken spawn
>
> atoms, fragile moth dust, sun motes.[24]

Henry tells me that his sense of belonging impinges on neither Aboriginal right nor Aboriginal privilege—unless they try to exclude him! He enters no claim beyond the personal to this place of distinctive wind and sun and star; his own children think of Tasmania as no more than a friendly holiday home. I ask if any psychic traces remain of the Black War against the Tasmanian Aboriginals, which culminated in the deportation of the survivors to Flinders Island. No: neither the dispossessor nor the dispossessed, he has felt no presences. Nor is a detached affection for the Australian mainland any more compromised than his feelings for Hobart. He loves the very look of the old settled country, *where the sheep have walked for a hundred years, the old worn footpaths. It's the conqueror's view but I can't help that; and so it's not a problem.* Flying down from Brisbane, he looks out on the stunning green landscape of forest and cleared land. *I find it beautiful.* One cannot construct oneself by logic alone, he reflects. It may not be reasonable to venerate the old Georgian houses of the Hunter Valley, but they remain just as beautiful. There's no point in telling himself, he explains, that the builders were dispossessors; that achieves nothing. *Settled valleys and wild hills, the mixture.* The onlookers change in time and circumstance, the viewed ever remains as it was. One of my favourite passages in his book *With the White People* reviews the actions of the many thousands of Aboriginals who as guides, pastoral workers and domestic servants worked alongside the Whites in furthering settlement. Were they traitors, he asks his readers, or were they the first multiculturalists?[25] Historically they are the same people, we cannot change what they did. It is we who come later who change our interpretations of their actions.

Henry puts a similar point in his 1999 autobiographical account of his professional life, *Why Weren't We Told?*

> In writing extensively about dispossession I haven't myself felt dispossessed. I am unable to share the view of those who feel they don't really belong in Australia, that they are barely tolerated guests or that they will always be so alienated from the land that they can't even contemplate being buried in Australian soil. I don't relate to Australia as a whole: it is much too large and much too diverse. But I cannot remember a time when I didn't feel at home in Tasmania. … Almost thirty years of writing revisionist history changed my views about many things, but never touched my sense of where I had come from, where I belonged and where since early childhood I had known the wind, the sky and the silver slanting light.[26]

I sense a connection between the secure belonging of Tasmanians and that of this famous son; between Henry's own considered serenity and the unruffled objectivity of Australia's most distinguished historian of Aboriginal Australia; between the relentless calm which distinguishes his historical works and this least complicated sense of belonging of almost anyone I have interviewed. *I've never felt a dispossessor, though I'm acutely aware of how it happened, and very personally engaged in it. But I have no immediate personal sense of guilt.*

Most of the troubling aspects of complex belonging he believes can equally be approached calmly and logically. Nationhood must give all its citizens that most important sense of belonging of equal citizenship within the polis. Those who in addition treasure an acute attachment to a particular place are merely lucky. Much of the feelings of dread at 'land claims' that many Australians feel, even though they live on land which cannot legally be challenged, stems from our failure to separate ideas of nation from those relating to state. Land claims slide from physical to metaphysical.

I now better understand Henry's histories in terms of his up-bringing and personality. Impassioned logic rather than moral outrage drives his histories, as it drives his life. 'I have often been incensed or angry about the cruelty and injustice involved, but even then I have felt under a professional obligation to try to understand and explain the behaviour of the perpetrators. To know why was more important and more challenging that simply to descry.'[27] From the revelation that the logical and rational British-Australian ethos in which he had been raised never extended to the Indigenous flowed the rationale of his histories. What he calls the tremendous Tasmanian sense of communal rejection of pretension and snobbery and hierarchy, the realisation that Australia was not the equal society he had assumed it to be, focused on the puzzlement at the little Murri girl of North Queensland cowering at the approach of the unknown white man. *I found it didn't apply to Black people in any sense of the word, a terrible shock.*

Historical facts must be accepted and accommodated in the world as surely as the sure emotions of belonging. All previous historical accounts, he wrote in *The Other Side of the Frontier*, must be drastically modified. The boundaries of historiography can be pushed back; the barriers which kept Aboriginal experience out of previous histories were not source material or problems of methodology but perception and preference. 'Deft scholarly feet avoided the embarrass-ment of bloodied billabongs.' A refurbished historiography must regard Aboriginals as equals, or our sudden interest in Black history will be seen as merely another phase of our intellectual usurpation of their tribal culture and traditions.[28] Obviously, he argues, there is a special and inescapable status, recognised by a good and continuing inter-national tradition, owing to first nations.

It is at this point that Henry asks again his first question about the Aboriginal dead. Black Australians will be our equals or our enemies. 'If', he wrote nearly twenty years ago, 'we are unable to embrace the other side of the frontier as part of our own heritage we will stand in the eyes of the world as a people still chained intellectually and emotionally to our nineteenth-century Anglo-Saxon origins, ever the transplanted Britishers.'[29] Obligations and duties continue towards the people whose country the colonist has acquired. These obligations do not include forgoing the right to belong in the new country.

WE HAVE TO RECOGNISE THAT IT'S ABORIGINAL COUNTRY

The Tasmania of the historian Lyndall Ryan could not be more divergent.

Lyndall tells me that she is a saltwater person who grew up near Bondi. She prefers to live close to the coast because she was made by the sea and the shore. Coastlines suggest expanding possibility, affirmation, excitement, familiarity, renewal. Bondi, though she does not often return to it, infused in her a particular configuration of headland and sand, cliff and beach, water temperature and shape, coastal scrubland fresh and green in midsummer, a benchmark by which to compare all other beaches and coastlines.

Almost all her special places are seamarks, none more than eastern and southern shores of Tasmania. After thirty years of association, arriving by plane over the shore gives her a 'gut-wrenching feeling'. *There's something about its hills and its coastline because I've done so much work on it I get quite overcome by it.*

In 1970 Lyndall enrolled at Macquarie University to study the history of the Tasmanian Aboriginals. She was a fourth- or fifth-generation Australian of some convict and Irish ancestry. Each previous generation had been homesick for Ireland, each felt guilty that they did not miss it enough. Lyndall, when abroad, is desperately homesick for Australia. *I'm a frightful simplistic patriot of the worst kind.* Though she thinks she probably was the first of her family to feel that her birthland was not alien, she does not feel that she has sprung from the Australian landscape. *I'm very conscious of my European roots.* Her reading about Aboriginals first indicated to her how much the non-Indigenous had still to learn.

Throughout the early 1970s Lyndall absorbed the nineteenth-century sources on Aboriginal history. She tried to perceive the landscape not as controlled or contained, but as the Oyster Bay Aboriginals —the same people who form the subject of Henry's *Fate of a Free People*—would have seen it. This, she believes, she never quite achieved, although she began to sense the special relationship between land and its Indigenous people.

The first principle was continuity. She wrote in the first edition of *The Aboriginal Tasmanians* that it was crucial to understand that they didn't die out; the first purpose of her history was 'to demolish the myth of "the last Tasmanian"'.[30] In the chapter 'The Tasmanian Aborigines in the Twentieth Century', Lyndall rejoiced that the story of the Tasmanian survival had become one of revival. Though in 1951 a government enquiry had recommended that the Islanders 'be gradually absorbed into the rest of the Tasmanian population', and that their plea for recognition as a 'special people' with Aboriginal ancestry should be dismissed, the self-identifying population had stabilised, then begun to increase. A 1971 conference of 200 Furneaux Group Islanders found that nearly 2000 of their people were scattered across Tasmania and Australia. The 671 people who identified as of Tasmanian Aboriginal descent had risen in 1976 to 2942.[31] Two new chapters were added for the extended 1996 edition of the book. Lyndall noted that in 1995 the Tasmanian premier announced the transfer of 3800 hectares of land to Tasmanian Aboriginals in twelve separate sites.[32] The cover of the new edition showed four young women smiling self-consciously and dressed in a contemporary Aboriginal costume, carrying out a ritual dance.

It is 1992. I've come to talk to Lyndall about her sense of belonging in relation to her book. We are in her home in Adelaide overlooking the grey waters of Spencer Gulf. A bottle of red wine arrives with the pasta, and we informally begin our conversation. It will be a difficult, almost an anguished, evening. The sense of belonging of Lyndall, the other major historian of Tasmanian Aboriginals, is as complex as Henry Reynolds' is uncomplicated. Lyndall loves the land Australia and its parts as passionately as anyone I have met; yet she feels that she can never belong.

At Cape Barren Island in 1971 she first met the Aboriginal community, 'whose problems were very similar to any Aboriginal group in south-eastern Australia'. More slowly emerged the differences. Early in her book she notes that Tasmania never experienced the levels of poisoning, trappings, ambushes and massacres that occurred in other parts of Australia. Not all kinds of European incursion were necessarily destructive.[33] Though Tasmania was still almost a foreign country, her journey of understanding had begun. The community accepted her and the first lessons were absorbed. Lyndall felt deeply moved that her hosts were so willing to share with her a coastline for which she, the outsider—the alien—already felt an affinity. Her attachment (though not her identity) in the landscape grew stronger. *I've been taken into another layer, though it's still a very superficial layer, but for me it's an enormous depth.* She watched the islanders pick berries at the edge of beaches, looking out for animals, pointing out particular trees or aspects of the country or even an important tribal physical boundary. She sensed that land had a much deeper significance for Aboriginal people than it could ever have for others. *I've been given a glimpse and I feel very privileged to have that glimpse. It's given me a greater sense that I can no longer live anywhere else.* I ask her if or how she communicates her arrival.

It doesn't really matter whether the trees are listening, it's more important that you speak or commune.

You've been introduced to the country by your Aboriginal friends?

Yes.

Was that important?

Yes. Yes.

And you wish that when you're somewhere else in Tasmania that you had someone to introduce you?

Yes. Absolutely. In fact I wouldn't go.

Lyndall explains that without formal introduction her acquaintance with new country would be superficial. If she visited country already familiar it would insult her friends, and herself, and the land itself.

I'd feel I shouldn't even properly look at it, it's not open to me. Maybe it's a bit unthought through and unconscious. If it means something to you, you have to abide by it. I feel I don't have the right to relate to it until they've given me their permission. I certainly couldn't go camping, they would be very offended because they've given me a certain trust in the first place to write about them, and it's a continuing trust.

Still she felt herself at some distance from true belonging. *I'd very much like to but I don't think I'd ever have the courage.* To the Tasmanian Whites also she felt that she remained an outsider. Lyndall feels that neither knowledge nor explanation of the past alone can provide expiation. She writes that until the Whites learn to cope with these problems and resolve them, they will remain a problem for Aborigines, that is, 'a shallow people in constant fear not only of the people whose land they have appropriated, but of the land itself'.[34]

Another glass of wine. I suggest that her intense associations with the indigenous people have brought her a little closer to belonging. Lyndall agrees that she is now very much accepted by many Aboriginal people in Tasmania, *who really go out of their way to make me feel at home, but I'm always conscious of being an outsider.*

The affinity she holds with aspects of the landscape seems dependent on people, yet the land itself has an independent life. Do you relate to both, I ask, independently? 'That's an interesting point. The people are part of that country, therefore for me to visit it would be to deny them. It recognises that Aboriginal society is alive and kicking, and that I wish to continue to respect that. I can't do it to all Australia, only the parts I know.' Evidently none of this deep personal relationship confers on Lyndall the right to belong to Tasmania. *I think I can argue that I have developed an understanding and love for it but that doesn't confer ownership. I'm not sure that it confers a right either.* I ask: How long does it take for the non-Indigenous to feel they belong, to feel that they have sprung from their birth land? *I'd like to feel that I've sprung from it, that would be wonderful, but I think that that's too bold a concept. I don't think that's legitimate.* Never will she be able to argue that she has a right to be there. I draw the melancholy but inevitable conclusion.

So, Lyndall, after all your work with Aboriginals, the places you've known and the people you've loved, the country that you were the first in five generations to feel homesick for—confer no more than that?

No. No. I still feel an outsider. [A long pause.] *It's interesting, isn't it? Maybe I had the audacity to say that I felt a strong affinity with that patch of the east coast.*

North-eastern Tasmania was different. There Lyndall felt like an outsider and was content with that status. She tells me that she didn't feel that she wanted it to become hers, she just learned to respect it. *You're asking a lot of very hard questions, Peter.*

Could we belong, then, collectively in some way, perhaps by a treaty between the federal government and senior Aboriginals? No, that would be cheap and cheating. We have to stop thinking in terms of the self-justificatory discourse of the coloniser, who seems to have refined the principle of individual ownership of land in order to sidestep indigenous people who did not so limit themselves.

If Jamie Grant and Henry Reynolds reject a sense of the past overshadowing the present, Lyndall is much closer to James Charlton. I think of his Koonya, the 'black girl' of Cape Barren Island:

> There in the Cape Barren dunes,
> under the midden shells,
> her chipped nails claw
> the evasive sand.[35]

This is no wallowing in guilt, which Lyndall reminds me is highly privileged and immobilising. The past is finished, but an act of infamy or wickedness cannot be undone.

I turn the tape over and we pause for another glass. Lyndall continues, saying that learning about being an Australian may be a more complex understanding than people think it is. Spiritual belonging is diverse and complex, which the non-Indigenous have yet to understand. Always she had thought her Irish culture of fairies and goblins an important cultural mythology. *I'm not a monolithic explanationist.* Aboriginal accounts of why the world is as it is draw their power from their precisely local origin built on local understandings. Her particular tools were the historian's, different from those of her parents who, though homesick for abroad, considered themselves absolutely Australian. *My mother loves the Murray; to me it's an Aboriginal river.* One can learn to understand and appreciate it and develop affinities with it.

Can Aboriginals give you the right to belong?

I've never asked.

But is it within their gift?

Yes, I've seen them do it.

A friend who lived on Cape Barren for longer periods than Lyndall was able to stay was invited to build a shack; she became more than a guest. I suggest that Lyndall too has gone beyond that status. Yes, perhaps; though belonging can never be simple, the experience of simply being was enriching. I ask: So we're bound to remain in that state forever?

Well it's part of being a colonial culture. The only way forward is to legitimise Aboriginals. Then we can relate to them legally in a different way, to rectify a great wrong. The relationship will never be perfect, for we must remain forever the descendants of the invaders. Understanding Aboriginal land is not the only way, but it's an enriching experience for the invaders who are the alien. I'd like to consider myself a good and trusted friend.

So an offer by Aboriginals to the rest of us must always, then, be rejected? Another silence. Surely it is dishonest, Lyndall proposes, to compare five generations of Australians with 40 000 years. We can respect, learn to understand, passionately defend, feel affinity, draw patterns of identity. Lyndall positions herself not far from Heather. *But we have to really recognise that it's Aboriginal country. Recognising that is in itself an enormous comfort. It does give you a place.*

Not much of this urgent and earnest thinking escapes into her book. Only in the conclusion does she allow that Europeans have never adjusted or adapted to the Indigenous presence in Australia, that Aboriginals from the first settlement exclaimed at their 'senseless brutality, their excesses of authoritarian control, and the drive for conformity'. She quotes with approval the judgement of Henry Reynolds, of the 'violence, the arrogant assertion of superiority, the ruthless single-mindedness and often amoral pursuit of material progress and the need to develop mature self-awareness'. In the last paragraph of the 1981 edition she writes what she takes to be Aboriginal feelings about non-Aboriginal Australians. I think Lyndall shares those feelings.

In Aboriginal eyes the Europeans may have had a superior technology, but they used this technology in a senseless obliteration of a landscape they did not understand. To Aborigines, therefore, Europeans are a shallow people who are in constant fear not only of the people whose land they have appropriated but of the land itself. They are also afraid of external forces who will in turn appropriate their ill-gotten gains.[36]

We can be accepted. That's a huge step. Lyndall wishes at her death to be cremated, not buried, and her ashes scattered over the ocean of south-eastern Tasmania. *Because it is a neutral territory over which no human may lay claim. And therefore I have the right to have a relationship with it because I'm not treading on anyone's toes.*

It has been a sombre but meditative evening. The recorder switched off, we have a final cup of coffee. The last thing Lyndall tells me is: *Peter, perhaps there are questions we don't yet have the right to ask, because there are questions which you don't ask until you know the answer. After 40 000 years we'd know the answers, and wouldn't need to ask the questions.*

CHAPTER 8

IN SEARCH OF THE PROPER COUNTRY

On Wednesday night Armidale airport was closed by the stormy wintry weather. Next morning it was cold, windy and clear. Returning to Sydney I flew over the northern Sydney beaches. Below me lay the whole seaboard side of Gai-mariagal country. Through the clouds emerged the dozens of clustered white boats moored at Akuna Bay. Opposite Akuna curved the indentation of Calabash Bay and the site of the clearing of William de Serve. To the north-east was Barrenjoey where Uncle William had been born, to the south-east Narrabeen Lake silver and dominating in the morning lights and shadows; there's the out-thrust arm of Long Reef and Collaroy, Dee Why Lagoon, narrow Harbord Beach hard by the Manly Lagoon, the long sweep down from Manly to Queenscliff, North Head in the distance. Tomorrow I begin exploring Gai-mariagal country with Dennis Foley. This squally weekend is to be one of the profound experiences of my life.

Friday night, dashing from Canberra to Sydney airport, Stoney Creek Road in the billowing rainy dusk to meet the 6.55 from Coolangatta. I arrive late; Dennis is waiting. Driving to dinner at the home of my daughter Jess, Dennis points out the flat sandy areas of south Sydney where pitched battles took place between the Sydney clans. After dinner I introduce Dennis to my mother-in-law Pat Arthur, born in Melbourne, but who has lived most of her life within Gai-mariagal country. Dennis and I are to stay with her. We discuss plans for tomorrow. Dennis says we should start where he began, his birthplace at the Royal North Shore Hospital. Here in 1953 his Gai-mariagal grandmother had burned the placenta and scattered the ashes in the trees outside.

We find the 1902 sandstone building but Dennis was born nearby in the maternity ward, now demolished, kept for the non-British. His birth was problematic: his tongue was attached to the roof of his mouth, preventing him from swallowing. Did Nanna Lougher spread the ashes of the placenta as acknowledgment of Dennis's imminent death, or to prevent it, or neither? There is much we don't know.

The maternity wing of Royal North Shore is a birthing place. Every mother, as Marivic Wyndham puts it, has spilled her life juices to conjoin not her child—for the child belongs already—but herself to this earth-site ever more marked as her own. An agitated sky darkens and lightens the playing field over the buried creek. Beside it and towards the overgrown cemetery Dennis points to several trees engraved with what he identifies as probably the markings of Gai-mariagal women.

We have seen in Randolph Stow's poem 'The Dark Women Go Down' the part-Aboriginal son of the first settler inherits the earth and dispossesses the Old People.

> I have robbed the starving women, I have gone down
> to the pool of children stolen, I have conceived
> a tall blond son, and the pool and the land are his …
>   The dark women come up
> barren from the dark water. The spirits die.[1]

In the early 1950s the divisions within urban Australia were less cruel. Although Dennis the short dark part-Aboriginal has not inherited any of the Gai-mariagal lands, and although the spirit progenitors of the Gai-mariagal sickened, they survived and so did he. His extended family kept their stories. Though they did not inherit their country, they lived in it and preserved their Aboriginality. But the pool and the land are not ours either, at least not by unquestioned right. Our journey to find a shared belonging in the dark water and in the wind-swept land has begun.

Near the site of the old maternity ward stands the stump of a huge Sydney blue gum. Though sawn down long ago, it shoots new leafy boughs from a trunk that otherwise appears dead. Dennis reminds me that regrowth after violent trauma symbolises also the survival of the Gai-mariagal. Of course the stump has been here always, of course it would have coppiced. Of course someone had dropped the lavender which Chas Read found and took to be a sign from Gulaga Mountain. But recall Peter Sutton's invitation to us all to make connections wherever they seem appropriate:

I don't believe in any great thing up there governing things, and I don't have an architect-of-the-universe view of the world, but I do think you've got to be opportunistic about gaining meaning, to link things that may appear to be unlike to each other, or linking things which are in fact like each other but which you've tried to forget are like each other. It's the connecting sensibility, and that's what Aborigines are doing talking about the dreaming and land. ... Connect Connect Connect. We [Westerners] tend to compartmentalise much more in a linear way.[2]

The trees carry their markings, the creek flows underneath the playing field, Dennis is here with me. That's a step to belonging.

From the shared birthing place Dennis and I follow the ridge-line which forms the modern Pacific Highway. Down the valley spur to Fullers Bridge, the ancient divide between dark and light, salt and fresh, the serpent from the serpent-free. Now sulphur-crested cockatoos, willy wagtails and grey herons, attracted by Dennis's whistles and calls, create what he describes to me as an 'amazing feeling of serenity'. The sun blazes, vanishes. *See that cave there, that's where Pemulwuy had a camp.* In the 1950s Dennis and I often played, picnicked, swam and paddled here. Quite possibly we were here on the same day.

> There, by that tree,
> Naked under the sun in simple joy
> We found our love; there on the sand our children
> Laughed, licking sea-salt from naked skin.
> We cannot ask forgiveness—but this site
> Bears our name now, our mark, as well as yours.[3]

Bob Brissenden, the poet, thought that southern Aboriginality was finished, and I'm sure now that he would rejoice to know that it isn't. Yet he would still hold the last point. So do I. We have to believe that the marks and names of our Australian humanity, theirs and ours, are indelible and valid.

Three hundred metres up the ridge is the Northern Suburbs Crematorium where the ashes of Clarice Lougher herself sustain a rose bush. Dennis cleans the plaque, speaks to her quietly, then introduces me to her. I tell her I'm proud to be here with this lad of yours, auntie. You raised him well. As we return to the car I think of my own father buried in the Northern Suburbs cemetery less than a kilometre away. Would it be appropriate, I ask myself, to introduce Dennis to him? I believe it is. As I stand before his grave I am unmindful of the distinctions between born of the land, on the land or from the land.

G'day, old man. I'm back again to see you. I want to introduce you to my mate Dennis. He's a Gai-mariagal custodian of this country. I've just met his nanna. Now I'd like him to meet you. You were born out of this land. So was she. So was I. So was he.

The stone cairn which Bill Insch dedicated to his father pointed to England. My father was born and buried on the North Shore of Sydney. His stone cairn points nowhere; he is already home. He would not have heard of Gai-mariagal land, nor perhaps been very interested in it. I suspect that his strongest loyalty and sense of belonging was to Australia. Dennis and Nanna are of Gai-mariagal country. My father and I are of the North Shore. It's the same country. To recognise that, as Lyndall explained, is a step to belonging.

Tom Griffiths suggested that the people who truly belong to a place are those who call it home. Having heard and pondered the words of so many Australians, I am more persuaded than ever that no Australian parent should be deprived of the right to bequeath their own sense of belonging to their descendants in their own birth country. No Australian should be forced from their land on the Darling if they care for it and want to stay. No Aboriginal should be deprived of the right to bequeath to their children the custodial rights to their country. Rene Diaz's 'poppa' in his 'Hard Times in Wonderland' is every man and woman of every Australian ethnicity:

> And every second home hangs its head in shame
> 'Cause poppa can't support his family.
> And all he says he needs is an honest day's work
> With his hard-earned pay at the end,

So he can offer his son the chance just like the one given him
When this was his father's land.[4]

But it's Aboriginal land. The right of Aboriginals to purchase
rural properties from a Land Fund subscribed to by federal and state
governments has more to recommend it than the present-day deeply
divisive and obstructive system which currently divides land claimants,
their opponents and themselves. In the 1970s and early 1980s the
purchase of properties by Aboriginals who could demonstrate native,
historic, moral or other title was the preferred federal model. Now,
regrettably, it is largely abandoned. Aboriginal ownership and joint
control of federal national parks like Uluru, Kakadu and Jervis Bay, and
most recently Namadgi in the Australian Capital Territory, have not yet
been adopted by the states with any enthusiasm. Why should not they
not follow a similar program of the return of national parks to their
original owners? Why should not the traditional custodians of the
Narrabeen Lagoon Recreation Reserve not share its management with
others whose name, whose mark, is now also upon it?[5] Narrabeen
Lagoon is where Dennis is taking me now.

Through rain, dark shadow and scudding sunshine we approach
the Gai-mariagal men's sacred site near the headwaters of Deep Creek:
the Oxford Falls. In the 1950s young Dennis tracked up here from the
lagoon with his male cousins and the older men. A few kilometres away
was a bora ground, now probably destroyed. When Dennis was a lad
the cataract was polluted by a piggery. Now it is a noisy crossing to the
new suburb of Oxford Falls. While we try to gain a sense of the site as
once it was, trucks crash their gears, cars splash and rev over the bumpy
ford. Exotic grass and weeds, the remains of a gravel heap and bits of
plastic contrast with the cleaner section of the falls below.

What does this abused site still hold of those old high mysteries?
Dennis himself has no doubt. He wrote this poem about a desecrated
sacred site in Brisbane:

Through solemn Gai-mariagal eyes I look across the reach of
the river at the city of Brisbane,
over the concrete cloak smothering the earth in its death shroud;
and I think of the Turrubul. …
Through those same saddened eyes

the concrete jungle of the Whiteman does not obliterate our land.
For the concrete is built on earth,
Murri earth,
Our mother,
and this they can never take
for we are of the earth and the earth of us.
Turrubul, may your dreaming never be lost.[6]

In Chapter 2 I wrote, 'It is the heart, not the brain, of Wright's casual horse rider which senses at an abandoned ceremonial ground a continuing Aboriginal spirit force tinged with unrequited violence. The man:

> halts at a sightless shadow, an unsaid word
> that fastens in the blood the ancient curse
> the fear as old as Cain.'[7]

In Chapter 4 Ian Green said, 'You feel that these details of the inner life of the country are always there, just waiting for the person with the right kind of vision to make them apparent to you.' I had asked: Do the people respond to the forces in the country already—or it is humankind which sacralises the country? Ian replied, 'I can't see you can have landscape independent of the human perception of it.' Heather Goodall has no need to feel the spirit forces. Chas Read holds that the Devas, the shining ones, are willing to give spiritual shape to any cultural or physical formation.

Five years after my own journey of belonging began, the question of whether the rider's heart still halts intuitively at the Oxford Falls interests me less. I'm ready to ask a different and more difficult question of myself. Why is it important whether the spirits of the Aboriginal landscape are there for me? Like Heather, I care about them because I care for Dennis, but in what sense are the creation ancestors actually relevant to Peter the non-Aboriginal? In seeking them, do I seek to expropriate the Indigenous spirits?

Manik Datar has helped me to realise that one can belong to and care for the land without a spiritual identification. She would, I think, acknowledge that the ancient life-forces, moribund in the crossing or whirling down the gorge, may well be perceived by Aboriginals, then or now, in the bright imported buffalo grass or amongst the sombre angophoras. Aboriginal belonging neither diminishes nor enlarges Manik's own sense of belonging in Australia.

Leave the spirits to the people who made them or were made by them. Let the rest of us find the confidence in our own physical and spiritual belonging in this land, respectful of Aboriginality but not necessarily close to it. Let's intuit our own attachments to country independently of Aboriginals. We can belong in the landscape, on the landscape, or irrelevantly to the landscape. We don't all have to belong to each other. To understand that is a step to belonging.

The Wakehurst Parkway runs parallel to the former foot track which Dennis took with the senior men, but on the other side of the creek. The steep descent takes us to the Narrabeen Lagoon, the very last of the big community life sites of the northern Sydney peoples. What do I call it? 'Mission' suggests church or government interference, 'camp' implies impermanence, 'fringe camp' suggests disreputability. There is no adequate Australian-English word for an Aboriginal community life site from which probably all the inhabitants leave at intervals, while the site itself remains always populated. 'Town camp' is the nearest equivalent.

As I drive down the valley for the first time in twenty years I comprehend how the town camp had been allowed to remain undisturbed for so long. At the saltwater end of the lagoon were the Whites, whose life on the Collaroy, Long Reef and Narrabeen beaches was oriented towards Sydney city. At the brackish end six or seven kilometres away, probably at the cusp of Ku-ring-gai and Gai-mariagal country, lived the northern Sydney Aboriginals in a secluded waterway of breathtaking fecundity and beauty. That's where we are now.

We cross the road to the main oval of the National Fitness Camp, once bisected, like that by the North Shore Hospital, by a creek. This is the very site. A whippy squall drives us back to the car. Uncle Willie's camp was over there on the left. Up behind us to the right, where the shots from the shooting range echo among the hills, the adults hunted for game in the swamp. On the rise in front of us stands the park administration. Here in the early 1960s I carried out morning inspections of the folded clothes and tidied beds of the young footballers of Knox Grammar School. Three years before then at this same site stood two or three huts of the Gai-mariagal elders, set aside from the others, which Dennis was not allowed to visit.

Dennis relates to me his vivid, though not very sentimental, memories of the village. His relatives lived on mullet and bream, prawn and cockle from the lagoon, duck and coot egg, parrot and seagull from the marshes, possum and spotted goanna from the hills. They never ate the young ones. The women made johnny cakes from flour when they had it and from seeds when they ran out of money. *You'd make yourself sick eating crabs.* The huts on the lower level were fibro, sailcloth, plastic, rubber sheeting and other materials scavenged from the Narrabeen tip. Some were built close enough to each other to be joined by a tarpaulin, others stood by themselves. *The seagulls used to be deafening. We'd throw rocks at the trees to keep them quiet.* The women cooked outside in drums, throwing casuarina needles on the fire to keep away the mosquitoes. In winter the whole valley was full of smoke. Watch out for the broken bottles, the jagged tins to cut your feet, the mangy-looking half breed dogs! *The older men caught ducks by covering a piece of corn in bacon fat: threading a fishing line through the corn they could in a day catch three or four ducks end to end! But maybe the old fellers just told us the story to keep us entertained.* There was not much alcohol, in Dennis's memory, because there wasn't much money. How many people lived here, Dennis? *I was told there were eighty, but I doubt it; but there would have been easily twenty.*

Usually Dennis came with his nanna or his uncles. She'd do a bake-up or bring out some flour. The one night he slept here occurred because he came with Uncle Gar to camp among the huge trees on the other side of the creek. *Or we'd fish all night and come in for breakfast.* Hunting was not with guns but with sticks, fish-hooks on twine, and bamboo fish spears. The men sold seafood at Narrabeen or travelled in the tram to sell the catch at Manly. Some were in regular employment on the railways and returned on weekends. Relatives mostly living along the northern beaches came to visit; they alighted at the tram terminus, walked or boated five kilometres up to the village. They treated the Whites with deference: there was no alternative.

On the saltwater side the White residents and picnickers were thickening. Of course they had heard about the people they referred to as 'only half-castes'. Most of the men they knew by sight and some by name. Probably, like the reserve which Elsie Chan visited near Armidale, the Gai-mariagal village remained a closed community that survived for a century because, securely out of sight, it did not challenge the Whites. They were able to pretend that it wasn't there. An 1885 tourist promotion maintained:

> It is saltbush and myall within fifty yards of the sea, and eight miles off Manly—what shall we see next? Half-a-dozen blackfellows starting up stark naked, with nullah nullahs and spears? It would hardly seem strange to those accustomed only to the grim aspects of the bush. ... No, there are no blacks, and, as yet, no whites, prone but to hack and hew and desecrate the bush. It is all a delightful wilderness. Take advantage of it now as it is, for surely as human nature will seek to surround itself with natural beauty, it will become an outpost of the great city ere long.[8]

The first outposts of the great city predicted in 1885 were the sand barges and trucks dredging the sand of Deep Creek. I can imagine the rest. Once it was visible to the casual onlooker, the camp was doomed. In the mid-1950s the Wakehurst Parkway snaked down through or past the Frenchs Forest bora ring, inviting more visitors to the Oxford Falls. Tourists and beach-goers peeped from their cars at the tin humpies amidst their smoky fires. By the middle 1950s caravan site proprietors at the head of the lagoon began to complain about the water quality and the dark men fishing with bamboo spears. Council began to plan the destruction of the camp. The horseman, the bridge builder, the sand truck, the property developer, the tourist, the fisherman, the health inspector, the welfare officer, the bulldozer, the dump truck. Uncle Gar and Uncle Alwyn, living in southern Gai-mariagal country at Manly, heard of the devastation of the Narrabeen camp when refugees began arriving at Manly later that night. To have protested would have almost certainly have invited the Welfare's attention to themselves. Next morning Dennis rushed to the site with his uncles:

I came here the morning after, everyone was crying. Some of them who had hidden up in the hill, women, fellers and two cousins and uncles, and smouldering smoke coming through the sand, the huts gone, bridge gone, all dug up, tins and bottles, just like a war zone. The lagoon and swamp filled in.

Recall Oodgeroo's meditation on the destruction of the Acacia Ridge Reserve in Brisbane, at about the same time:

White men, turn quickly the earth of Acacia Ridge,
Plough the guilt in, cover and hide the shame;
These are black and so without right to blame
As bulldozers brutally drive, ruthless and sure
Through and over the poor homes of the evicted poor.[9]

Very soon the cottages along the Manly foreshore will suffer the same fate. One by one the Aboriginal families living on Brisbane Water, Pittwater, Scotland Island, the obscure bays and reaches of the Hawkesbury inaccessible by road will be obliterated. In this way the Gai-mariagal ceased at last to associate with each other as a living and working community almost independent of the Whites. What determination they had shown to endure for 170 years after the invasion in this region first and most densely settled.

Besides the catastrophe there were the insults to be daily endured. Dennis reflects upon how Nanna Lougher, who was noticeably Aboriginal, let the children scamper upstairs to get the front seat on the double-decker bus which ran the coastal route to Manly after the trams stopped. Protesting that her bag was too heavy to carry upstairs, she'd stand or sit beside the door outside on the platform at road level. She did not know for certain that a passenger or the conductor would complain about her presence inside, but the risk of humiliation and shame was real enough to prevent its possibility.

Let's paraphrase Henry Reynolds' question to ask: How, if we wish to belong to this land, shall we deal with such Aboriginal pain?

Manik and Marivic argued fiercely that the search for knowledge of the past should never be relinquished. I suggested to Manik that perhaps we had heard enough bad history. She replied, 'Don't cover it up. We haven't finished with history, it's not a report-collecting exercise. We can't say "let's stop, we have enough for the datum now".' Marivic said:

That's such dangerous country. You're denying the role of truth. Suppose the Jews took that attitude, 'Let's forget about it.' If you could give the whole world a cup of amnesia, fine. But you can't, and in the gap some will create their own truth—lies—and they will teach the nation's children and grandchildren the 'truth' that they want—and they won't be armed with their own information to fight it. There are people who say the Holocaust didn't happen! Imagine if you take away the facts. It's the burden of the historian. As a people Aboriginals have a right to survive by forgetting, but we don't have that privilege as historians. We cannot allow the truth to die with the generation that holds the kernel of that truth.

These strong opinions do not resolve the issue of what sense of belonging, imparted through which history, should we teach the next generation. Listening to embarrassed silence and giggles of students asked to name some Australian achievements of which they were proud, I've worried at some possibly over-negative history curriculums circulating in our schools. The students' reluctance to take pride in our history may invite social as well as educational disquiet. Australian society in reality has achieved much: very many communities and cultures living in a fair degree of harmony, a stable democracy, a fundamental decency, a tolerance of each other and a respect for Indigenality are features most obvious to Australians who have come from those parts of the world which do not enjoy them. These achievements are as much our history as this needless destruction of Gai-mariagal community life. Mature belonging to the present neither conceals past violence nor minimises past achievements.

Let's make no secret, then, of the destruction of the Gai-mariagal town camp. It was no catastrophe on the scale of the Coniston Massacre, but tragedy enough. Simultaneously let's admit that some of the Gai-mariagal had already left it voluntarily. Some were dissatisfied with their life on the lagoon. Good-hearted Whites were indignant that Aboriginals should have to live without power, water or sewerage. The descendants of the scattered inhabitants today are not the starving homeless like those on the outskirts of hundreds of the 'great' cities of the world. They live now in Housing Commission houses in the Sydney suburbs of Campbelltown, St Marys and Penrith.

What memorial, then, what sign will commemorate the life and death of the community of Narrabeen Lagoon? We can draw encouragement from the historian summarising new Victorian site-memorials for those 'who want to share in Aboriginal heritage by visiting reminders of their past so that we can build a future together based on respect and understanding'.[10] The original nineteenth-century sign at Merri Creek where John Batman concluded a treaty with the Wurundjeri reads: '[Batman] entered Port Phillip Heads 29 May 1835 as leader of an expedition which had been organised in Launceston, Van Diemen's Land, to form a settlement and founded one on the site of Melbourne then unoccupied.' In 1992 the Wurundjeri did not destroy the old sign, but added a new plaque inviting a renegotiated sense of belonging to the descendants of both sides: 'When the monument was erected in 1881 the Colony considered that Aboriginal people did not occupy land. It is now clear that prior to the colonisation of Victoria, the land was inhabited and used by Aboriginal people.'

The recent past is much more difficult. Prime Minister John Howard has said:

> I sympathise fundamentally with Australians who are insulted when they are told that we have a racist, bigoted past. Australians are told this quite regularly. … Of course we treated Aboriginals very badly in the past—very very badly—but to tell children whose parents were no part of that maltreatment, to tell children who themselves have been no part of it that we're all part of a sort of racist, bigoted history is something that Australians reject.[11]

I regret that the prime minister evidently has not had the opportunity to learn the acts of racism and bigotry that occurred, as public policy, within our own times. The destruction of the Narrabeen village (rather than the alternative of new houses and facilities on the same site) was one such act. To acknowledge its destruction is the mark of the maturity of a nation. We've made our mark here, not for good or ill but for good and ill. We non-Indigenous are Les Murray's lush trees who both add to and subtract from the subtle fire landscape they found:

> And they called lush water-leaved trees
> like themselves to the stumpholes of gone rainforest
>
> to shade with four seasons the tattered evergreen
> oil-haloed face of a subtle fire landscape …
> It was this shade in the end, not their coarse bottling fruit
> that mirrored the moist creek trees outward,
> as a culture
> containing the old gardener now untying and heaping up
> one more summer's stems and chutneys.[12]

For a decade during her Christmas school holidays in the 1920s, my mother stayed in a house in the Collaroy Basin not far from where the Narrabeen Lagoon debouches to the sea. I have dozens of photos of the house and beach. Surely in one of them, just in or just out of sight, must have gathered the Gai-mariagal, Dennis's aunts and great aunts and cousins, carrying out their invisible pursuits of picnicking, fishing and yarning. My mother never mentioned them to me, as her aunts and great-aunts and cousins never mentioned them to her. In 1960 I spent a magical holiday at the same beach. Like that travel writer of 1885, and my own elders, I never saw an Aboriginal face sharing the beach with me, not once. Everyone knew that Aboriginals had disappeared— well, years ago. But they saw us. They could not but be acutely aware of the Whites.

Belonging-in-parallel does not imply that the majority cultures pretend that the Aboriginals don't exist. A plaque commemorating the Narrabeen site, and its destruction, will remind the visitor that Aboriginality is around us and beside us. That's a step to mature belonging. Now Dennis and I, the one Indigenous, the other native-born, each respecting the past and present cultures of the other, are together travelling the northern beaches of Gai-mariagal lands in search of the proper country. That's another step.

We cross the creek to explore the site among the mighty angophoras where Dennis camped for the night with Uncle Gar. Dennis is able to locate the exact site. A squall blows over, the sky clears. We return to the edge of the lagoon. Dennis takes off his shoes to enter the water, produces a notebook and recites some Gai-mariagal phrases. Instantly we are enveloped in a stormy sun shower. Dennis invites me to follow him into the water, where he places water scooped from the Narrabeen Lagoon on to my cheeks and forehead in a ceremony of welcome and acceptance into Gai-mariagal country.

The wind has risen to a roaring easterly at Narrabeen Beach as Dennis points to the penguin rookeries of his nanna's early memory. We head south down the coast. At each beach Dennis recounts the stories of Nanna Lougher, learned in the first thirteen years of his life. At Dee Why she chose picnic spots protected from the nor'-easter along the huge, but now buried, shell midden. The yarns began when Dennis and his cousins, emerging tired and sunburnt from the mid-afternoon surf, lay down while Nanna had another cuppa. From the midden she might extract a bone, a shell or a piece of charcoal and tell the kids about the Old People. At Long Reef, she said, they summoned the dolphins to help catch schools of fish by slapping the water with their spears. The southern cliff is red from the blood of Gai-mariagal women who have their own strong story and relationship with that place. Just where the children lay listening, two female Aboriginal skeletons had been excavated by a team from the Australian Museum. In another story from Forty Baskets Beach, Nanna explained that several children were attacked by a harbour whaler shark. A huge man, a great hunter and father of the Cadigal, went to rescue them; holding the children aloft he strode from the water, the shark tearing his legs off at the knee; on the beach he fell down and died. The body was burned and the bones placed in a cave above the beach. Nanna told the children the rumour that bones taken from the cave and held in the Australian Museum bore the marks of shark teeth. No Gai-mariagal had been allowed to see them. At every picnic spot the spirits of Aboriginal adults would appear to share the day to tell or listen to stories of the deep and recent past.

At Curl Curl, Nanna said, the men would sharpen their barnacle hooks on sandstone, bring a kangaroo thigh bone to a fine point, attract the tuna with pieces of fish, then feed them the baited bone. At Freshwater the early sailors would anchor offshore and row the longboats in to refill their casks. In the hot sandy rockpools Gai-mariagal women placed the skin and bones of fish to distil the fish oil to grease their bodies. Huge sand dunes used to run the length of the Manly Beach. At king tides the channel that became the whitefellers' Corso ran deep and South Head became an island. Once when the dunny overflowed at the Loughers' home near the beach front on Sydney Road, fourteen-year-old Alwyn, digging a new hole, found a huge turtle shell concealing spear points and stone tools. They became his first hunting weapons. From that time, as Dennis's mother put it disapprovingly, Alwyn 'was away with the blackfellers', messing around with lines and fish spears and nets and boats on the Manly foreshores. Alwyn didn't bother too much about school after he found those spear points.

The children's heads drooped. A feed of hot chips and sleep on the bus all the way home. Nanna sat outside.

Late in the day Dennis and I came to Wyandra Avenue, Harbord, where he lived until Nanna Lougher died in 1966. Dennis was sent first to his eldest sister's, then the Welfare took him. His memories of this country are very strong.

Constantly there were visitors to the Lougher home. During the war, his mother told him, Nanna would prepare scones and tea for the soldiers manning the gun emplacement at the end of the road. In Dennis's own time most of the visitors were Aboriginal; knowing the routine, they would wash in the laundry outside before presenting themselves for a feed. One was so dark that Dennis cried in fright before being scolded for being scared of a Black man. It was an easy walk through the bush to Manly, Harbord or Curl Curl.

Clarice Malinda married Garfield Lougher in the 1920s. Their mutual tough-mindedness kept the Aborigines Welfare Board at bay while they reared their children, Dennis's mother, and his uncles Gar and Alwyn. Those three children grew up on the Manly seaboard while many an expansive Federation bungalow of the north shore of Sydney bustled with an Aboriginal housegirl who had progressed from the Cootamundra Aboriginal Girls Home to 'disposal' (to use the official phrase) as teenage maid and child-minder. Certainly Dennis and his mother would have passed them playing with young White children in the parks or the northern beaches. Assimilation was at its peak. In the 1950s, Nanna reared a second family of grandchild, grand-nieces and nephews. At Wyandra Avenue, Dennis more than survived: he flourished and grew culturally strong within this secure, loving and defended family home.

How did two generations of children survive this period when the Aborigines Welfare Board was at its most vicious? Nanna Lougher was a strong woman. Outdoors she dressed in stockings, hat and gloves; in winter she added a long coat and a fox fur. She kept her dignity. If challenged, she maintained that she and her relatives were a darker variety of Welsh coal miner. Sometimes they were Greeks or Maltese. No, those dark Aboriginal visitors were not relations. Nanna Lougher understood the Welfare Board all too well. If she failed, her family was doomed.

The integrity of the family was not maintained by the strength of Nanna alone. She married a good man, the son of a Welsh miner who built his house with the help of his Aboriginal brother-in-law. The determination and strength of Garfield senior, equal to that of his wife, upheld the family too. If he too had faltered, gambled or drunk his pay, lost his job or vanished, the Aborigines Welfare Board must have seized the children. Dennis' mother would have been raised in an institution, and Dennis surely would have been lost to the Gai-mariagal, like his own cousins who vanished from the family's ken in the late 1950s and are lost to this day. The survival of Aboriginality, which for so many individuals and families in the 1950s balanced on the razor's edge, has depended also on good White people.

It's a strong kind of belonging that out of trauma creates descendants who, understanding that the world is unfair, want to change it for the better. Sharing human life as partners, friends, colleagues, mates or lovers demands no land, does not see through or ignore the other nor seeks to own its spirituality. Indigenous and non-Indigenous people like Dennis' grandparents pooled their humanity, abilities, emotions and affections. They belonged to each other, but their union belonged to the constructive and optimistic history of this country. We met it first in Troy Cassar-Daley's song 'Dream out Loud':

> There's two people in love, one black and one white,
> Who's to say who's wrong and who's right.
> Both standing tall, both standing proud, both not afraid
> To dream out loud.
>
> Dream out loud, it's up to me and you,
> Dream out loud, it's not too hard to do.
> So if you see your brother/sister falling on the ground
> Don't be afraid to dream out loud.[13]

The band Goanna reinforced it:

> We sat down upon the earth,
> Talked of reason and of fear,
> Sang our songs into the night,
> Stars rained down on black and white.[14]

The strong characters of individuals, united in a respect for cultural difference, may affect three or four generations of Aboriginal descent. Clarice and Garfield bequeathed to their children that more optimistic model of Oodgeroo, who explained to her own son Denis:

> But I'll tell you instead of brave and fine
> When lives of black and white entwine,
> And men in brotherhood combine—
> This would I tell you, son of mine.[15]

Garfield the elder died first. His son Garfield, the youngest, left the family home in the early 1960s. Alwyn moved to a house in Manly. Dennis's great-uncle, who lived next door, left with his family at about the same time. By the time Dennis was twelve, all his cousins and their older relatives had gone. Dennis does not know where they went or where they are.

Dusk turned to night.

Next morning Jessie and her husband Tony arrived to accompany us, with Dennis's agreement, to Uncle Willie's house in Coal and Candle Creek. Five minutes after we embarked from Cottage Point a sea eagle appeared. It dived for a fish, followed us for a hundred metres, flew ahead, alighted on a branch to watch us as we putt-putted underneath. Across the stone steps of Uncle Willie's garden flew a crescent-crested grey heron. *That's a spirit bird. And three ravens to talk to us.* The house site which our party had found in March 1998 Dennis identified as the shed in which William De Serve kept his fishing and boating supplies. Of the larger building that Dennis remembered standing on a cleared slope above the shed site, we now found no trace. Sheets of tin and the bottles probably were cleared by the park authorities. The furrows and ridges—still yielding melons and cucumbers at the time of Dennis's first visit—were now densely overgrown, but the fertile soil that once supported the garden still trickled beneath the roots of the bracken. After hunting fruitlessly for artefacts, the four of us returned to the cement floor of the store shed, scratched at the leaf mould, pushed aside the fish bones, dug in the ash of long-dead fires. From a square hole Dennis unearthed the stump of a hardwood pole which once had supported the roof.

> The fish-bones smoulder in the cooling fire.
> The spear shines in the moonlight. In the cave

Behind the sleeping lovers the earth floor
Minutely shifts and settles,

Drifts over the other bones, the other spears—
The fish-hooks carved from shell, the flakes of stone,
The bones of birds and animals and fish,
The blood, the long-dead fires.[16]

Though the site inherits to Dennis—not to me, nor to us—I shall return. In the present absence of a Ku-ring-gai guardian, my peace of mind is in knowing that the site belongs morally to someone who knew and loved it. Like Lyndall Ryan, I would find it unthinkable to visit the site without the endorsement of its de facto custodian who also is my friend. Belonging grows more intense.

That night Dennis showed me an article which traces the best anthropological guesses at pre-invasion Gai-mariagal movement patterns.[17] One track started at the head of the Narrabeen Lagoon, followed Deep Creek up the plateau to Oxford Falls, across the sandstone through Belrose, Terrey Hills, the Ku-ring-gai Chase National Park, touched the headwaters of Coal and Candle Creek less than 400 metres from Uncle Willie's camp site, to end two kilometres away at Castle Lagoon. It was from Castle Lagoon where Anna, Jay and I had set out to search for the lost Aboriginal rock carving; Castle Lagoon where I'd begun the first night of my marriage; Castle Lagoon where I hear still my mother's squeak of delight as she woke to see the bush swinging past our windy anchorage; Castle Lagoon where I had already asked for my own ashes to be scattered onto the green-black waters of the deep sandstone gorges.

Over lunch we talk of Refuge Bay, the wide expanse of shoaling water, a waterfall that cascades over the ever-diminishing midden, and the prettiest beach on Broken Bay. I know it to be a place of much White interaction. Many a coastal steamer used to run for shelter to the bay before an approaching southerly storm. Yacht crews wrote the names of their boats on the cliffs. A recent plaque informs the visitor that from this exact point the little *Krait* left Australia on its heroic journey to destroy Japanese shipping in Singapore Harbour. Visitors splash in the waterfall, scuff away the midden with their bare feet and sunbake. My own memories are of helpless pleasure, lazy lunches, rowing boat races, damming the creek, cricket and badminton, long walks.

Dennis tells us that he didn't come here with his uncles. Too many whitefellers and too many bad associations, of timber-getters keeping Aboriginal women as slaves. Like Barren Island, Refuge Bay in the early nineteenth century was a place of exploitation, sexual violence and murder:

> Still she coughed up oyster pulp;
> and those white barnacles she grew
> inflamed Dan Smith with their hot rasp.
> He buttoned up his trousers,
> trussed up her legs,
> took her out the back,
> fired a flintlock in her ribs …

Randolph Stow wrote of the haunted West Australian landscape:

> Only I, riding the flat-topped hills alone,
> feel in the inland wind the sing of desert,
> and under alien skin the surge, the singing,
> a wisdom and a violence, the land's dark blood.[18]

In the sandstone gorges I have felt neither wisdom nor violence. Like Heather Goodall, I have intuited nothing. Yet what Dennis tells me historically is perfect sense. Captain John Hunter marked the bay clearly on the coastal chart he surveyed in the colony's first year.[19] It coincides with records of how busy was the waterway last century. Coastal ships often unloaded their cargo in Broken Bay rather than in Sydney Harbour. Yet on this lovely beach I've never felt anything but merriment and fun. How then do we deal with the Aboriginal dead who lived and perished horribly on this same sandy cricket pitch and picnic place? How can we belong in places of our own intense pleasure but others' intense pain?

After sixty thousand years, surely almost every square metre of habitable Australia has been drenched with the blood of birth as well as death. On every Gai-mariagal site people have made love—and been raped. Children have played, and cried; adults have argued and yarned, gathered food, picnicked, lazed about, telephoned, cooked fish, played cricket, lost their car keys, smacked their kids, been generous and mean, loved and hated. All the wide intensity of human passion, for many thousands of years, has been expressed at Manly and Calabash Bay, Narrabeen Lagoon and Fullers Bridge, Collaroy and Curl Curl; and Refuge Bay.

> Ashes
> Of cooking fires that warmed us while we talked
> And touched, slept, wrestled with love and grief,
> Cried out or wept beneath indifferent stars
> Cold dawns and leaching rains: these—yours and ours—
> Have mingled with this soil. ...

I cannot share the despair of Adrian Caesar discovering that the Wirraweena of his attachment had been occupied by Adnyamathanha people for thirty thousand years,

> I'm put in my stranger place,
> returning to suburbia
> try to know it more nearly where it is
> I both belong and don't.[20]

If I did not already know and love this site, I should not visit it now. Yet to Veronica Brady, and to me, profound attachments derive from many sources: from literature, awe, fear and fascination, respect for spirituality. They derive from listening rather than speaking, sharing rather than competing, the self flowing into and part of the whole, a sadness at the violation of what we first encountered.[21] And belonging derives partly from law. Lyndall Ryan, reviewing a draft of the previous chapter, writes to me of the Mabo decision: 'Mabo has made me feel more at ease. I felt a huge burden fall from my shoulders that day. It was as if the decision gave me the right to breathe as an Australian for the first time. I stopped feeling like a colonial, a secondhand person.'[22]

Refuge Bay, once known and loved, cannot be unloved by mental fiat. My emotions and memories already are cemented deep into this sand and beach and creek. Yes, our country is a war grave, but it is not only a war grave. Some of the powerful and terrible sweep of human life transacted at this place I now know; the rest I do not. Dennis's story enriches the site, not subtracts from it. I hold it in new respect. But I shall go back again. Belonging grows more intense.

On Monday morning we travel first to Balmoral, where Dennis tells me that the deadly smallpox epidemic first appeared, transmitted through government blankets. Next, to the Spit, where the creeks and tides of Middle Harbour wash into the northern part of Sydney Harbour. In the 1960s the entrance was narrower than now, and densely grown in mangroves. Dennis's relations walked down from Manly above to sit on the beach, boil the billy and supervise the catching and gathering of the mangrove snails, mud crabs, bream and shellfish. Never were the children allowed to enter the water. This is why not.

The Gai-mariagal story concerns the shark known as the harbour whaler, and the dangerous, hairy little people known as Gubjas—a word long in use, Dennis explains, before the Whites wrongly concluded that the word which Aboriginals use for them was derived from 'Gubna'. Gubjas were evil, ever on watch for solitary Gai-mariagal to kill the men, rape the women, rip open the stomach and eat the eyes. Part of their weaponry was their excrement-like stink, which was so debilitating that the Gai-mariagal found alone, vomiting and overcome, stood paralysed until captured and slain. The back country of the creeks and gullies of Bantry Bay, Sailors Bay, Castlecrag, and Middle Harbour were the home of the Gubjas. Watching from the foreshores, the Gai-mariagal judged that the sailors climbing the rigging of the ships of the First Fleet were the Gubjas themselves, long known for their agility in the trees, now daringly visible in broad daylight.

Amongst the people of Forty Baskets Beach, long before the harbour was flooded by the melting of the last ice age, three girls were learning their women's business. The Gubjas, knowing the men seldom entered the area, raided this women's place. They killed the older ones, kidnapped the girls and dragged them to their hideaway in Middle Harbour. The Gai-mariagal men tracked them through the tea-tree to The Spit where they found their canoe tracks by the water, then the canoes themselves hidden in the trees. Months later they located the girls, tied up, pregnant and abused, in a gully near Castlecrag. They stole down to rescue them, but as they made their way back to the water the Gubjas discovered them. They attacked the fugitives with spears which, mysteriously, could break bones at great distance. The paddling men were hit and fell out, three canoes overturned, the women pitched into the blood-red water. Their bellies burst to reveal the first harbour whaler sharks, which savagely attacked and killed the escaping swimmers and their own mothers. Other Gai-mariagal, watching from the cliffs, threw their spears in desperation. None was able to reach the sharks. The entire party died. The watchers inscribed the tragedy in stone above the site where the people perished, the women gave birth and the harbour whalers were born. To this day in the green-black waters above The Spit the harbour whalers breed and cruise, awaiting the arrival of the incautious swimmer to be captured and slain.

What is the meaning of this fathomless story? Mourning the death of a female kangaroo, Eve Langley wrote:

> Beside her in the ashes I sat deep
> > And mourned for her, but had no native song
> To flatter death …[23]

Though we have no explanations for local creation except the Indigenous, Langley was wrong in imagining she had no native song. We do. Indigenous creation stories are part of the deep inheritance that Tom Griffith hopes we will eventually embrace. Like Lyndall Ryan I am no monolithic explanationist. All accounts of why the world is as it is are to some degree metaphorical. As so many of the strong thinkers in this book confirm, explanations satisfy the emotional, imaginative and visceral natures as well as the merely intellectual. I'm drawn to this account because it is a local explanation of a local phenomenon by people who lived beside The Spit, and kept their children from its waters for twenty-six thousand years while the sea levels rose and fell by 40 metres. We don't need to claim it as 'our' story, but to treasure its explanation of this country of our own close belonging. Whichever explanation is 'correct' is irrelevant: all are appropriate for the humans who create them and are prepared to share them with those who value their culture.

A linguist found that an area slightly larger than Gai-mariagal country near Cairns had about ninety place names, of which two-thirds had etymologies and some, like The Spit, had stories about ancestral creation figures who had given them their names.[24] A tiny proportion of the Sydney stories survive. The Spit will never be the same for me again. Belonging grows more intense.

We go on to Forty Baskets Beach, and Dennis shows me where Uncle Gar in the 1960s had argued with archaeologists excavating skeletal remains from the midden now invisible. We go to the western end of the Manly Cove where Governor Phillip landed, to the spot near the art gallery where the Aboriginal people gathered to keep an eye on the kids swimming in the enclosure, to the eastern end where Dennis dived for coins, to Ivanhoe Park above the oval, recently re-landscaped to reduce the native bushland. Fish and chips at the ferry terminal. To Collins Beach, where Governor Phillip was speared by an Aboriginal from Broken Bay. We return to the park where in the 1950s stood the Fairlight gasworks, whose strong odour had protected the Aboriginals and others from removal from the foreshores. We gaze across to Spring Cove, where Nanna Watson had her dwelling. There were perhaps six cottages on the beach, better built than the Narrabeen huts because of the more plentiful material floating about the harbour. Perhaps only one of them was inhabited by Aboriginals. Nanna Watson's house had proper windows and doors, a shellgrit floor, massive timber supports which looked like sleepers of bridge work, a corrugated iron roof. Outside, under another piece of tin, was the fuel stove on a cement slab, surrounded by piles of firewood. *She was a big woman. Big hands. For a young kid she had sort of a yucky smell. Smother you in kisses.*

The wintry afternoon is darkening as we approach the last point of our journey, the country of the Gatlay clan of the Gai-mariagal at Manly Lagoon, discovered by Governor Phillip in April 1788. Here at last is the proper country of Dennis Foley. Once it was also a site of wonder to Governor Phillip's exploration party, which, walking northwards from Manly Cove towards Queenscliff, 'fell in with a small salt-water lagoon, on which we found nine birds, that, while swimming, most perfectly resembled the *rara avis* of the ancients—a black swan'.[25]

By the time Dennis swam and fished in the lagoon as a lad, the Gai-mariagal no longer lived here. White people building their houses here since the 1900s had no desire to share their country with the Gai-mariagal. Probably at the time of the first constructions, the Aboriginals, as at Narrabeen, moved permanently to the freshwater end of their huge reedy lagoon, which extended almost to Brookvale and Curl Curl. Like the Narrabeen community they remained secure in their swampy refuge until the invaders appeared in their rear: at Narrabeen by way of the Wakehurst Parkway, at Manly by the Italian market gardeners and the road to Brookvale. Dennis's people continued to fish with line and net, though whenever Uncle Alwyn used a fishing spear the police moved him on. When Dennis was a lad, the Gai-mariagal still came here to picnic. Today it remains the favourite coastal site of Dennis's mother.

From about 1960 the Manly Council authorities began to exploit the swamp as a huge dump. For more than a decade unknown chemicals joined the plastics, oils and metals, old cars and fridges, batteries, sump oil, noxious substances from the clothing factories and building rubble swept into the marsh. Finally it was covered over with clay, topsoil, parks and two golf courses. Today the lagoon is one-quarter of its former size. All the natural vegetation is gone.[26] It is heavily polluted. Mandy Martin and Tom Griffiths hold that true belonging carries responsibility for present and future. So did the Warumpi Band:

> I believe the time will come when everyone will join in
> And understand our way of life and know we care for this land.[27]

This once-wondrous lagoon which supported hundreds of generations of Gai-mariagal, whose thickets and swamps twice stopped Governor Phillip from northwards exploration, is useless now for anything except as a place to walk the dog.

In the 1920s the Italian market gardeners living on the Brookvale edge of the swamp confronted the 'madmen with matted hair hanging over their eyes'.[28] They were Dennis's own great-grandparents, the cousins and uncles and aunties of Nanna Lougher, the Indigenous people of northern Sydney pushed back from Queenscliff Beach at their penultimate community refuge. *God only knows where they went to.* Some, it is easy to surmise, moved up to Narrabeen, where they remained undisturbed for two generations.

Those migrants were Australians too, bearing their own deepening sets of hard-won belonging. The first generation of Australians like Salvatore Zofrea and Elsie Chan probably felt that belonging was not a matter of sharing land but of finding acceptance of their cultural and social difference. Marivic Wyndham:

Renegotiating Australia is always a struggle to convince people I have a right to be here, to have an Australian voice, not just an Australian place. I need to insist on that in asking to become an Australian. The exile will always belong at a price. That's the price for belonging. To me a line was drawn when I was born somewhere else. I'll never have the sense of security that this land sees and recognises me as her own. If there's no price to pay, you just know you belong.

Nor is the sense of belonging of the children of migrants entirely secure. In Chapter 3 Damian says:

'Always was, always will be Aboriginal land?' It's a tough question. It is their land, because it's a part of them, but by the same token because I'm a first-generation Australian, this is all I've ever wanted, it's all I've ever known.

Whether we forgive or even understand the men of the 1950s who dumped the filthy rubbish of northern Sydney into the Manly Lagoon doesn't matter. To Bill Insch and Neil Murray, ethical belonging implies the protection of the land Australia from this moment:

Australia, where are your caretakers gone?
I am just one who has been battered
By the damage within your shores.
Australia I will not sell you for a price,
I will not strip you of your forests
Or pollute your clear blue skies,
I will not desecrate your sacred lands
I will not plunder on your shores
I would not foul your precious waters
For I am native born.[29]

During this chapter I've used for the first time the phrase 'native-born' about myself. Though no very energetic conservationist, I've gained confidence—not only from the words of Neil Murray; not only through listening or through my journey with Dennis; not only in being here at the Manly Lagoon or hearing the stories; not only through understanding the past, attaching plaques, writing history; not only through disturbing the ash of long-dead fires. I've engaged with my fellow

Australians, who have convinced me that, though there are many ways to belong to this land and to this nation, none should be taken for granted. All come at a cost. We need the reassurance that we will not sell Australia at a price; that we will carry sufficient confidence in our own cultures to find belonging in thinking and acting and being; that stars rain down on Black and White; that wherever lives of Black and White entwine, all of us can dream out loud. We need the metaphors, the connections, the songs and the art. I need the Gai-mariagal stories, I need to believe that the voices in the river will never be silent, that the land bears our mark now as well as theirs. Though the journey matters more than the arrival, I think now that I'm almost ready to belong.

But not quite. Dennis and thousands of Aboriginals like him still are denied the custodianship of their proper country. He and his family are largely unrecognised, both by the non-Indigenous people of Gai-mariagal country and by many Aboriginals of Sydney, as a true descendant of the Gai-mariagal. We cannot share the land with Aboriginals until they have their land to share with us. Dennis Foley needs to hold his own country as custodian, inheritor and guardian before he can share it with others. We cannot fully belong in our own culturally specific fashion if that fashion excludes others from belonging within their own cultures. This our own country is not the far horizon of the nameless pastoralists, but here; neither commodity nor the idealised, inscrutable, unpossessable, arid sublime, but the very land we walk on.[30] Non-Indigenous Australia currently excludes urban Aboriginals from belonging in the country of their cultural inheritance. Dennis is excluded from his, which a simple declaration of ownership and joint custodianship of the parks and bush reserves of Gai-mariagal country would begin to provide.

I have no right to claim on behalf of non-Aboriginal Australia that all the non-Indigenous are now part of Australia's deep past, nor do I wish to. Belonging ultimately is personal. There are as many routes to belonging as there are non-Aboriginal Australians to find them. My sense of the native-born has come—is coming. It comes through listening but with discernment; through thinking but not asserting; through good times with my Aboriginal friends but not through wanting to be the same as them; through understanding our history but being enriched by the sites of past evil as well as good. It comes from believing that belonging means sharing and that sharing demands equal partnership.

Judith Wright wrote:

> Let us go back to that far time,
> I riding the cleared hills,
> plucking blue leaves for their eucalypt scent,
> hearing the call of the plover,
>
> in a land I thought was mine for life ...
>
> But we are grown to a changed world:
> over the drinks at night
> we can exchange our separate griefs
> but yours and mine are different ...
>
> The knife's between us. I turn it round,
> the handle to your side,
> the weapon made from your country's bones,
> I have no right to take it.
>
> But both of us die as our dreamtime dies,
> I don't know what to give you
> for your gay stories, your sad eyes,
> but that, and a poem, sister.[31]

Yes, Dennis, our griefs are different, but your dreamtime is not dead. Neither we nor our peoples are dying. The deep future lies before us.

NOTES

INTRODUCTION

1 P. Read, *Returning to Nothing*, 1996, p. xi.
2 Epigraph to Roslynn Haynes, *Seeking the Centre*, 1998.
3 Haynes, 1998, pp. 16–17.
4 David J. Tacey, *Edge of the Sacred*, 1995, p. 129.
5 R. Dessaix, in G. Papaellinas, ed., *Homeland*, 1991, p. 153, quoted in Read, 1996, p. 22.
6 Robert Levitus, introduction to R. Levitus, ed., *Lying About the Landscape*, 1997, pp. 8–10.
7 Smith quoted by Denis Byrne, 'Deep Nation: Australia's Acquisition of an Indigenous Past', *Aboriginal History* 20, p. 95.
8 V. Brady, 'Truth, Illusions and Collisions', *Australian Book Review*, July 1999, pp. 23–6.
9 V. Brady, 'The Ambiguities of Place', in *Sense of Place Colloquium II*, 1997, pp. 41–2.

1 DEEP IN THE SANDSTONE GORGES

1 Douglas Stewart, 'Rock Carving', in D. Stewart, *Douglas Stewart*, 1963, pp. 21–3.
2 Quoted by V. Brady, 1999, from Gelder and Jacobs, *Uncanny Australia: Sacredness and Identity in a Postcolonial Nation*, 1998.
3 David Campbell, 'Letters to a Friend II: Rock-engravings', in Leonie Kramer, ed., *David Campbell: Collected Poems*, 1989, p. 153.
4 J. Brook and J. L. Cohen, *The Parramatta Native Institution and the Black Town: A History*, 1991, p. 89.
5 Brook and Cohen, 1991, pp. 2–3.
6 H. C. Coombs, 1983, interviewed for a public radio series 'The Aboriginal Treaty Proposal'.

7   Manning Clark, 'Australia, Whose Country Is It?', in M. Clark, *Speaking out of Turn*, 1997, p. 144.

8   Cassandra Pybus, *Community of Thieves*, 1991, p. 15.

9   Judith Wright, 'South of My Days', in J. Wright, *Collected Poems 1942–1985*, 1985, p. 20.

10 Judith Wright, *The Cry for the Dead*, 1981, pp. 277–80.

11 'The Broken Links', republished in J. Wright, *Born of the Conquerors*, 1991, p. 30.

12 Anthony Moran, 'Aboriginal Reconciliation: Transformations in Settler Nationalism', in *The Reconciliation Issue, Melbourne Journal of Politics*, 1998, p. 120.

13 Tacey, *Edge of the Sacred*, 1995, pp. 132–3 .

14 Anonymous poet, 'Our Political System Is Best', in *Integration*, April–July 1996, back cover.

15 'Our Man in Bunyah' in Les Murray, *A Working Forest*, 1977, pp. 82–3: 'In what many see as a particularly nauseous lie, we alone are blamed for the dispossession of the Aborigines and continuing occupation of stolen land. Immigrants of any but British antecedents are immune from charges of complicity.'

16 S. Zofrea (woodcuts) and S. McInerney (text), *The Journeyman*, 1992.

17 Mick Dodson in 'Unfinished Business', prod. Bill Bunbury, Radio National, ABC, 1996.

18 Noel Pearson, 'An Australian History for All of Us', Address to the Chancellor's Club Dinner, UWS, 20 November 1996, photocopy, pp. 9–11.

19 Anne Pattel-Grey 1991, quoted in Eugene Stockton, *The Aboriginal Gift: Spirituality for a Nation*, 1995, p. 67.

20 Council for Aboriginal Reconciliation, *Sharing History*, Key Issue Paper No. 4, 1994.

21 Eleanor Dark, *The Little Company*, 1945, p. 177. I thank Marivic Wyndham for showing me this extract.

22 Stewart Hall, epigraph to Gelder and Jacobs, 1998.

23 Tacey, *Edge of the Sacred*, 1995, pp. 71, 142.

24 Stockton, 1995, pp. 4, 9.

25 Isabel McBryde, 'Dream the Impossible Dream? Shared Heritage, Shared Values, or Shared Understanding of Disparate Values', *Historic Environment*, 1993, p. 11.

26 McBryde, 1993, p. 12.

27 M. Rose, 'Dadirri', in Stockton, 1995, pp. 179ff.

28 J. H. Wootten, *Report of the Enquiry into the Death of David Gundy*, 1991.

29 Council for Aboriginal Reconciliation, 1994, p. 9.

30 Maria Nugent, 'La Perouse Versus Larpa: Contesting Histories of Place', *Public History Review* 1996–7, pp. 192–9.

31 Meyer Eidelson, *The Melbourne Dreaming: A Guide to the Aboriginal Places of Melbourne*, 1997, p. 1.

32 Veronica Brady, 'The Ambiguities of Place', in *Sense of Place Colloquium II*, 1997, pp. 42–3.

33 Anon. [Richard Baker] in P. Read, 'Post-Colonialism and the Native Born', *Canadian Journal of Native Studies*, 1994, p. 385.

34 Pearson, 1996, p. 14.

35 Gelder and Jacob, 1998, pp. 138–9.

36 Nadine Gordimer, *The Essential Gesture*, 1989, pp. 32–3.

37 Michael King, *Being Pakeha*, 1985.

38 Pers. comm. and recorded interview, Dennis Foley, August 1998.

39 Judith Wright, 'Two Dreamtimes', in Wright, 1985, pp. 316–18.

40 Deborah Bird Rose, *Nourishing Terrains*, 1996, p. 10; italics in the original.

41 Pers. comm., Stephanie Lindsay-Thompson; see also Ruth Longdin and Elida Meadows, 'Catalina: Wild Heart of Katoomba', *Public History Review* 7, 1998, pp. 103–16.

42 Kath Walker, 'Acacia Ridge', in K. Walker, *We Are Going*, 1964, p. 31.

43 Ossie Ingram, 'The Proudest People on Earth', in B. Gammage and P. Spearritt, eds, *Australians 1938*, 1987, pp. 117–24.

44 L. Ingram in P. Read, ed., *Down There With Me on the Cowra Mission*, 1984.

45 Zofrea and McInerney, 1992.

46 Judith Wright, 'Two Dreamtimes', in Wright, 1985, 316–18.

2 VOICES IN THE RIVER

 1 Colin Johnson, 'They Give Jacky Rights', in K. Gilbert, ed., *Inside Black Australia*, 1988, p. 41.

 2 Molly Kruger, 'The Lost Race: My Father's Story', in R. Bennett, ed., *Voices from the Heart*, 1995, p. 35.

 3 Mudrooroo Narogin [Colin Johnson], 'Country Dog in the City', in B. Dibble, D. Grant and G. Phillips, eds, *Celebrations*, 1988, p. 176.

 4 Gavin Gleeson, 'Without No Stars', in Bennett, 1995, p. 26.

 5 John Khan, 'Put Up or Shut Up', in Bennett, 1995, p. 34.

 6 Kenny Laughton, 'Made My Bed', in Bennett, 1995, p. 40.

 7 Jack Davis, 'My Mother the Land' [*sic*], in J. Davis, *Black Life*, 1992, p. 6.

 8 Tony Birch, 'Daisy Bates', in *Melbourne Historical Journal* 23, 1995, pp. 17–18. I am grateful to Dr Paula Byrne for showing me this poem.

 9 Aileen Corpus, 'Taxi Conversation', in S. Hampton and K. Llewellyn, eds, *The Penguin Book of Australian Women Poets*, 1988, p. 226.

10 Paddy Biran, 'Paddy Biran's Song' [trans. from Girramay by R. W. Dixon], in R. Hall, ed., *The Collins Book of Australian Poetry*, 1981, p. 376.

11 Robert Walker, 'Solitary Confinement', in Gilbert, 1988, p. 128. Walker died at Fremantle Prison in 1984, aged 25, from 'Misadventure'.

12 Jack Davis, 'To Ron and Catherine Berndt', in Davis, 1992, p. 71.

13 Kath Walker, 'Then as Now', in K. Walker, *We Are Going*, 1964, p. 18.

14 Katharine Susannah Prichard, 'The Earth Lover', in William Grono, ed., *Margins*, 1988, p. 188.

15 Eve Langley, 'Native Born', in Hampton and Llewellyn, 1986, pp. 50–1.

16 Gwen Harwood, 'Oyster Cove', in G. Harwood, *Selected Poems*, 1985, p. 81.

17 Randolph Stow, 'The Dark Women Go Down', in R. Stow, *A Counterfeit Silence*, 1969, p. 58.

18 David Campbell, 'Sugarloaf', in D. Campbell, *Collected Poems*, 1989, p. 238.

19 R. Brissenden, 'Rock Climbers, Uluru, 1985', *Sacred Sites*, 1990, p. 14.

20 Peter Lugg, 'The Early History of Canberra', in P. McKenzie, ed., *The Poetry of Canberra*, 1990, p. 4.

21 M. Mackay, 'To the Kooris', unpublished, 1997.

22 David Campbell, 'Weapons', in Campbell, 1989, p. 116.

23 Judith Wright, 'Two Old Men', in J. Wright, *Collected Poems 1942–1970*, 1971, p. 149.

24 Judith Wright, 'Bora Ring', in Wright, 1971, p. 8.

25 Randolph Stow, 'There was a Time', in Stow, 1969, p. 59.

26 R. F. Brissenden, 'South Coast Midden', in Brissenden, 1990, p. 15.

27 R. F. Brissenden, 'Sea Beach and Cave, Durras', in Brissenden, *Building a Terrace*, 1975, p. 42.

28 James Charlton, 'Koonya, a Black Girl', in V. Smith and M. Scott, eds, *Effects of Light: The Poetry of Tasmania*, 1985, p. 130.

29 J. Wright, 'The Broken Links', in Wright, 1991, p. 31.

30 Alec Choate, 'Custodians No Longer', in Choate, *Mind in Need of a Desert*, 1995, pp. 102–3 .

31 A. Caesar, 'Landscapes', in A. Caesar, *Life Sentences*, 1998, p. 3.

32 Les Murray, 'Louvres', in L. Murray, *Selected Poems*, 1986, p. 134.

33 Les Murray, 'Towards the Imminent Days', in Murray, 1986, p. 15.

34 Les Murray, 'The Bulladeelah-Taree Holiday Song Cycle', in Murray, 1986, p. 60.

35 Les Murray, 'The China Pear Trees', in Murray, 1986, p. 139.

36 Les Murray, 'On the Present Slaughter of Feral Animals', *Subhuman Redneck Poems*, 1996, pp. 41–2.

37 Kath Walker, 'We Are Going', in Hall, 1981, p. 208.

38 Kath Walker, 'The Past', in K. Walker, *My People*, 1970, p. 93.

39 David Rowbotham, 'Mullabinda', in Hall, 1981, pp. 224–5.

40 Ian Mudie, 'Retreat of a Pioneer', in I. Mudie, *Selected Poems 1934–1974*, 1976, p. 11.

41* David Campbell, 'Bora Ring', in Campbell, 1989, p. 115.

42 Dorothy Hewett, 'Legend of the Green Country', in D. Hewett, *A Tremendous World in Her Head*, 1989, p. 8.

43 Judith Wright, 'Old House', in Wright, 1971, p. 83.

44 Mark O'Connor, 'Sister of the Moon', in M. O'Connor, *Selected Poems*, 1986, p. 139.

45 Claude N. Lee, 'Burragorang Valley', in C. N. Lee, *A Place to Remember: Burragorang Valley, 1957*, 1971, p. 28.

46 Judith Wright, 'Two Dreamtimes', in Wright, *Collected Poems 1942–1985*, 1985, pp. 316–18.

47 Bruce Dawe, 'Nemesis', in *Sometime Gladness*, 1988, p. 212.

48 Jamie Grant, 'Sunlight at Montacute', in Smith and Scott, 1985, pp. 144–5 .

49 Robert Adamson, 'Canticle for the Bicentennial Dead', in R. Adamson, *Selected Poems, 1970–1989*, 1990, p. 266.

50 Bruce Dawe, 'Exiles', in Dawe, 1988, p. 210.

51 Geoff Page, 'Ballad for Joseph Hartmann', in G. Page, *Selected Poems*, 1991, p. 130.

52 Bruce Dawe, 'Beggar's Choice', in Dawe, 1988, p. 213.

53 Unfortunately, the executors of Kevin Gilbert's literary estate declined permission to quote any of his work in this chapter.

54 Kath Walker, 'Son of Mine', in Walker, 1970, p. 59.

55 Charmaine Papertalk-Green, 'Are We the Same', in *Inside Black Australia*, 1988, p. 74.

56 Les Murray, 'Letters to the Winner', in Murray, 1986, p. 136.

57 Jack Davis, 'Our Land', in Davis, 1992, p. 79.

58 Ouyang Yu, 'Alien', in O. Yu, *Moon Over Melbourne and Other Poems*, 1995, p. 28.

59 Errol West, Untitled, in Gilbert, 1988, pp. 166–7.

60 Les Murray, 'A Brief History', in Murray, 1996, p. 11.

61 Les Murray, 'On the Present Slaughter of Feral Animals', in Murray, 1996, pp. 41–2.

62 Bruce Dawe, 'Phase to Phase', in Dawe, 1988, p. 233.

63 Geoff Page and Pooaraar, 'Bandjalang', in *The Great Forgetting*, 1996, pp. 154–7.

3 GROWING

1 Geoff Levitus, 'Introduction', in G. Levitus, ed., *Lying About the Landscape*, 1997, p. 8.

4 MEN'S BUSINESS

1 P. Sutton in P. Read, ed., 'Eleven O'clock on the Last Night of the Conference', *UTS Review* 3/1, May 1997, pp. 151–2.

2 Cf. Read, ed., 'Eleven O'clock on the Last Night of the Conference'.

3 Deborah Bird Rose, *Dingo Makes Us Human*, 1992, p. 122.

4 Rose, 1992, p. 177.

5 Read, ed., 'Eleven O'clock on the Last Night of the Conference'.

6 Rose, 1992, p. 56.

7 Insch to Read, June 1999.

8 Verses supplied by Chas Read for this chapter.

9 D. B. Rose, *Gulaga: A Report on the Cultural Significance of Mt Dromedary to Aboriginal People*, 1990, p. 1.

10 Rose, 1990, p. 55.

11 J. Mulvaney, quoted in Rose, 1990, p. 15.

5 SINGING THE NATIVE-BORN

1 Norma O'Hara Murphy, 'Tamworth', *The Winners 1*, 1993.

2 Lou Bennett, sleeve note on *Our Home Our Land*, 1995.

3 *Country Music in Australia, 1936–1959*, c. 1997.

4 'Belong', *Abo Call* [journal], August 1938, p. 3.

5 John Williamson, 'My Oath to Australia', *The Winners 4*, 1996.

6 John Williamson, 'Shivering', *True Blue*, 1995, p. 91.

7 Slim Dusty, 'I've Been, Seen and Done That', *The Winners 2*, 1994.

8 John Williamson, 'This Is Australia Calling', *The Winners 1*.

9 Slim Dusty, 'Song of the West', *Songs from Down Under*, 1976.

10 Michael O'Sullivan, 'Blue Outback Skies', *A Big Country*, c. 1990.

11 John Williamson, 'Chain around My Ankle', *John Williamson Live*, c. 1987.

12 Grant Luhrs, 'The Men without Shoes', *The Best of Australia*, 1992.

13 Ted Egan, 'Tjandamara', *The Aboriginals*, 1993.

14 Brian Young, 'Kakadu', *The Winners 1*.

15 Eric Bogle, 'Hard Hard Times', *The Eric Bogle Songbook*, LP, 1982.

16 J. Williamson, 'Rip Rip Woodchip', 1995, p. 110.

17 G. Connors, 'Sicilian Born', in *North*, 1987.

18 Slim Dusty, 'Wild Rugged Land that I Love', *Songs from Down Under*.

19 Lee Kernaghan, 'The Outback Club', *The Winners 3*.

20 Graeme Connors, 'Songs from the Homeland', *The Winners 3*.

21 Lee Kernaghan, 'High Country', *The Outback Club*.

22 Slim Dusty, 'I've Been, Seen and Done That', *The Winners 2*.

23 Michael Gant, 'Under the Southern Cross', *The Winners 2*.

24 John Williamson, 'I Can't Feel these Chains Any Longer', *John Williamson Live*, c. 1987.

25 Les Murray, 'The Bulladeelah-Taree Holiday Song Cycle', in L. Murray, *Selected Poems*, 1986, p. 60.

26 Traditional; reproduced, for example, in A. Lloyd, M. Wyndham-Reade and T. Lucas, *The Great Australian Legend*, LP, Topic Records, 1973.

27 The Flying Emus, 'It's a Sunburnt Country', *A Big Country*, c. 1990.

28 James Blundell and James Reyne, 'Way Out West', *The Winners 1*.

29 Slim Dusty, 'Ringer From the Top End', *The Winners 2*.

30 Lee Kernaghan. 'The Outback Club', *The Winners 3*.

31 Lee Kernaghan, 'Boys from the Bush', *The Best of Australia*.

32 P. Read and M. Wyndham, 'The Farmer and the Bushman', in *Environmental History*, forthcoming.

33 Pat Drummond, 'Gamblers on the Land', *The Best of Australia*; The Bushwackers, 'Henry's Men', *The Winners 4*.

34 Rene Diaz, 'Hard Times in Wonderland', *The Winners 2*.

35 Rene Diaz, 'Hard Times in Wonderland', *The Winners 2*.

36 John Williamson, 'It's Good to Be Me', *John Williamson Live*, c. 1983.

37 Big Red, 'Tough Country', *The Winners 3*.

38 Pat Drummond, 'Gamblers on the Land', *The Best of Australia*.

39 Slim Dusty, 'Ringer From the Top End', *The Winners 2*.

40 Brian Letton, 'The Brumbies', *The Winners 3*.

41 John Williamson, 'My Oath to Australia', *The Winners 4*.

42 Eileen Ryan, 'Wild Franklin River', *The Tassie Songs*, c. 1989.

43 Big Red, 'Tough Country', *The Winners 3*.

44 Michael Fix, 'Laughter Like a Shield', *The Winners 2*.

45 Michael Fix, 'Laughter Like a Shield', *The Winners 2*.

46 Noel Watson, 'Tom's Woman', *The Winners 2*.

47 Colin Buchanan, 'A Drover's Wife', *The Winners 1*.

48 John Williamson, 'Back at the Isa', *Mallee Boy*, 1986.

49 Lee Kernaghan, 'Outback Club', *The Winners 3*.

50 Bank of New South Wales, *January the Twenty-Sixth*, 1967.

51 John Williamson, 'Back at the Isa', *Mallee Boy*.

52 Rogers and Hammerstein, *Oklahoma!*.

53 United Artists, 'Our Home, Our Land', *Our Home Our Land*, 1995.

54 Warumpi Band, 'Fitzroy Crossing', *Sing Loud Play Strong*, 1990.

55 Ceddy McGrady, 'The Mission', *Culture Country*, c. 1988.

56 Archie Roach, 'There is a Garden', *Jamu Dreaming*, 1993.

57 Peter Yamada McKenzie, 'Koiki, Father Dave and James', *Our Home Our Land*.

58 Kev Carmody, 'From Little Things Big Things Grow', *The Winners 2*.

59 Bobby McLeod, 'Magic Mountain', *Culture Up Front*, c. 1984.

60 Yothu Yindi, 'Homeland Movement', *Homeland Movement*.

61 Frank Yamma, 'Blackman's Crying', *From the Bush*, 1989.

62 B. McKenzie, 'Big Mountain Wilpena Pound', *Our Home Our Land*.

63 Archie Roach, 'Charcoal Lane', *Charcoal Lane*, 1990.

64 Ceddy McGrady, 'Bright Lights in the City', *Culture Country*, c. 1988.

65 Tiddas, 'My Sister', *Sing About Life*, 1993.

66 Jimmy Little, 'Yorta Yorta Man', *The Winners 3*.

67 Archie Roach, 'Native Born', *Charcoal Lane*.

68 Amunda, '1788', *Sing Loud Play Strong*.

69 Sunrize Band, 'Land Rights', 1990.

70 Warumpi Band, 'Wayathul', *Too Much Humbug*, 1995.

71 Coloured Stone, 'Forgotten Tribe', written by Robert Buna Lawrie, 1994, about the Yirgala Miruing people of the Nullarbor, *Our Home Our Land*, 1995.

72 The Wedgetail Eagles, 'Black Boy', *From the Bush*.

73 'The Land's Worth More than Gold and Silver', *Our Home Our Land*.

74 Our Home Our Land (dedicated to the Meriam people).

75 Blekbala Mujic, 'Nitmiluk' [the Jawoyn name for the Katherine River Gorge], *Our Home Our Land*.

76 Yothu Yindi, 'Mainstream', *Homeland Movement*, 1989.

77 Troy Cassar-Daley, 'Dream Out Loud', *The Winners 3*.

78 'The Swaggies Have All Waltzed Matilda Away', in A. Hulett, *Dance of the Under Class*, 1991. I thank Debbie Rose for introducing me to this musician.

79 Midnight Oil, 'One Country', *Blue Sky Mining*, 1989.

80 Midnight Oil, 'Wara Kurna', *Diesel and Dust*, 1987.

81 Paul Kelly, 'Nakkanya', *Our Home Our Land*. Kelly is described as a non-Aboriginal having 'a long association with indigenous culture'.

82 Paul Kelly, 'Special Treatment', *Yella Mundi*, 1996.

83 Tiddas, 'Malcolm Smith', *Sing About Life*, 1993.

84 The song is dedicated to Margaret Tucker, the author of the first of the stolen generations autobiographies, *If Everyone Cared*.

85 Goanna, 'Sorry', *Spirit Returns*, 1998.

86 Goanna, 'Children of the Southern Land', *Spirit of Place*, 1982.

87 Spoken introduction, 'Black Mary', Penny Davies and Roger Ilott, *Backbone of a Nation*, 1992.

88 Goanna, 'Solid Rock', *Spirit of Place*.

89 Goanna, 'Spiritual Thing', *Spirit Returns*, 1998.

90 Goanna, 'Poor Fella My Country', *Spirit Returns*.

91 Ian Mudie, *This Is Australia*, n.d. [c. 1941], pp. 7, 15, 19, 30.

92 Eileen Ryan, 'Save the Earth', *The Tassie Songs*.

93 Council for Aboriginal Reconciliation, *Sharing History*, Key Issue Paper No. 4, 1994.

94 Neil Murray, 'Tjapwurrung Country', *Yella Mundi* and *Dust*, ABC Music, 1996.

95 CD insert, *Yella Mundi*.

96 Neil Murray, *Sing for Me Countryman*, 1993, p. 43.

97 Archie Roach, 'Native Born', *Charcoal Lane*.

98 Warumpi Band, 'Blackfella Whitefella', *Too Much Humbug*.

99 Warumpi Band, 'We Shall Cry', *Our Home Our Land*.

100 Neil Murray, 'Native Born', *Dust*, ABC Music, 1996.

6 WOMEN'S BUSINESS

1 The names of Ida, her husband and her daughter are fictitious.

2 Manik Datar, 'My Sister's Mother', *Quadrant*, October 1995, pp. 75–6.

3 Manik Datar, 'Point of No Return', *Voices,* Summer 1995-6, pp. 83–8.

4 Mandy Martin, 'This El Dorado of Pure Recognition and Desert of Pure Non-Recognition', paper presented to Visions of Future Landscapes, Canberra, 2–5 May 1999, typescript, p. 6.

5 Bean, *On the Wool Track*, 1945, pp. 60–1.

6 Bean, 1945, p. 6.

7 Bean, 1945, p. 7.

8 Guy Fitzhardinge, 'A Sense of Knowing, a Sense of Place and a Sense of Caring', in Mandy Martin and Paul Sinclair, *Tracts: Back o' Bourke*, n.d., p. 5.

9 Paul Sinclair, in Martin and Sinclair, n.d., pp. 37, 39.

10 P. Haynes, 'Mandy Martin: The Continuing Narrative', in Martin and Sinclair, n.d., pp. 7–8.

11 P. Sinclair, 'Feral', in Martin and Sinclair, n.d., p. 40.

12 Martin, 1999, p. 2.

13 Quoted by M. Holloway, 'In the Boiler Room of Art: Mandy Martin, Painting and the Industrial Landscape', in Mandy Martin, *Latrobe Valley Series*, Latrobe Valley Arts Centre, 1990, p. 5.

14 Bean, *Dreadnought of the Darling*, 1956, cited by J.Beckett, 'George Dutton's Country', *Aboriginal History* 2, 1978, p. 10.

15 J. Beckett, 'George Dutton's Country', *Aboriginal History* 2, 1978, p. 29.

16 Evelyn Crawford as told to Chris Walsh, *Over My Tracks*, 1993, pp. 47, 61.

17 Heather Goodall, *Invasion to Embassy*, 1996, p. 18.

18 Max Kamien, *The Dark People of Bourke*, 1978, p. 17.

19 Martin, 1999, p. 3.

20 Coral Hull, 'Concentric Circles', in *Broken Land: Five Days in Bre, 1995*, 1997, p. 22.

21 Martin, 1999, p. 6.

22 Geoff Page and Pooaraar, 'Bandjalang', in *The Great Forgetting*, 1996, pp. 154–7.

23 M. Wyndham, unpublished paper presented to Biennial Conference of the Australian Historical Association, Melbourne, 1996.

7 FOUR HISTORIANS

1 Heather Goodall, *Invasion to Embassy*, 1996, introduction.
2 Interview with Heather Goodall, 1992.
3 Goodall, 1996, p. 195, 199, 357.
4 Quoted by P. Read, review of *Invasion to Embassy*, in *Aboriginal Law Bulletin*, November 1996, p. 15.
5 Goodall, 1996, pp. 61–5.
6 Goodall, 1996, p. 200.
7 Goodall, 1996, p. 359.
8 Goodall to Read, August 1999.
9 Tom Griffiths' first sustained scholarly work was a study of the emotional effects of the end of mining on residents of the gold-mining town of Beechworth: *Beechworth: An Australian Country Town and Its Past*, 1987.
10 Tom Griffiths, 'The Outside Country. An Elemental History', Catalogue essay for Mandy Martin and Tom Griffiths, *Watersheds: The Paroo to the Warrego*, 1999, p. 52.
11 Griffiths, 1999, p. 52.
12 Tom Griffiths, 'Legend and Lament', review article, *The Australian's Review of Books*, March 1999, pp. 11–13.
13 Tom Griffiths, *Hunters and Collectors*, 1996, p. 5.
14 Griffiths, 1996, pp. 269–72.
15 Henry Reynolds, *The Other Side of the Frontier*, 1981, p. 1.
16 Reynolds, 1981, pp. 1–3.
17 Henry Reynolds, *Why Weren't We Told?*, 1990, p. 20.
18 Reynolds, 1981, pp. 164–5.
19 Henry Reynolds, *Fate of a Free People*, 1995.
20 Reynolds, 1995, p. 197.
21 Reynolds, 1995, pp. 210–13.
22 Reynolds, 1995, pp. 1–3.
23 Reynolds, *Why Weren't We Told*, 1999, p. 244.
24 Jamie Grant, 'Sunlight at Montacute', in Smith and Scott, *Effects of Light*, pp. 144–5.
25 Henry Reynolds, *This Whispering in Our Hearts*, 1998, pp. 245–9.
26 Reynolds, 1999, p. 247.
27 Reynolds, 1999, p. 244.
28 Reynolds, 1981, p. 163.
29 Reynolds, 1981, p. 166.
30 L. Ryan, *The Aboriginal Tasmanians*, 1981, introduction.
31 Ryan, 1996 [revised edition of 1981], pp. 247–53.
32 Ryan, 1996, pp. 310.
33 Ryan, 1996, pp. 2–3.

34 Ryan, 1996, p. 261.

35 James Charlton, 'Koonya, A Black Girl', in V. Smith and M. Scott, eds, *Effects of Light: The Poetry of Tasmania*, 1985, p. 130.

36 Ryan, 1996, pp. 260–1 (also in the 1981 edition).

8 IN SEARCH OF THE PROPER COUNTRY

1 Randolph Stow, 'The Dark Women Go Down', *A Counterfeit Silence*, 1969, p. 58.

2 P. Sutton in P. Read, ed., 'Eleven O'clock on the Last Night of the Conference', *UTS Review*, pp. 151–2.

3 R. F. Brissenden, 'South Coast Midden' in R. F. Brissenden, *Sacred Sites*, 1990, p. 15.

4 Rene Diaz, 'Hard Times in Wonderland', *The Winners 2*, 1994.

5 Brissenden, 1990, p. 15 .

6 Dennis Foley, 'Turrubul', in 'Koori Men Can Cry!', unpublished ms, p. 34. Dennis notes that 'Turrabul is the original people from the Brisbane River Maroochy Baramba and Auntie Connie Isaacs mob'.

7 Judith Wright, 'Bora Ring', in J. Wright, *Collected Poems 1942–1970*, 1971, p. 8.

8 Francis Myers, *A Traveller's Tale: From Manly to the Hawkesbury*, 1885, p. 35.

9 Kath Walker, 'Acacia Ridge', in K. Walker, *We Are Going*, 1964, p. 31.

10 Meyer Eidelson, *The Melbourne Dreaming: A Guide to the Aboriginal Places of Melbourne*, 1997, pp. 3, 32.

11 John Howard, radio interview with John Laws, quoted by Noel Pearson, 'An Australian History for All of Us', Address to the Chancellor's Club Dinner, UWQS, 20 November 1996, photocopy.

12 Les Murray, 'The China Pear Trees', in L. Murray, *Selected Poems*, 1986, p. 139.

13 Troy Cassar-Daley, 'Dream Out Loud', *The Winners 3*, 1995.

14 'Spiritual Thing', Goanna, *Spirit Returns*, 1988.

15 'Son of Mine', in K. Walker, *My People*, 1970, p. 59.

16 R. F. Brissenden, 'Sea Beach and Cave, Durras', in Brissenden, 1990, p. 42.

17 Anne Ross, 'Inter-Tribal Conflict—What the First Fleet Saw', BA (Hons) thesis, University of Sydney, 1976.

18 Randolph Stow, 'There Was a Time', in Stow, 1969, p. 59.

19 J. Cobley, ed., *Sydney Cove 1788*, 1962, p. 120.

20 A. Caesar, 'Landscapes', in A. Caesar, *Life Sentences*, 1998, p. 3.

21 V. Brady, 'The Ambiguities of Place', in *Sense of Place Colloquium II*, 1997, pp. 41–2.

22 Ryan to Read, 5 August 1999, quoted with permission.

23 Eve Langley, 'Native Born', in Hampton and Llewellyn, 1986, pp. 50–1.

24 M. Walsh, 'The Land Still Speaks? Language and Landscape in Aboriginal Australia', in D. B. Rose and A. Clarke, eds, *Tracking Knowledge*, 1997, p. 106.

25 Cobley, 1962, pp. 118–19.

26 D. Benson and J. Howell, *Taken For Granted: The Bushland of Sydney and its Suburbs*, 1990, p. 18.

27 Warumpi Band, 'We Shall Cry', *Our Home Our Land*.

28 S. Zofrea (woodcuts) and S. McInerney (text), *The Journeyman*, 1992.

29 Song by Neil Murray, formerly of the Warumpi Band, reproduced in Martin Flanaghan, *Good Weekend, Sydney Morning Herald*, 8 February 1997, p. 35; see also *Dust*, cassette album, 1997.

30 Cf. Ross Gibson, *South of the West*, 1992, pp. 14–18.

31 Judith Wright, 'Two Dreamtimes', in J. Wright, *Collected Poems 1942–1985*, 1985, pp. 316–18.

WORKS CITED

Abo Call [journal], August 1938.

Adamson, Robert, *Selected Poems 1970–1989*, University of Queensland Press, St Lucia, 1990.

Amunda, *Sing Loud Play Strong*, CD, Central Australian Aboriginal Media Association, 1990.

Anonymous poet, 'Our Political System Is Best', *Integration*, vol. 4, no. 10, April–July 1996.

Bank of New South Wales, *January the Twenty-Sixth*, devised and produced by George Patterson Pty Ltd, Sydney, 1967.

Bean, Charles, *On the Wool Track*, Angus and Robertson, Sydney, 1945 [1911].

Beckett, Jeremy, 'George Dutton's Country', *Aboriginal History* vol. 2, 1978, pp. 2–31.

Bennett, R., ed., *Voices from the Heart*, Institute for Aboriginal Development, Alice Springs, 1995.

Benson D., and J. Howell, *Taken for Granted: The Bushland of Sydney and its Suburbs*, Kangaroo Press, Kenthurst, NSW, 1990.

The Best of Australia, CD, ABC Country, 1992.

A Big Country, CD, ABC Country, 1992.

Birch, Tony, 'Daisy Bates', *Melbourne Historical Journal*, vol. 23, 1995.

Bogle, Eric, *The Eric Bogle Songbook*, LP, Larrikin/EMI, 1986; reprinted by kind permission of Larrikin Music Publishing Pty Ltd.

Brady, Veronica, 'The Ambiguities of Place', in Pre-Colloquium Papers, 'Sense of Place. The Interaction Between Aboriginal and Western Senses of Place', University of Western Sydney, 1997.

—— 'Truth, Illusions and Collisions', *Australian Book Review*, July 1999, pp. 23–6.

Brissenden, Robert, *Building a Terrace*, Australian National University, Canberra, 1975.
—— *Sacred Sites*, Phoenix/Bistro, Canberra, 1990.
Brook, Jack, and J. L. Cohen, *The Parramatta Native Institution and the Black Town: A History*, NSW University Press, Kensington, 1991.
Buchanan, Colin, 'Drover's Wife', CD, Wanaaring Road Music/Rondor Music, 1995.
Bygrave, Rose, 'Spiritual Thing', CD, Jointed Venture, 1997.
Byrne, Denis, 'Deep Nation: Australia's Acquisition of an Indigenous Past', *Aboriginal History*, vol. 20, 1996.
Caesar, A., *Life Sentences*, Molonglo Press, Canberra, 1998.
Campbell, David, *Collected Poems*, Angus and Robertson, Sydney, 1989.
Carmody, Kev, 'From Little Things Big Things Grow' reprinted by kind permission of Larrikin Music Publishing Pty Ltd.
Cassar-Daley, T., 'Dream out Loud', Warner Chappell Music Australia, 1997.
Choate, Alec, *Mind in Need of a Desert*, Fremantle Arts Centre Press, 1995.
Clark, Manning, *Speaking Out Of Turn*, Melbourne University Press, 1997.
Cobley, J., ed., *Sydney Cove 1788*, Hodder and Stoughton, London, 1962.
Connors, Graeme, 'Sicilian Born', *Songs from the Homeland*, CD, Panama Music/Rondor Music, 1987.
Coombs, H. C. 1983, interviewed for a public radio series, 'The Aboriginal Treaty Proposal'.
Corbett, Roger, 'Tough Country', Warner Chappell Music Australia, 1993.
Council for Aboriginal Reconciliation, *Sharing History*, Key Issue Paper No. 4, AGPS, Canberra, 1994.
Country Music in Australia 1936–1959, CD set, EMI, c. 1997.
Crawford, Evelyn, as told to Chris Walsh, *Over My Tracks*, Penguin, Ringwood, Vic., 1993.
Dark, Eleanor, *The Little Company*, Collins, Sydney, 1945.
Datar, Manik, 'My Sister's Mother', *Quadrant*, October 1995, pp. 75–6.
—— 'Point of No Return', *Voices*, 1995, pp. 83–8.
Davies, Penny, and Roger Ilott, *Backbone of the Nation*, cassette, Restless, 1992.
Davis, Jack, *Black Life*, University of Queensland Press, St Lucia, 1992.
Dawe, Bruce, *Sometime Gladness*, Addison Wesley Longman Australia, Melbourne, 1988.
Dibble, B., D. Grant and G. Phillips, eds, *Celebrations*, UWA Press, Nedlands, 1988.
Dodson, Mick, speaker in 'Unfinished Business', ABC production, prod. Bill Bunbury, Radio National, 1996.
Drummond, Pat, 'Gamblers on the Land', 1995.
Dusty, Slim, *Songs From Down Under*, LP, CBS/Sony, 1976.

—— and Stan Coster, 'Wild Rugged Land that I Love', EMI Music Publishing Australia, 1994.

Egan, Ted, 'Tjandamara', *The Aboriginals*, Central Australian Aboriginal Media Association, c. 1988.

Eidelson, Meyer, *The Melbourne Dreaming: A Guide to the Aboriginal Places of Melbourne*, Aboriginal Studies Press, Canberra, 1997.

Fitzhardinge, Guy, 'A Sense of Knowing, a Sense of Place and a Sense of Caring', in Mandy Martin and Paul Sinclair, *Tracts Back o' Bourke*, M. Martin, n.d.

Flanaghan, Martin, 'Native Poet', *Sydney Morning Herald Good Weekend*, 8 February 1998.

Foley, Dennis, 'Koori Men Can Cry!', unpublished ms.

Gelder, Ken, and Jane M. Jacobs, *Uncanny Australia: Sacredness and Identity in a Postcolonial Nation*, Melbourne University Press, 1998.

Gibson, Ross, *South of the West*, Indiana University Press, Bloomington, 1992.

Gilbert, Kevin, ed., *People Are Legends*, University of Queensland Press, St Lucia, 1978.

—— ed., *Inside Black Australia*, Penguin, Ringwood, Vic., 1988.

Goanna, *Spirit of Place*, CD, Platinum Productions/Warner Bros, 1982.

—— *Spirit Returns*, CD, EMI, 1998.

Goodall, Heather, *Invasion to Embassy*, Allen and Unwin, St Leonards, NSW, 1997.

Gordimer, Nadine, *The Essential Gesture*, ed. Stephen Clingman, Penguin, London, 1989.

Griffiths, Tom, *Beechworth: An Australian Country Town and Its Past,* Greenhouse, Melbourne, 1987.

—— *Hunters and Collectors*, Cambridge University Press, Melbourne, 1996.

—— 'The Outside Country. An Elemental History', catalogue essay for Mandy Martin and Tom Griffiths, *Watersheds: The Paroo to the Warrego*, M. Martin, Mandurama, 1999.

—— 'Legend and Lament', review article, *The Australian's Review of Books*, March 1999, pp. 11–13.

Grono R., ed., *Margins*, Fremantle Arts Centre Press, 1988.

Hall, Rodney, ed., *The Collins Book of Australian Poetry*, Collins, Sydney, 1981.

Hampton S., and K. Llewellyn, eds, *The Penguin Book of Australian Women Poets*, Penguin, Ringwood, Vic., 1986.

Harwood, Gwen, *Selected Poems*, Angus and Robertson, North Ryde, NSW, 1985; ETT Imprint, 1996.

Haynes, Peter, 'Mandy Martin: The Continuing Narrative', in Mandy Martin and Paul Sinclair, *Tracts Back o' Bourke*, M. Martin, n.d.

Haynes, Rosslyn, *Seeking the Centre*, Cambridge University Press, Melbourne, 1998.

Hewett, Dorothy, *A Tremendous World in Her Head*, Kangaroo Press, Sydney 1989.

Holloway, M., 'In the Boiler Room of Art: Mandy Martin, Painting and the Industrial Landscape', in Mandy Martin, *Latrobe Valley Series*, Latrobe Valley Arts Centre, 1990.

Hulett, Alistair, *Dance of the Under Class*, tape cassette, Red Rattler, 1991.

Hull, Coral, *Broken Land: Five Days in Bre, 1995*, Five Islands Press, Wollongong, NSW, 1997.

Ingram, Ossie, 'The Proudest People on Earth', in B. Gammage and P. Spearritt, eds, *Australians 1938*, Fairfax Syme and Weldon, Melbourne, 1987, pp. 117–24.

Kamien, Max, *The Dark People of Bourke*, Australian Institute of Aboriginal Studies, Canberra, 1978.

Kane, John, and Jenny Kane, 'It's a Sunburnt Country', Rondor Music Australia, 1994.

Kernaghan, Lee, and Garth Porter, *The Outback Club*, ABC Music/Warner Chappell Music Australia, 1992.

King, Michael, *Being Pakeha*, Hodder and Stoughton, Auckland, 1985.

Kirk, Rob, 'Hard Times in Wonderland', 1994.

Kramer, Leonie, ed., *David Campbell: Collected Poems*, Angus and Robertson, Sydney, 1989.

Lloyd, A. L., M. Wyndham-Reade and T. Lucas, *The Great Australian Legend*, LP, Topic Records, 1973.

Longdin, R., and Elida Meadows, 'Catalina: Wild Heart of Katoomba', *Public History Review*, vol. 7, 1998, pp. 103–16.

Lee, Claude, *A Place to Remember: Burragorang Valley, 1957*, C. Lee, Bowral, NSW, 1971.

Mackay, M., 'To the Kooris', unpublished ms, 1997.

McBryde, Isabel, 'Dream the Impossible Dream? Shared Heritage, Shared Values, or Shared Understanding of Disparate Values', in Historic Environment, Australia ICOMOS Conference, Darwin, December 1993, selected papers published by Australia ICOMOS, vol. 11, nos 2 and 3, 1995.

McGrady, Ceddy, *Culture Country*, CD, Enrec, c. 1988.

McKean, Joy, 'I've Been, Seen and Done That', *Ringer from the Top End*, Slim Dusty Enterprises Pty Ltd, n.d.

McKenzie, P., ed., *The Poetry of Canberra*, Polonius, Canberra, 1990.

McLeod, Bobby, *Culture Up Front*, CD, Larrikin, c. 1984.

Martin, Mandy, 'This El Dorado of Pure Recognition and Desert of Pure Non-Recognition', paper presented to Visions of Future Landscapes, Canberra, 2–5 May 1999.

—— and Paul Sinclair, *Tracts Back o' Bourke*, exhibition catalogue, M. Martin, n.d.

Midnight Oil, *Diesel and Dust*, CD, CBS/Sony, 1987.

—— *Blue Sky Mining*, CD, CBS/Sony, 1989.

Moran, Anthony, 'Aboriginal Reconciliation: Transformations in Settler Nationalism', *The Reconciliation Issue, Melbourne Journal of Politics*, vol. 25, 1998.

Moyses, Barry, 'Where Country Is', 1981.

Mudie, Ian, *This Is Australia*, Frank E. Cork, Adelaide, n.d. [c. 1941].

—— *Selected Poems, 1934–1974*, Nelson, Sydney, 1976.

Murray, Les, *A Working Forest*, Duffy and Snellgrove, Potts Point, NSW, 1977.

—— *Selected Poems*, Carcanet, Manchester, 1986.

—— *Subhuman Redneck Poems*, Duffy and Snellgrove, Potts Point, NSW, 1996.

Murray, Neil, *Sing for Me Countryman*, Sceptre, Rydalmere, NSW, 1993.

—— *Dust*, CD, ABC Music, 1996; lyrics reprinted with permission, Rondor Music Australia.

Myers, Francis, *A Traveller's Tale: From Manly to the Hawkesbury 1885*, facsimile edition compiled by Colleen Cook, View Productions, Sydney, 1984.

Nugent, Maria, 'La Perouse Versus Larpa: Contesting Histories of Place', *Public History Review*, vol. 5–6, 1996–7, pp. 192–9.

O'Connor, Mark, *Selected Poems*, Hale and Iremonger, Sydney, 1986.

Our Home Our Land, CD, Central Australian Aboriginal Media Association, 1995.

The Outback Club, CD, ABC Music, 1992.

Page, Geoff, *Selected Poems*, Angus and Robertson, North Ryde, NSW, 1991.

—— and Pooaraar, *The Great Forgetting*, Aboriginal Studies Press, Canberra, 1996.

Pearson, Noel, 'An Australian History for All of Us', Address to the Chancellor's Club Dinner, University of Western Sydney, 20 November 1996, photocopy.

Pybus, Cassandra, *Community of Thieves*, Heinemann, Melbourne, 1991.

Read, Peter, ed., *Down There with Me on the Cowra Mission*, Pergamon, Sydney 1984.

—— Review of *Invasion to Embassy, Aboriginal Law Bulletin*, November 1986, pp. 15–16.

—— 'Eleven O'clock on the Last Night of the Conference', *UTS Review*, vol. 3, no. 1, May 1997, pp. 142–59.

—— *Returning to Nothing*, Cambridge University Press, Melbourne, 1997.

—— and Marivic Wyndham, 'The Farmer and the Bushman', *Environment and History*, forthcoming.

Reynolds, Henry, *The Other Side of the Frontier*, James Cook University, Cooktown, 1981.

—— *Fate of a Free People*, Penguin, Ringwood, Vic., 1995.

—— *This Whispering in Our Hearts*, Allen and Unwin, St Leonards, NSW, 1998.

—— *Why Weren't We Told?*, Viking, Melbourne, 1999.

Roach, Archie, *Charcoal Lane*, CD, Aurora, 1990 .

—— *Jamu Dreaming*, CD, Aurora, 1993.

Rose Deborah Bird, *Gulaga: A Report on the Cultural Significance of Mt Dromedary to Aboriginal People*, [commissioned report] 1990.

—— *Dingo Makes Us Human*, Cambridge University Press, 1992.

—— *Nourishing Terrains*, Australian Heritage Commission, Canberra, 1996.

Ross, Anne, 'Inter-Tribal Conflict—What the First Fleet Saw', BA (Hons) thesis, University of Sydney, 1976.

Ryan, Eileen, *The Tassie Songs*, CD, Hadley Records/Yeldah Music, 1992.

Ryan, Lyndall, *The Aboriginal Tasmanians*, Allen and Unwin, St Leonards, NSW, 1981; second edition 1996.

Sinclair, Paul, 'Back o' Bourke', in Mandy Martin and Paul Sinclair, *Tracts Back o' Bourke*, M. Martin, n.d., pp. 31–42.

Smith, Broderick, 'Way out West', 1985.

Smith, V., and M. Scott, *Effects of Light: The Poetry of Tasmania*, Twelvetrees Publishing Co., Hobart, 1985.

Stewart, Douglas, *Douglas Stewart*, Angus and Robertson, Sydney, 1963.

Stockton, Eugene, *The Aboriginal Gift: Spirituality for a Nation*, Millennium Books, Alexandria, NSW, 1995.

Stow, Randolph, *A Counterfeit Silence*, Angus and Robertson, Sydney, 1969.

Sunrize Band, *Darwin Aboriginal Music Festival*, ABC, 1990.

Tacey, David, *Edge of the Sacred*, HarperCollins, North Blackburn, Vic., 1995.

Tiddas, *Sing about Life*, CD, Phonogram, 1993.

Walker, Kath [Oodgeroo of the Tribe Noonuccal], *We Are Going*, Jacaranda Press, Brisbane, 1964.

Walsh, Michael, 'The Land Still Speaks? Language and Landscape in Aboriginal Australia', in D. Rose and A. Clarke, eds, *Tracking Knowledge*, North Australian Research Unit, Australian National University, Darwin, 1997.

Warumpi Band, *Sing Loud Play Strong*, CD, Central Australian Aboriginal Media Association, 1990.

—— *Too Much Humbug*, CD, Central Australian Aboriginal Media Association, 1995; lyrics reprinted with permission, Rondor Music Australia.

Watson, Noel, and Ren Thorpe, 'Tom's Woman', Warner Chappel Music Australia, n.d.

The Wedgetail Eagles, *From the Bush*, cassette, Central Australian Aboriginal Media Association, 1989.

West, Errol, untitled poem, in Ida West, *Pride against Prejudice: Reminiscences of a Tasmanian Aboriginal*, Australian Institute of Aboriginal Studies, Canberra, 1984.

Williamson, John, *John Williamson Live*, CD, EMI, 1983.

—— *Mallee Boy*, CD, Festival, 1986.

—— *True Blue*, Angus and Robertson, Pymble, NSW, 1995.

The Winners 1, CD, EMI, 1993.

The Winners 2, CD, EMI, 1994.

The Winners 3, CD, EMI, 1995.

The Winners 4, CD, EMI, 1996.

Wootten J. H., *Report of the Enquiry into the Death of David Gundy*, AGPS, Canberra, 1991.

Wright, Judith, *Collected Poems, 1942–1970*, Angus and Robertson, Sydney, 1971.

—— *Born of the Conquerors*, Aboriginal Studies Press, Canberra, 1991.

—— *Collected Poems, 1942–1985*, Carcanet, Manchester, 1994.

Yamma, Frank, *From the Bush*, CD, Central Australian Aboriginal Media Association, 1989.

Yella Mundi, CD, Jimaru Records/BMG Australia, 1996.

Yothu Yindi, *Homeland Movement*, CD, Mushroom, 1989.

Yu, Ouyang, *Moon Over Melbourne and Other Poems*, Papyrus Publishing, Upper Ferntree Gully, Vic., 1995.

Zofrea, Salvatore (woodcuts) and Sally McInerney (text), *The Journeyman*, Picador, Chippendale, NSW, 1992.

INDEX

DATE DUE

			Printed In USA

HIGHSMITH #45230